Marilyn D

G br 165 K
4

Germany   p.225

Gebruder Krauss Doll

p.5
Movies
    mag.
April.82
Doll world
Clues to the
  Germany
      Dolls.

A.M-5-DEP   370
    Armand Marseille

25"

ABOVE: 21in (53.3cm) Kestner "Gibson Girl." *Mary Lou Rubright Collection.*

FRONT COVER: 23in (58.4cm) Kley and Hahn #526 character girl. *Jan Foulke Collection.*

TITLE PAGE: Bébé Phenix. *Richard Wright Collection.*

4th
Blue Book
Dolls & Values
by Jan Foulke

photographs by *Howard Foulke*

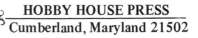

Published by

HOBBY HOUSE PRESS
Cumberland, Maryland 21502

Other Titles by Author:

Blue Book of Dolls & Values
2nd Blue Book of Dolls &·Values
3rd Blue Book of Dolls & Values
Focusing on Effanbee Composition Dolls
Focusing on Treasury of Mme. Alexander Dolls
Focusing on Gebruder Heubach Dolls

The doll prices given within this book are intended as value guides rather than arbitrarily set prices. Each doll price recorded here is actually a compilation. The retail prices in this book are recorded as accurately as possible but in the case of errors, typographical, clerical or otherwise, the author and publisher assume no liability nor responsibility for any loss incurred by users of this book.

**ADDITIONAL COPIES AVAILABLE @ $10.95 FROM
HOBBY HOUSE PRESS
900 FREDERICK STREET
CUMBERLAND, MARYLAND 21502**

Printed in the United States of America

ISBN 0–87588–162–9

Introduction

In this 4th BLUE BOOK OF DOLLS AND VALUES, our objectives are the same as they were for the very first BLUE BOOK, although we have greatly expanded from the original 194 pages.

Our first objective is to present a book which will help collectors identify dolls and learn more about them: dolls which they already own, those that they might like to own among the large variety pictured, those that are offered to them for purchase, or those which they just might be curious about.

The dolls are listed alphabetically in the text by the maker, the material, the type of doll, or the name of the individual doll. An extensive index has been provided at the back of the book for the reader's convenience in locating a specific doll. Of course, in a volume of this size, it would be impossible to include every doll, but we have tried to include those which were either available, desirable, interesting or popular, and even a few which are very rare. For each doll, we have provided historical information, a description of the doll, and in most cases, a photograph. For your further study we have also included a glossary, a selected bibliography, and an additional section on doll bodies. The historical information given for some of the dolls would have been much more difficult to compile were it not for the original research already published by Dorothy, Elizabeth, and Evelyn Coleman and Johana G. Anderton.

Our second objective is to list the actual retail prices of the dolls discussed to provide a guide for the prospective buyer and seller. The data on the prices was gathered from January to August 1980, and was obtained from antique shops and shows, auctions, doll shops and shows, advertisements in collectors' periodicals, lists from doll dealers, and purchases reported by friends. For some of the rarer dolls we had to dip back a little further into late 1979. The information was sorted, indexed, cataloged and finally computed into the range of prices shown in this book. Hence, the figures used here are not merely our own valuations and judgments—they are the results of our research as to the actual retail prices at which these dolls were either sold or offered for sale.

In setting down a price, we used a range to allow for the variables discussed later which necessarily affect the price of any doll. All prices given for antique dolls are for those of good quality and condition, appropriately dressed, but showing normal wear, unless specifically noted in the description accompanying that particular doll. Bisque and china heads should not be cracked or broken. The especially outstanding doll in absolutely mint condition, never played with, in the original box, or with original clothes, would command a price far higher than those quoted. Prices given for modern dolls were for those in overall good to better condition with original hair and clothes except as noted. Again, a never-played-with doll in original box with tagged clothes would bring a higher price than noted.

LEFT: 8in (20.3cm) Heubach "Bonnie Babe". *Jan Foulke Collection.*

BELOW: 18in (45.7cm) SFBJ #238. *Mary Lou Rubright Collection.*

22in (55.9cm) A.T. *Mary Lou Rubright Collection.*

K★R 114, S&H 151, K★R 101. *Richard Wright.*

Certain dolls are becoming increasingly difficult to find and are seldom offered at a show or advertised since most dealers usually have a list of customers waiting for these desirable dolls. If we did not find a sufficient number of these rare dolls offered to be sure of giving a reliable range, we reported the information which we could find and marked those prices with a "**". In a very few instances we would find none of a certain doll offered, so we resorted to estimates from reliable established dealers and collectors. These, too, are noted individually with an "**".

The users of this book must keep in mind that no price guide is the final word–it cannot provide the absolute answer of what to pay. It should be used only as an aid in purchasing a doll. The final decision must be yours, for only you are on the scene actually examining the specific doll in question. No book can take the place of actual field experience. Before you buy, do a lot of looking. Ask questions. You will find that most dealers and collectors are glad to talk about their dolls and pleased to share their information with you.

With these thoughts in mind, we are proud to present to you our 4th BLUE BOOK OF DOLLS AND VALUES.

Determining Doll Prices

Doll collecting is an exciting hobby, but deciding whether or not to buy a specific doll to add to your collection, can be difficult when you begin to consider the many variable factors which affect the value of a doll. Some of these have already been outlined by Janet Johl and Dorothy Coleman, but they are important enough to bear restatement and amplification. Hopefully, you will find in this chapter some helpful suggestions about what to look for and what to consider when purchasing a doll.

I have found very few people who buy dolls strictly as an investment. Although many collectors rationalize their purchases by saying that they are making a good investment, they are still actually buying the doll because they like it—it has appeal to them for some reason: perhaps as an object of artistic beauty, perhaps because it evokes some kind of sentiment, perhaps it fills some need that they feel, or perhaps it speaks to something inside them. When my daughter and I go doll shopping, we look at them all, but we only stop to examine closely and consider buying those which have some appeal for us. Thus, we more often find ourselves buying first with our hearts and second with our heads. Anyway, it is this personal feeling toward the doll that makes it of value to you.

Marks

After you decide that you like a doll, find out what it is. Certainly, the *marks* on dolls are important in determining a price, for with a little luck, they might tell what the doll is, who made it, where, and sometimes when. A 20in (50.8cm) doll marked A.M. 390 even though she is in good condition and well dressed, is plentiful and should not cost as much as the harder-to-find S&H 1279 girl in the same size and condition. Likewise, if the doll is tagged "Jane Withers", you know it is a rare one; a "Patsy" would be far more common. Of course, many dolls are unmarked but after you have seen quite a few dolls, you begin to notice their individual and special characteristics, so that you can often determine what a doll possibly is.

Quality

But even the mark does not tell all. Two dolls, from exactly the same mold could carry vastly different prices (and look entirely different) because of the *quality* of the work done on the doll. To command top price, a bisque doll should have lovely bisque, decoration, eyes and hair. As you examine many dolls, you will see that the quality varies from head to head, even with dolls made from the same mold by one firm. Choose the best example that you can find of the type for which you are looking. The bisque should be smooth and silky, not grainy, rough, peppered (tiny black specks), or pimply. The tinting should be subdued and even, not harsh and splotchy, although the amount of color acceptable is often a matter of personal preference, some collectors liking very pale white bisque and others preferring a little more pink. Since doll heads are hand-painted, one of good quality should show artistic skill in the portrayal of the expression on the face and in details, such as the mouth, eyebrows and

18in (45.7cm) Lenci #1500 face, all original. *Beth Foulke Collection.*

18in (45.7cm) S&H #1358 Black Girl. *Mary Lou Rubright Collection.*

18in (45.7cm) Celluloid Boy with turtle mark, all original. *H&J Foulke.*

19in (48.3cm) 1958 vinyl "Shirley Temple", all original. *H&J Foulke.*

F & B "Tommy Tucker", all original. *Glenn Mandeville/Chip Barkel Collection.*

iv

eyelashes. On a doll with molded hair, deep molding, an unusual hair style and brush marks to give the hair a more realistic look would be details which are desirable. If a doll has a wig, the hair should be appropriate, if not original—a lovely human hair wig or good quality mohair. The eyes should have a natural and lifelike appearance, whether they are glass or painted. If a doll does not meet these standards, it should be priced lower than one that does.

Condition

Another factor which is important when pricing a doll is the *condition.* A doll with a crack on the face or extensive professional repair would sell for considerably less than a doll with only normal wear; a hair line or a small professional repair in an inconspicuous place would decrease the value somewhat, but not nearly so much. Sometimes a head will have a factory flaw which occurred in the making, such as a cooking crack, scratch, piece of kiln debris or a ridge not smoothed out. Since the factory was producing toys for a profit, not works of art, they did not discard all heads with slight flaws, especially if they were in an inconspicuous place or could be covered. If these factory defects are slight and not detracting, they have little or no effect on the value of the doll, and whether or not to purchase such a doll would be a matter of personal opinion. You almost have to expect an old doll to show minor wear; perhaps there is a rub on the nose (a vulnerable spot) or cheek, a chipped earring hole, wear on the hair of an old papier-mache or china head doll, or scuffed toes or missing fingers on an old composition body—these are to be expected and do not affect the value of the doll. Certainly, an old doll in never-played-with condition, all-original hair and clothes, labeled, in its original box is every collector's dream—and would carry the highest of all prices for that type. Unless the doll is rare and you particularly want it, do not pay top price for a doll which needs extensive work: restringing, setting eyes, replacing body parts, new wig, dressing—all these repairs add up to a considerable sum at the doll hospital. As for the composition dolls, you should expect a more nearly perfect condition if you are paying top price—original hair, clothes, little or no crazing, good coloring and tag, if possible. However, dolls in this condition are becoming harder to find. Pay less for a doll which does not have original clothes; even less for a damaged one. On the hard plastics and vinyls, you should expect mint condition for top price; original clothes would be a must.

Body

Check over the *body* of the doll. For a top price, an old doll should have the original or an appropriate old body in good condition. If a doll does not have the right body, you could conceivably end up not with a complete doll, but with two parts—head and body—not worth as much as one whole doll. Minor damage or repair to an old body scarcely affects the value of the doll. An original body carefully repaired is preferable to a new one. If you have a choice, a good quality ball-jointed composition body is more desirable than a crudely made five-piece body or a stick-type body with just pieces of wood for upper arms and legs, but unfortunately many of the small German character heads came on these crude bodies, and collectors just have to live with them. Occasionally the body adds value to the doll. For instance, in the case of bisque heads, a small doll with a completely jointed body, a French fashion-type with jointed toddler-type body would all be higher in price because of their special bodies. On the all-composition dolls, a body in poor condition, cracked and peeling, greatly reduces the value of the doll. The same is true of a vinyl doll with stains on the body.

Clothing

Look at the *clothing* critically in considering the value of the doll. Because as the years go by fabrics deteriorate, it is becoming increasingly difficult to find dolls in old clothes. As a result, many collectors are willing to pay more for an antique doll if it has old clothes. When the clothing has been replaced on an antique doll, it should be appropriate for the age of the doll, made in types of fabrics and styles which would have been in vogue when the doll was produced. Original clothes are, of course, highly desirable and even carefully mended ones would be preferable to new clothes. However, it is often difficult to determine whether or not the clothes are original or simply just old. Many old dolls came undressed or clad only in a chemise and were dressed at home. A doll with original clothes is certainly more valuable, but whether or not these clothes are retained on the doll seems to be a matter of personal preference among collectors, many of whom enjoy dressing their own dolls. If you do feel that you want to redress your dolls, show respect for the original clothes and keep them in a labeled bag or box for giving to the next owner should you ever sell your doll, or pass it down to a younger member of the family, for dolls are heirlooms and you are only the keeper for a short time in history. Again, to bring top price, a modern doll must have original clothes; replaced clothing would greatly affect the price. Also without the clothing it is often impossible to identify a modern doll as so many were made using the same face mold.

Total Originality

Having already discussed body, wig, eyes and clothes, this would seem to be a good place to put in a word about the *total originality* of an antique doll. Some collectors feel that an antique doll which they are sure has all original parts and clothes is much more valuable than one which has replaced wig, body parts, eyes, pate, clothes, and so on. They try to be sure that the head and body and all other parts are not only appropriate, but have always been together. Of course, this is not always possible to determine when a doll has seen hard play for several generations or has passed through many hands before reaching the collector. But sometimes if you know the original source of the doll, you can be reasonably sure by using a little knowledge as well as common sense. Again, this is a matter of personal preference and totally original dolls nowadays are few and far between.

15in (38.1cm) Oriental #220. *Mary Lou Rubright Collection.*

16in (40.6cm) French Fashion. *Mary Lou Rubright Collection.*

19in (48.3cm) A.M. 1894, all original with label. *H&J Foulke.*

16in (40.6cm) French Fashion. *Mary Lou Rubright Collection.*

Size

Take into account the *size* of the doll in determining the price. Usually price and size are related for a certain type of doll—a smaller size is lower, a larger size is higher. The greatest variances of price to size occur at the extremes, either a very small or a very large doll. On the large side, bisque head dolls, especially over 30in (76.2cm) are in demand and rising in price; the large 36in (91.4cm) vinyl Shirley Temple and the 30in (76.2cm) composition Patsy Mae are very difficult to find. On the tiny side, the small closed-mouth Jumeau and the composition Wee Patsy are examples in the opposite direction, bringing higher prices than comparable average-sized dolls.

Age

Another point to consider in pricing your doll is the *age* of the doll. An early Queen Anne wood doll is more greatly valued than a late 19th century penny wooden. However, curiously enough to some, the oldest dolls do not necessarily command the highest prices. A lovely old china head with exquisite work and very unusual hairdo would bring a good price, but not as much as a 20th century, S.F.B.J. 252 Pouty. Many desirable composition dolls of the 1930s and fairly recent but discontinued Alexander dolls are selling at prices higher than older bisque dolls of 1900—1920. So, in determining price, the age of the doll may or may not be significant, according to the specific type.

So far, except for the aspect of personal appeal, the factors which we have considered in pricing a doll have been physical and tangible—the marks, the quality of craftsmanship, condition, clothing, size and age. But here are still several others; these might be called the intangible factors.

Availability

Perhaps most important here would be the *availability* of the doll— how easy to difficult it is to find. Each year brings more new doll collectors than it brings newly-discovered desirable old dolls; hence, the supply is diminished. As long as the demand for certain antique and collectible dolls is greater than the supply, prices will rise. This explains the gigantic increase in the prices of less common dolls, such as the Brus, K★R and S.F.B.J. characters, googlies, and some Alexanders which were made for only a limited period of time, and the more gentle rise in dolls which are fairly common, primarily, the German girl or child dolls which were made over a longer period of time. The price you pay should be consistent with the availability of the doll.

Popularity

Sometimes, however, it is the *popularity* of a certain doll which makes the price rise. This is currently true with dolls such as Shirley Temples, Jumeaus, Bye-los and Alexanders which still seem to be fairly plentiful, yet rising in price, because they are popular and many collectors want them enough to be willing to pay a price that might be higher than the availability factor warrants.

Uniqueness

Sometimes the *uniqueness* of a doll makes price determination very difficult. If you never have seen a doll exactly like it before, and it is not given in the price guide or pictured in any books, deciding what to pay can be a problem, especially if you are not sure of the reliability of the seller. In this case, you have to use the knowledge you have as a frame of reference in which to place the doll. For instance, you find a doll which you really like, an 18in (45.7cm) girl marked A.M. 2000. It is not pictured anywhere and you cannot find it in the price guide—yet you have looked at hundreds of dolls and have never seen one before, so you know from experience it is not common. The dealer is asking $50 more than the price of a common number A.M. girl in the same size and condition. You have to decide on your own whether or not the doll is worth the price to you. (I think it would be!)

Selling Price

Of course, another important factor which helps determine what price goes on the doll in the shop, is the price the dealer had to pay for it. In buying a doll, a dealer has to consider everything discussed here, in addition to whether or not there is the possibility of making a reasonable profit on the doll. Contrary to what many collectors believe, dealers in antique dolls do not make enormous profits. Their margin of profit is not nearly so high as that of the proprietor of a shop which sells new items. This is primarily due to the availability factor already discussed. Old dolls cannot be ordered from a wholesale catalog. Most are coming from estates or collections, whose owners, understandably enough, want to get as much as they can for their dolls. To the price which he must pay a dealer adds his percentage of profit and comes up with a dollar amount for the tag.

Buying Price

The last factor to consider about doll prices is that the price guide gives the retail price of a doll if obtained by a collector from a dealer, whereas actually a doll might have several types of buying prices. This idea is pointed out by Ceil Chandler. First, a dealer when buying stock could not pay the prices listed; he must buy somewhat lower if he expects to sell at a profit. In order to obtain stock, a dealer looks to disbursement of estates, auctions, collectors and other dealers as possible sources—all of which are also available to collectors who can purchase from these sources at the same prices that dealers can. Second, a dealer would expect to pay less per doll if he bought a collection or a large lot than if he purchased them individually. A third type of price would prevail if a collector buys from another collector; in this case, you would probably pay less than when buying from a dealer. The fourth type of price is the "lucky" price you might find at a shop, garage sale, flea market or just about anywhere that there might be an old doll!

Hopefully, in this chapter, we have presented some ideas which might be of help to you in purchasing your next doll or in evaluating dolls which you already own. And we hope that you will enjoy many, many hours of pleasure as you build your doll collection.

Acknowledgements

A book of this type is the result of not only the author's own talents and energies, but also the encouragement, assistance, and cooperation of friends, associates, and family.

My thanks and appreciation, therefore, is given - -

To my husband, Howard, not only for his lovely photographs, but also for believing in me.

To my daughter, Beth, for her help in filing and clerical work as well as her understanding and patience.

To the many doll collectors, friends, and dealers whose encouragement and support have made this edition possible.

To those friends who allowed us to photograph their dolls to be used in this book: Mary Lou Rubright, Joanna Ott, Richard Wright, Mike White, Betty Harms, Marjorie Yocum, Vivian Flagg, Maxine Salaman, Edna Black, Rosemary Dent, Virginia Slade, The Doll Royalle, Barbara Doyle, Barbara Crescenze, Grace Dyar, Miriam Blankman, Glenn Mandeville, Chip Barkel, Jan Naibert, Ann Lloyd, William Crandall, Nancy Smith, Barbara Steiker, Emma Wedmore, Becky Roberts, Gail Hiatt, Jilda Sallade, Old Curiosity Shop, Louise Ceglia, Betty Ferrell, Esther Schwartz, Mary Goolsby, Gordon Hitchings, Nancy Schwartz Blaisure, Elizabeth McIntyre, Violet Mackemull, Joan Kindler, and Barbara Foster.

To friends who sent photographs of their own dolls: Jane Sheetz, Eileen Wincklhofer, Sheila Needle, Alma Wolfe, and Anarene Barr.

To the Colemans who allowed some of the doll marks to be reproduced from their book, *The Collector's Encyclopedia of Dolls.*

To Virginia Heyerdahl and Donna Felger, my editors, and Gary Ruddell, my publisher.

Without all of these people, this 4th BLUE BOOK OF DOLLS AND VALUES would not be a reality.

ABG

MAKER: Alt, Beck & Gottschalck, Nauendorf, Thüringia, Germany
DATE: 1893—on
MATERIAL: Bisque head, composition body
SIZE: Various
MARK:

Child Doll: Ca. 1893—on. Mold number 1362. Bisque head, good wig, sleep eyes, open mouth; ball-jointed body; dressed, all in good condition.

Size		
16—18in	(40.6—45.7cm)	$200-225
20—22in	(50.8—55.9cm)	250-275
24—26in	(61.0—66.0cm)	325-350
32in	(81.3cm)	550
40—42in	(101.6—106.6cm)	1000-1200

Character Baby: 1910—on. Mold numbers 1361, 1352. Bisque head, open mouth, sleep eyes, good wig, open nostrils; composition body; suitably dressed; nice condition with bent-limb baby body.

10—12in	(25.4—30.5cm)	$225-250*
15—18in	(38.1—45.7cm)	300-350*
21—24in	(53.3—61.0cm)	400-450*

    *Allow extra for toddler body

ABOVE: 19in (48.3cm) ABG 1361 character girl, all original. *Mary Lou Rubright Collection.*

LEFT: 11in (27.9cm) ABG 1352 character baby. *Joanna Ott Collection.*

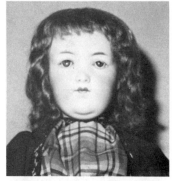

A.M.
(Armand Marseille)

MAKER: Armand Marseille of Köppelsdorf,
Thüringia, Germany

DATE: Ca. 1890—on

MATERIAL: Bisque socket and shoulder
head, composition, cloth or
kid body

SIZE: Various

MARK: Armand Marseille
Germany
990
——————— A 9/0 M ———————

Child Doll: Ca. 1890—on. Mold numbers such as 390, 1894, 370, 3200.
Also sometimes horseshoe mark.
Bisque head, composition ball-jointed body or jointed kid body with
bisque lower arms, nice wig, set
or sleep eyes, open mouth, pretty
clothes; all in good condition.

#390

8—9in (20.3—22.9cm) Five-piece body	$100-125
8—10in (20.3—25.4cm) Fully jointed body	125-150
14—16in (35.6—40.6cm)	180-200
18—20in (45.7—50.8cm)	200-225
22—24in (55.9—61.0cm)	250-325
28—30in (71.1—76.2cm)	400-450
34—36in (86.4—91.4cm)	650-750
40—42in (101.6—106.6cm)	1000-1200

#370, 3200

20—22in (50.8—55.9cm)	225-250

#1894

15—18in (38.1—45.7cm)	275-300
20—22in (50.8—55.9cm)	325-350

Florodora (Ball-jointed composition or
kid body): Ca. 1901—on.

16—18in (40.6—45.7cm)	200-225
25—26in (63.5—66.0cm)	350-375

Queen Louise: Ca. 1910—on.

24—26in (61.0—66.0cm)	325-375
28—30in (71.1—76.2cm)	400-425
34—36in (86.4—91.4cm)	650-750

TOP: 24in (61.0cm) A.M. #400
character. *Esther Schwartz Collec-*

MIDDLE: 8½in (21.6cm) A.M.
390, all original. *H&J Foulke.*

BOTTOM: 22in (55.9cm) A.M.
1894. *H&J Foulke.*

Character Baby: 1910–on. Mold numbers such as 990, 992, 985, 971, 996, etc. Bisque head, composition bent-limb body, sleep eyes, open mouth some with teeth, good wig, suitably dressed; all in nice condition.

Mold #990, 985, 971, 996, and other common numbers:

10–12in (25.4–30.5cm)
$225-250*
15–17in (38.1–43.2cm)
300-350*
21–24in (53.3–61.0cm)
400-450*

#233

15in (38.1cm) $325-375

*Allow extra for toddler body

23in (58.4cm) "Queen Louise". *Mary Lou Rubright Collection.*

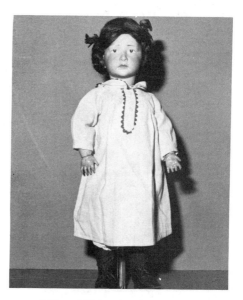

15in (38.1cm) A.M. pouty girl with intaglio eyes. *Esther Schwartz Collection.*

14in (35.6cm) A.M. 985. *H&J Foulke.*

10in (25.4cm) A.M. 248, closed mouth with tongue between lips. *H&J Foulke.*

Character Children: 1910—on. Mold numbers such as 500, 550, 590, 600, etc. Bisque head, glass or painted eyes, molded hair or wig, open or closed mouth. Composition body. Dressed. All in good condition.

#500
10—12in (25.4—30.5cm) $300-350
550
16—18in (40.6—45.7cm)1500-1600
560a
16—18in (40.6—45.7cm)   450-550
590
16—18in (40.6—45.7cm)1250-1350
248, open/closed mouth
10—12in (25.4—30.5cm)   800**
Fany #231, wigged
15—18in (38.1—45.7cm)   2200**

**Not enough price samples to compute a reliable range

18in (45.7cm) A.M. 590 character toddler. *Esther Schwartz Collection.*

15in (38.1cm) A.M. 560a. *Mary Lou Rubright Collection.*

19in (48.3cm) A.M. 550. *Richard Wright Collection.*

Lady: 1910–1930. Mold number 401. Bisque head with mature face, mohair wig, sleep eyes, open or closed mouth; composition lady body with molded bust, long slender arms and legs; appropriate clothes; all in good condition.

#401
14in (35.6cm) $650-1300*
    Painted bisque, 14in (35.6cm) $400-450**
#400, closed mouth
24in (61.0cm) $2200**

10in   (25.4cm)
A.M. G.B. 250.
Betty Harms Collection.

*Prices on this doll are not stable.

**Not enough price samples to compute a reliable range

Infant: 1924—on. Mold numbers 351 (open mouth) or 341 (closed mouth). Solid-dome bisque head with molded and/or painted hair, sleep eyes; composition body or hard-stuffed jointed cloth body or soft-stuffed cloth body; all in good condition. Dressed.

351 and **341**
Head circumference:

8—10in (20.3—25.4cm)	$225-275
12—13in (30.5—33.0cm)	325-375
15in (38.1cm)	425

16in (40.6cm) A.M. 341 infant. *H&J Foulke.*

ABOVE: 13in (33.0cm) A.M. 401 lady. *Mike White Collection.*

RIGHT: 13in (33.0cm) A.M. 351 infant. *H&J Foulke.*

A.T.

MAKER: Probably by A. Thuillier, Paris, France
DATE: 1875–1890
MATERIAL: Bisque socket head on wooden, kid, or composition body
SIZE: Size 2 is usually 12in (30.5cm); size 14 is 29in (73.7cm)
MARK: A. T. and size number (2–14 known) incised as shown or with size number between the A and T

AT·N° 8

Marked A. T. Child: Perfect bisque head, paperweight eyes, pierced ears, closed mouth, cork pate, good wig. Body of wood, kid or composition in good condition. Appropriate clothes.

20in (50.8cm) $10,000**up
**Not enough price samples to compute a reliable range

22in (55.9cm) A.T., composition body. *Mary Lou Rubright Collection.*

A.W.

MAKER: Adolf Wislizenus of Waltershausen, Thüringia, Germany
DATE: About 1890—on
MATERIAL: Bisque head, composition ball-jointed body
SIZE: Various
MARK: "A. W.", "A. W." over "W", "A. W. SPECIAL", sometimes with
"Germany" added, sometimes "OLD GLORY" etc.

Germany
A.W.
0

Wislizenus Child Doll: Marked bisque head, composition ball-jointed
body, blue or brown sleep eyes, open mouth, good wig, dressed. All in
good condition. 22—25in (55.9—63.5cm) $250-325

24in (61.0cm) A.W. *Mary Lou Rubright
Collection.*

Alabama Indestructible Doll

MAKER: Ella Smith Doll Co., Roanoke, Ala.
DATE: 1904–on
MATERIAL: All-cloth
SIZE: Various
MARK: On torso:

PAT. NOV. 9, 1912.
NO. 2
ELLA SMITH DOLL CO.

Alabama Baby: All-cloth painted with oils, tab-jointed shoulders and hips, painted hair and features, molded face, applied ears, painted stockings and shoes. Appropriate clothes, all in good condition.
$450-500**
**Not enough price samples to compute a reliable range

Alabama Baby, 14in (35.6cm) tall. *Mary Merritt's Doll Museum.*

Madame Alexander

MAKER: Alexander Doll Co., New York, N.Y., U.S.A.

DATE: 1923–on

MARK: Dolls themselves marked in various ways, usually "ALEXANDER". Clothing has a white cloth label with blue lettering sewn into a seam which says "MADAME ALEXANDER" and usually the name of the specific doll.

CLOTH

Alice In Wonderland: Ca. 1930. All-cloth with one-piece arms and legs sewed on. Flat face with hand-painted features, large round eyes, O-shaped mouth, yellow yarn hair. Original blue and white dress with apron. All in good condition. 16in (40.6cm) $250-300**

**Not enough price samples to compute a reliable range

Cloth Character Dolls: Ca. 1933 through the 1930s. All cloth with one-piece arms and legs sewed on. Molded mask face of felt or flocked fabric, painted eyes to side, mohair wigs. Original clothes tagged with name of particular doll. Produced characters from *Little Women,* Charles Dickens, Longfellow and other literary works as well as storybook characters.

16in (40.6cm) $250-300

ABOVE: 16in (40.6cm) "David Copperfield" and "Little Emily", all original. *Marjorie Yocum Collection.*

LEFT: 20in (50.8cm) cloth "Alice in Wonderland", all original. *Vivian C. Flagg Collection.*

Little Shaver: 1942. Stuffed pink stocking body, curved arms, tiny waist, mask face with large painted eyes to side, tiny mouth, floss wig glued on; original clothes, all in good condition. Various sizes.

MARK: Cloth dress tag:
"Little Shaver
Madame Alexander
New York
All Rights Reserved."

10–12in (25.4–30.5cm) $150
16in (40.6cm)   200-225

ABOVE: 10in (25.4cm) "Little Shaver", all original. *H&J Foulke.*

LEFT: "Pinky", all original. *Maxine Salaman Collection.*

BELOW: 18in (45.7cm) "Baby McGuffey", all original except booties. *H&J Foulke.*

COMPOSITION

Babies: 1936—on. Composition head, hands and legs, cloth bodies, sleep eyes, molded hair or wigged, open or closed mouth. Original clothes. All in good condition. Various sizes.

MARK: On dolls:
ALEXANDER
On clothing: "Little Genius", "Baby McGuffey", "Pinky", "Precious", "Butch", "Bitsey", etc.

16–18in (40.6–45.7cm) $125-175

11in (27.9cm) Tony Sarg Marionette. *Edna Black Collection.*

10in (25.4cm) Dionne Baby "Cecile", all original. *H&J Foulke.*

Tony Sarg Marionettes: 1934. Composition character faces, composition torso, arms, and legs with painted shoes, cloth upper limbs; original clothes; all in good condition.

10–12in (25.4–30.5cm)
$100-125

MARK: on torso:

TONY SARG
ALEXANDER
on head: TONY
SARG
on clothing: Madame   Alexander sometimes with the name of the character.

9in   (22.9cm) "Swiss",   all original.   *H&J Foulke.*

Dionne Quintuplets: 1935.   All-composition with swivel head, jointed hips and shoulders, toddler or bent-limb legs, sleep or painted eyes, wigs or molded   hair,   original clothing. All in good condition.

MARK: "ALEXANDER", sometimes "DIONNE"
Clothing Label:
GENUINE
DIONNE QUINTUPLET DOLLS
ALL RIGHTS RESERVED
MADAME ALEXANDER, N.Y.
OR
DIONNE QUINTUPLET
(her name)
EXCLUSIVE LICENSEE
MADAM ALEXANDER DOLL CO. [sic]

7–8in (17.8–20.3cm)	$100-110
10–11in (25.4–27.9cm)	175-200
13in (33.0cm)	200-225
16in (40.6cm)	225-250

Foreign and Storyland:
7–9in (17.8–22.9cm). Ca. 1935 to mid 1940s. All-composition with one-piece head and body on smaller ones and separate head on larger ones, painted eyes, mohair wig, jointed shoulders and hips. Original tagged clothes. All in good condition. Made children to represent foreign lands as well as storybook characters.
MARK: On back:
    Mme. Alexander
7–9in (17.8–22.9cm)
            $100-125*
*More for special characters

13in (33.0cm) "Little Colonel", all original. *H&J Foulke.*

Dopey: 1938. Composition character head, cloth body, original felt outfit.
13in (33.0cm) $125

Little Colonel: 1935. All-composition with swivel head, jointed hips and shoulders, sleep eyes, dimples, closed mouth, mohair wig, original clothing. All in good condition.
MARK: ALEXANDER
13–14in (33.0–35.6cm)
            $400-450**

**Not enough price samples to compute a reliable range

13in (33.0cm) "Dopey", all original. *H&J Foulke.*

Baby Jane: 1935. All-composition with swivel head, jointed hips and shoulders, sleep eyes, open mouth, mohair wig. Original clothes. All in good condition.
MARK: On head:
    Baby Jane
    Reg Mme. Alexander
16in (40.6cm) $300**
**Not enough price samples to compute a reliable range.

Princess Elizabeth: 1937. All-composition jointed at neck, shoulders and hips; mohair wig, sleep eyes, open mouth; original clothes. All in good condition. Various sizes.
MARK: On head:
    PRINCESS ELIZABETH
    ALEXANDER DOLL CO.
On dress tag:
    "Princess Elizabeth"

13in (33.0cm) $150-175
18in (45.7cm)   225-250

16in (40.6cm) "Princess Elizabeth", all original. *Mary Lou Rubright Collection.*

16in (40.6cm) "Snow White", all original. *Mary Lou Rubright Collection.*

Snow White: 1937. All-composition jointed at neck, shoulders and hips; black mohair wig, brown sleep eyes, very pale complexion, closed mouth. Original clothes. All in good condition. Various sizes.
MARK: On head:
    PRINCESS ELIZABETH
    ALEXANDER DOLL CO.
On dress tag: "Snow White"
13in (33.0cm) $150-175
16in (40.6cm)   200-225

Flora McFlimsey: 1938. All-composition jointed at neck, shoulders and hips, sleep eyes, open mouth, freckles on nose, human hair wig with bangs; original clothes. All in good condition. Various sizes.
MARK: On head:
    PRINCESS ELIZABETH
    ALEXANDER DOLL CO.
On dress: "Flora McFlimsey
        of Madison Square
    by Madame Alexander, N.Y."

13—15in (33.0—38.1cm) $250-300

Kate Greenaway: 1938. All-composition with swivel head, jointed shoulders and hips, blonde wig, sleep eyes, with lashes, open mouth; original clothes. All in good condition. Various sizes.
MARK: On head:
PRINCESS ELIZABETH
ALEXANDER DOLL CO.
On dress tag:
"Kate Greenaway"

15–18in (38.1–45.7cm) $300-350

RIGHT: 20in (50.8cm) "Kate Greenaway", all original. *Maxine Salaman.*

McGuffey Ana: 1937. All-composition jointed at shoulders, hips and neck, sleep eyes, open mouth, human hair or mohair pigtails. Original clothes. All in good condition. Various sizes.
MARK: On head:
PRINCESS ELIZABETH
ALEXANDER
On dress tag: "McGuffey Ana"

9in (22.9cm) $125
12–13in (30.5–33.0cm)   150
16–18in (40.6–45.7cm)175-200
20in (50.8cm)   250

11in (27.9cm) "McGuffey Ana", closed mouth, all original. *H&J Foulke.*

Wendy–Ann: 1936. All-composition with swivel head, jointed at neck, shoulders, hips and waist, sleep eyes, closed mouth, human hair wig, original clothing; all in good condition.
MARK: "WENDY-ANN
MME ALEXANDER"

14in (35.6cm) $200-225
9in (22.9cm) Painted eyes   125

RIGHT: 16in (40.6cm) "McGuffey Ana", all original. *H&J Foulke.*

Karen Ballerina: 1946. All-composition jointed at neck, shoulders and hips, closed mouth, sleep eyes, blonde wig with coiled braids and flowers; original clothes. All in good condition. Various sizes.

MARK: On head:
     ALEXANDER
on Dress tag:
     "Madame Alexander"

18–21in (45.7–53.2cm) $250-300

Scarlet O'Hara: 1937. All-composition jointed at neck, shoulders and hips; original black wig, green sleep eyes, closed mouth; original clothes. All in good condition. Various sizes.

MARK: On dress tag:
     "Scarlet O'Hara
     Madame Alexander
     N.Y. U.S.A.
     All rights reserved"

11in (27.9cm)	$200
18in (45.7cm)	300-350

LEFT: 21in (53.2cm) "Karen Ballerina", all original. *H&J Foulke.*

BELOW: 11in (27.9cm) "Scarlett O'Hara", all original. *H&J Foulke.*

14in (35.6cm) "Fairy Princess", all original. *H&J Foulke.*

Fairy Princess: 1942. Composition jointed at neck, shoulders and hips, closed mouth, sleep eyes, mohair wig; original clothes including tiara and necklace. All in good condition. Various sizes.
MARK: On head:
MME. ALEXANDER
On dress:
"Fairy Princess"

14in (35.6cm) $200-225

Madelaine: 1940. All-composition jointed at neck, shoulders, and hips, closed mouth, sleep eyes, dark wig, original clothes; all in good condition.
MARK: On head:
ALEXANDER
On dress tag: Madelaine or Madelaine Du Baine

14in (35.6cm) $225-250
18in (45.7cm)   275-300

Bride and Bridesmaids: 1940–on. All-composition jointed at neck, shoulders and hips, closed mouth, sleep eyes, mohair wigs; original clothes. All in good condition. Various sizes.
MARK: On head:
MME ALEXANDER
On dress: ·
"Madame Alexander"

14in (35.6cm) $125-150
18in (45.7cm)   200
21in (53.3cm)   250

Alice in Wonderland: 1947. All-composition jointed at neck, shoulders and hips, closed mouth, sleep eyes, blonde wig; original clothes. All in good condition. Various sizes.
MARK: On head:
ALEXANDER
On dress tag: "Alice in Wonderland"

Composition:
13–14in (33.0–35.6cm)
                    $150-175
18in (45.7cm)   225-250

From 1948–on, in hard plastic:
14–15in (35.6–38.1cm)
                    $200-225

UPPER RIGHT: 18in (45.7cm) "Alice in Wonderland"; Wendy face on left, Margaret face on right. *H&J Foulke.*

BOTTOM RIGHT: 14in (35.6cm) Bridesmaid, all original. *H&J Foulke.*

Carmen (Miranda):   1942. Composition jointed at neck, shoulders and hips, closed mouth, sleep eyes, black mohair wig; original clothes including turban and gold-hoop earrings. All in good condition.Various sizes.

MARK: On head: MME. ALEXANDER
       On dress: "Carmen
              Madame Alexander, N.Y. U.S.A.
                 All Rights Reserved"
13—16in (33.0—40.6cm) $200-225**   **Not enough price samples to
                                          compute a reliable range.

Portrait Dolls: 1940s. All-composition jointed at neck, shoulders and hips, closed mouth, sleep eyes, mohair or human hair wigs, painted fingernails, original clothes; all in good condition. Came with green cloverleaf wrist tag.

MARK: None on doll; label inside dress:
              "Madame Alexander"
21in (53.3cm) $400-450

Jeannie Walker: 1941. Composition jointed at neck, shoulders and hips with walking mechanism; sleep eyes, closed mouth, human hair or mohair wig; original clothes. All in good condition.

MARK: On body:
ALEXANDER/PAT. NO. 2171281
On dress: "Jeannie Walker—
Madame Alexander—N.Y., U.S.A.
All rights reserved"

13—14in (33.0—35.6cm) $200

Jane Withers: 1937. All-composition with swivel head, jointed shoulders and hips, dark mohair wig, sleep eyes, open smiling mouth. Original clothes. All in good condition. Various sizes.

MARK: On dress:

              "Jane Withers
           All Rights Reserved
         Madame Alexander, N.Y."

18in (45.7cm) "Jeannie Walker",
all original. *Rosemary Dent Collection.*

15—16in (38.1—40.6cm) $650
20in (50.8cm)   750-850

Sonja Henie: 1939. All-composition jointed at neck, shoulders and hips, smiling open mouth with teeth, sleep eyes, human hair or mohair wig; original clothes; all in good condition. Various sizes. 14in (35.6cm) can be found on the WENDY ANN body with swivel waist.

MARK: On back of neck:
MADAME ALEXANDER—SONJA HENIE
On dress: "Sonja Henie"

13—14in (33.0—35.6cm) $200-225

18in (38.1cm)   275-300

21in (53.3cm) "Sonja Henie", replaced clothes. *Mary Lou Rubright Collection.*

Special Girl: 1942. Composition head, shoulder plate, arms, and legs; cloth torso; blonde braids. Doll unmarked; clothing tagged "Madame Alexander".
22in (55.9cm) tall. $250

Margaret O'Brien: 1946. All-composition jointed at neck, shoulders and hips, closed mouth, sleep eyes, dark wig in braids; original clothes. All in good condition. Various sizes.
MARK: On head: ALEXANDER
On dress tag: Madame Alexander
          "Margaret O'Brien"

18—21in (45.7—53.3cm) $550-650

HARD PLASTIC

18in (45.7cm) "Margot Ballerina", all original. *H&J Foulke.*

Margaret Face: 1948—on. All-hard plastic jointed at neck, shoulders, and hips, closed mouth, sleep eyes, lovely wig; original clothes tagged with name of doll; all in excellent condition. All prices for the 14in (35.6cm) size except Wendy Ann, which is 18in (45.7cm).

Nina Ballerina, 1949—1951. $175-200	Wendy Ann, 1947—1948.		
Fairy Queen, 1947—1948.	200-225		$225-250
Babs, 1948—1949.	200-225	Cinderella, 1950.	400
Margaret Rose, 1948—1953?	200-225	Prince Charming, 1950.	500
Margaret O'Brien, 1948.	400-450	Cynthia (black), 1952—1953.	500

ABOVE: 17in (43.2cm) "Wendy Ann", all original. *H&J Foulke.*

LEFT: 17in (43.2cm) "Margaret Rose", all original. *H&J Foulke.*

ABOVE: 14in (35.6cm) Little Women "Meg", all original. *H&J Foulke.*

RIGHT: 14in (35.4cm) "Cinderella", all original. *Edna Black Collection.*

Little Women: 1948–1956. All-hard plastic jointed at neck, shoulders and hips, closed mouth, sleep eyes, synthetic wigs; original clothes. All in good condition.

MARK: On head: ALEXANDER (used both "Maggie" and "Margaret" faces)
On clothes tag: "Meg", "Jo", "Beth", "Amy" and "Marme"

14–15in (35.6–38.1cm) $175-225
Amy with loop curls   275-300
Little Men   500

Godey Ladies: 1950. All-hard plastic, jointed at neck, shoulders, and hips; sleep eyes, lovely wigs; original period costumes; all in excellent condition.   14in (35.6cm) $400

Glamour Girls: 1953. All-hard plastic, jointed at neck, shoulders, and hips; walkers; lovely human hair wigs; original period costumes; all in excellent condition.
18in (45.7cm) $400-500

RIGHT: 15in (38.1cm) Little Men "Nat", all original. *Maxine Salaman Collection.*

BOTTOM LEFT: 14in (35.6cm) Godey Lady, all original. *Maxine Salaman Collection.*

BOTTOM RIGHT: 18in (45.7cm) Glamour Girl, all original. *Maxine Salaman Collection.*

Maggie Face: 1948–1956. All-hard plastic, jointed at neck, shoulders, and hips; closed mouth, sleep eyes, good quality wig; original clothes tagged with the name of the doll; all in excellent condition.

Maggie, 1948–1953.
   14in (35.6cm) $150-175
Polly Pigtails, 1949.
   14in (35.6cm)   200-225
Kathy, 1951.
   14in (35.6cm)   300
Alice in Wonderland, 1950–1951.
   14in (35.6cm)   200-225
Annabelle, 1952.
   14in (35.6cm)   200-225

17in (43.2cm) "Maggie", all original. *Maxine Salaman Collection.*

18in (45.7cm) "Alice in Wonderland", all original. *H&J Foulke.*

14in (35.6cm) "Polly Pigtails", all original. *H&J Foulke*

Winnie and Binnie: 1953–1955. All-hard plastic, walking body, later with jointed knees and vinyl arms; closed mouth, sleep eyes, lovely wig; original clothes; all in excellent condition.

15in (38.1cm) $125-150
18in (45.7cm)   200-225

18in (45.7cm) "Binnie Walker", all original. *Edna Black Collection.*

Cissy: 1955–1959. Head, torso and jointed legs of hard plastic; jointed vinyl arms; synthetic wig, sleep eyes, pierced ears, closed mouth; original clothes; all in good condition.
MARK: On head:
       ALEXANDER
    On dress tag: "Cissy"
21in (53.3cm) $150-250*

*Depending upon costume

21in (53.3cm) "Cissy", missing hat. *Mary Lou Rubright Collection.*

Elise: 1957–1964. All-hard plastic with vinyl arms, completely jointed; closed mouth, sleep eyes, lovely wig; original clothes; all in excellent condition.

16½in (41.9cm) $150-225*

*Depending upon costume

17in (43.2cm) "Elise", all original. *H&J Foulke.*

Sleeping Beauty: 1959. All-hard plastic with vinyl arms, completely jointed; closed mouth, sleep eyes, blonde wig; original clothes; all in excellent condition. 16½in (41.9cm) $350

Shari Lewis: 1959. All-hard plastic with slim fashion body; closed mouth, auburn hair, brown eyes; original clothes; all in excellent condition.

14in (35.6cm)	$250
21in (53.3cm)	400

Maggie Mixup: 1960–1961. All-hard plastic, fully jointed; red straight hair, freckles, green eyes, closed mouth; original clothes; all in excellent condition. 16½in (41.9cm) $225

14in (35.6cm) "Shari Lewis", all original. *H&J Foulke.*

RIGHT: 17in (43.2cm) "Maggie Mixup", all original. *H&J Foulke.*

Lissy: 1956–1958. All-hard plastic jointed at neck, shoulders, hips, elbows and knees; sleep eyes, synthetic wig, closed mouth; original clothes; all in good condition.

MARK: None on doll
On dress tag: "Lissy"
or name of character
12in (30.5cm) $275-300

12in (30.5cm) "Lissy", all original. *H&J Foulke.*

Little Women, 1957–1967. $200
Laurie, 1967.   400
Kelly: 1959. Same doll as Lissy but does not have jointed elbows and knees; original clothes; all in excellent condition.   12in (30.5cm) $300
Cissette: 1957–1963. All-hard plastic jointed at neck, shoulders, hips and knees; sleep eyes, synthetic wig, closed mouth, pierced ears; original clothes; all in good condition.

MARK: None on doll
On dress tag: "Cissette"
        10in (25.4cm) $125 up*
        *Depending upon costume
Portrettes (Cissette face)

Jenny Lind	$400
Melinda	350-400
Godey	350-400
Southern Belle, 1968	300
Margot	350
Gibson Girl	550-600
Scarlett	250
Jacqueline	450-500

10in (25.4cm) "Cissette", all original. *Edna Black Collection.*

10in (25.4cm) "Southern Belle", all original. *Doll Royalle.*

10in (25.4cm) "Jacqueline", all original. *Virginia Slade Collection.*

Alexander-Kins: 1953. All-hard plastic jointed at neck, shoulders and hips, sleeping eyes, closed mouth, synthetic wig; original clothes. All in good condition. 1954–Walking mechanism added; discontinued in 1965. 1956–jointed knees were added.

MARK: On back of torso: ALEX
On dress tag: "Madame Alexander", "Alexander-Kins" or specific name of doll   7½–8in (19.1–20.3cm) $125*
        *More for special outfits

Little Genius: 1956–1962. Hard plastic head with short curly wig, sleep eyes, drinks and wets; vinyl torso, arms and legs. Original clothes; all in good condition. 8in (20.3cm) $100-125

VINYL

Sonja Henie: 1951. Character face with open smiling mouth and dimples; rooted hair; body of hard plastic; original clothes; all in excellent condition. 18in (45.7cm) $350-400**

**Not enough price samples to compute a reliable range.

Madelaine: 1952, 1953, 1961. Character face with rooted hair, ball-jointed hard plastic body; original clothes; all in excellent condition. 18in (45.7cm) $150-175

Kelly Face: 1958–on. Character face with rooted hair, vinyl arms, hard plastic torso and legs, jointed waist; original clothes; all in excellent condition. Mark on head:

Kelly, 1958–1959.
15in (38.1cm) $150-175
Pollyana, 1960–1961.
15in (38.1cm) $150-175   1958
Marybel, 1959–1965.
15in (38.1cm) In case $150-175
Edith, 1958–1959.
15in (38.1cm) 150-175

Miss Melinda: 1962–1963. Character face with smiling open/closed mouth and two painted upper teeth, swivel waist, vinyl arms, hard plastic torso and legs. Original clothes; all in excellent condition.

16in (40.6cm) $150-200

Mark on head: ALEXANDER
19©62

Smarty: 1962–1963. Hard plastic and vinyl; smiling character face with rooted hair; knock-kneed and pigeon-toes; original clothes; in excellent condition. 12in (30.5cm) $100-125

Portrait Dolls: 1965 to present. Vinyl and hard plastic, rooted hair with elaborate hair styles; lovely original clothes; all in excellent condition. 21in (53.3cm) $200 up*

*Depending upon individual doll.

16in (40.6cm) "Edith", all original. *Barbara Doyle.*

7½in (19.1cm) Early Alex-
ander-Kin. *H&J Foulke.*

ABOVE: 12in (30.5cm) "Smarty",
with original clothes. *Barbara
Doyle.*
RIGHT: 21in (53.3cm) 1967
Godey Portrait. *Edna Black Collec-
tion.*

Coco: 1966. Vinyl and hard plastic, rooted blonde hair, jointed waist,
     right leg bent slightly at knee; original clothes; all in excellent condi-
     tion. This face was also used for the 1966 portrait dolls. 21in
          21in (53.3cm) $1350-1500

LEFT: 21in (53.3cm) "Coco"
Maxine Salaman Collection.
MIDDLE: 21in (53.3cm) "Jacque-
line", all original. *Edna Black
Collection.*

Jacqueline: 1961–1962. Vinyl and
hard plastic, closed mouth, sleep
eyes, rooted dark hair; original
clothes; all in excellent condition.
          21in (53.3cm) $600-650

Mary Ann Face: Introduced in
1965 and used widely to present a
variety of dolls. Only discontinued
dolls are listed here. Vinyl head
and arms; hard plastic torso and
legs; appropriate synthetic wig,
sleep eyes.

MARK: On head: ALEXANDER
                    19 © 65

14in (35.6cm) Easter Doll
with Mary Ann face; 8in
(20.3cm)   Alexander-Kins
Easter Doll. *Maxine Salaman
Collection.*

14in (35.3cm) only:

Madame, 1967–1975.	$200
Mary Ann, 1965.	250
Orphant Annie, 1965–1966.	
	225-250
Gidget, 1966.	250**
Little Granny, 1966.	150
Riley's Little Annie, 1967.	250
Renoir Girl, 1967–1971.	150-175
Scarlett #1495, 1968.	300**
McGuffey Ana #1450, 1968–1969	
	150
Jenny Lind & Cat, 1969–1971.	
	250
Jenny Lind, 1970.	400
Peter Pan, 1969.	275-300
Wendy, 1969	250
Grandma Jane, 1970–1972.	150
Disney Snow White to 1977.	300

          **Not enough price samples to
compule a reliable range.

15in (38.1cm) "Caroline", all original.
Rosemary Dent Collection.

Caroline: 1961–1962. Hard plastic and vinyl, smiling character face, rooted blonde hair; original clothes in excellent condition.
15in (38.1cm) $250

Polly Face: All-vinyl with rooted hair, jointed at neck, shoulders, and hips; original tagged clothes; all in excellent condition.
17in (43.2cm) tall

Polly, 1965. $125-150
Leslie, black, 1965–1971.   150

17in (43.2cm) "Polly", all original. *Edna Black Collection.*

Kathy: 1956–1962. All-vinyl jointed at neck, shoulders and hips; sleep eyes, molded or rooted hair, drinks and wets; original clothes; all in good condition. MARK: On dress tag: "Kathy"; also called "Kathy Cry Dolly" and "Kathy Tears" Various sizes.
15in (38.1cm) $65-75

Elise: 1966 to present. Vinyl face, rooted hair; original tagged clothes; all in excellent condition.
17in (43.2cm) $75-100*
Portrait Elise, 1973   200-225
*Discontinued styles only

Marlo, 1967. $500**

17in (43.2cm) "Marlo", all original. *Maxine Salaman Collection.*
**Not enough price samples to compute a reliable range.

Janie: 1964–1966. Vinyl and hard plastic with rooted hair, impish face, pigeon-toed and knock-kneed; original tagged clothes; all in excellent condition. 12in (30.5cm) $125   **Lucinda** $175

12in (30.5cm) "Lucinda", with Janie face, all original. *Vivian Flagg Collection.*

Littlest Kitten: 1963–1964. All-vinyl with rooted hair, jointed at neck, shoulders and hips; original tagged clothes; all in excellent condition. 8in (20.3cm) $100-125

8in (20.3cm) "Littlest Kittens". *Rosemary Dent and Barbara Crescenze Collections.*

Sound of Music: Large set 1965–1970; small set 1971–1973. All dolls of hard plastic and vinyl with appropriate synthetic wigs and sleep eyes; original clothes; all in good condition.

Sound of Music Prices   MARK: Each doll tagged as to character.

Small Set		Large Set	
8in (20.3cm) Friedrich	$95	11in (27.9cm) Friedrich	$135
8in (20.3cm) Gretl	95	11in (27.9cm) Gretl	135
8in (20.3cm) Marta	95	11in (27.9cm) Marta	135
10in (25.4cm) Brigitta	125	14in (35.6cm) Brigitta	150
12in (30.5cm) Maria	150	17in (43.2cm) Maria	200
10in (25.4cm) Louisa	250	14in (35.6cm) Louisa	200
10in (25.4cm) Liesl	250	14in (35.6cm) Liesl	200

ALL—BISQUE DOLLS

(German)

MAKER: Various German firms
DATE: Ca. 1880—on
MATERIAL: Bisque
SIZE: Various small sizes, most under 12in (30.5cm)
MARK: Some with Germany and/or numbers; some with paper labels on stomachs

---

All-Bisque with molded clothes: Ca. 1880—on. Jointed only at shoulders, molded and painted clothes or underwear; molded and painted hair, sometimes with molded hat; painted eyes, closed mouth, molded shoes and socks (if in underwear often barefoot); good quality work; all in good condition.

4in (10.2cm)	$65-85
5in (12.7cm)	100-115
6—7in (15.2—17.8cm)	125-175

4½in (11.5cm) Girl with molded underwear. *H&J Foulke.*

Girl with molded clothes made in a variety of small sizes. *H&J Foulke.*

3½in   (8.9cm)
Child,   molded
dress   covered
with green flock-
ing. *H&J Foulke.*

3in (7.6cm) jointed clown. *H&J Foulke.*

All-Bisque French-type: Ca. 1880—on. Jointed usually by wire or pegging at shoulders and hips, slender arms and legs, glass eyes, good wig, closed mouth, molded shoes or boots and stockings, dressed or undressed; all in good condition.

    3¼—4in (8.3—10.2cm) $125-150
      swivel neck   225-250
    6in (15.2cm)   225-250
    Black, 4-5in (10.2—12.7cm) 225

3¾in (9.6cm) French-type black bisque. *H&J Foulke.*

4in (10.2cm) French-type boy with swivel neck, all original. *Betty Harms Collection.*

4½in (11.5cm) French-type mulatto, brown bisque with molded arm and leg bracelets. *H&J Foulke.*

4in (10.2cm) French-type girl with tan stocking-painted legs, all original. *H&J Foulke.*

All-Bisque with glass eyes: Ca. 1890—on. Jointed at shoulders and hips, glass eyes, good wig, closed mouth, molded and painted shoes and stockings; dressed or undressed; all in good condition.

4—5in (10.2—12.7cm) $125-150
6—7in (15.2—17.8cm)   175-225
8in (20.3cm)   275-300

LEFT: 4in (10.2cm)   Girl with glass eyes, all   original. *H&J Foulke.*

RIGHT: 6in (15.2cm)   Girl with glass eyes. *H&J Foulke.*

All-Bisque with swivel neck and glass eyes: Ca. 1890—on. Jointed at neck, shoulders and hips, glass eyes, good wig, closed mouth, molded and painted shoes and stockings; dressed or undressed; all in good condition.

4—5in (10.2—12.7cm) $200-250
6—7in (15.2—17.8cm)   300-400
Bare feet
5—6in (12.7—15.2cm)   650-750

ABOVE: 4½in (11.5cm) Girl incised 620, swivel neck. *H&J Foulke.*

LEFT: 5in (12.7cm) Girl with swivel neck incised K★R, all original. *H&J Foulke.*

All-Bisque with swivel neck and glass eyes: Ca. 1890. Jointed at neck, shoulders and hips, glass sleep eyes, good wig, open mouth with teeth, molded brown shoes and molded long black or blue stockings; dressed or undressed; all in good condition. Sometimes marked S & H 886 or 890.

5—6in (12.7—15.2cm) $350-400
8—9in (22.9—25.4cm)   900-950

6in (15.2cm) Girl with swivel neck, long blue stockings. *Betty Harms Collection.*

All-Bisque with glass eyes: Ca. 1915. Jointed at shoulders and hips, glass eyes, good wig, closed or open mouth, molded and painted black one-strap shoes and stockings. Undressed or dressed; all in good condition.

4—5in (10.2—12.7cm) $100-125
7in (17.8cm)   150-175
11—12in (27.9—30.5cm) 750-850
Character face
5—5½in (12.7—14.0cm) 225-250

6in   (15.2cm)   Girl
incised 150.   *H&J*
Foulke.

4½in (11.5cm) Girl with painted eyes, black bootines. *H&J Foulke.*

All-Bisque with painted eyes: Ca. 1880—on. Jointed at shoulders and hips, stationary neck, painted eyes, molded and painted hair or mohair wig, molded and painted shoes and stockings, closed mouth, fine quality work, dressed or undressed; all in good condition.

1½–2in (3.8–5.1cm)
$35-40
4–5in (10.2–12.7cm)
75-85
4–5in (10.2–12.7cm),
swivel neck $110-125

All-Bisque with painted eyes: Ca. 1920. Jointed at shoulders and hips, stationary neck, painted eyes, mohair wig, molded and painted brown one-strap shoes and white stockings, closed mouth; dressed or undressed; all in good condition.
4½–5in (11.5–12.7cm) $55

3½in (8.9cm) Boy with painted eyes, all original. *H&J Foulke.*

LEFT: 4in (10.2cm) Girl with painted eyes, tan stocking-painted legs, all original. *H&J Foulke.*
RIGHT: 4in (10.2cm) Girl with swivel neck, molded hair and bow, all original, very unusual. *H&J Foulke.*

All-Bisque "Flapper": Pink bisque with wire joints at shoulders and hips; molded bobbed hair and painted features, painted shoes and socks; original factory clothes; all in good condition.

3in (7.6cm) $40

6–7in (15.2–17.8cm), long yellow stockings, naked $225-250

All-Bisque Baby: 1900–on. Jointed at shoulders and hips with curved arms and legs, molded and painted hair, painted eyes, very good workmanship; not dressed; all in good condition.

2½–3½in (6.4–8.9cm) $40-45

5in (12.7cm)   75-85

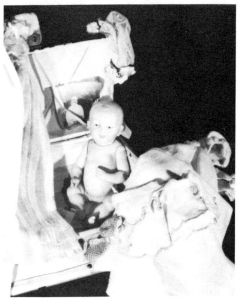

3in (7.6cm) Flapper, all original.   *H&J Foulke.*

All-Bisque Baby: Pink bisque, jointed at shoulders and hips, curved arms and legs, painted hair, painted eyes; original factory clothes; all in good condition.

3in (7.6cm) $40-45

All-Bisque Baby with glass eyes: Jointed at shoulders, hips, and neck; curved arms and legs, mohair wig, glass eyes, character face. Not dressed; all in good condition.

5–6in (12.7–15.2cm)
$350

4½–5½in (11.5–14.0cm) stiff neck
225-250

9½in (24.2cm) Baby with character face, swivel neck, painted eyes; labelled F.A.O. Schwarz trunk with original layette. *H&J Foulke.*

All-Bisque Character Dolls: 1913—on. Character faces with painted features and molded hair, usually jointed only at arms. Also see individual listings.

Heubach child, 7in (17.8cm)	
page-boy hairdo	$550
with bows	750
Baby Bud, 5—7in (12.7—17.8cm)	150-200
Heubach girl, 4in (10.2cm)	175-200
Chin Chin (Heubach), 4in (10.2cm)	175
Little Imp, 5in (12.7cm)	200
Our Fairy, 9in (22.9cm)	1250
7in (17.8cm)	850
Small pink bisque characters, up to 3in (7.6cm)	25-35
Thumbsucker, 3in (7.6cm)	65

2½in (6.4cm) Pink bisque character girl, all original. *H&J Foulke.*

ABOVE: 8in (20.3cm) Girl by Gebruder Heubach. *Richard Wright Collection.*

All-Bisque Nodder Characters: Ca. 1920. Nodding heads, elastic strung, molded clothes; all in good condition.

3—4in (7.6—10.2cm)	$35
German Comic Characters	
3—4in (7.6—10.2cm)	$50 up

3½in (8.9cm) Elf Nodder. *H&J Foulke.*

LEFT: 3½in (8.9cm) Child Nodder. *H&J Foulke.*

RIGHT: 3½in (8.9cm) Comic Character "Auntie Blossom". *H&J Foulke.*

All-Bisque Immobiles: Ca. 1920. All-bisque figures with molded clothes, molded hair and painted features. Decoration is not fired, so it wears and washes off very easily.

Children
  1½in (3.8cm) $15-18
Adults
  2¼in (5.7cm) 20-22
Children with animals on string
  3in (7.6cm) 35-40

2¼in (5.7cm) Immobile Indians. *H&J Foulke.*

All—Bisque Dolls

(French)

MAKER: Various French firms
DATE: Ca. 1880—on
MATERIAL: All-bisque
SIZE: Various small sizes, under 12in (30.5cm)
MARK: None, sometimes numbers

All-bisque French Doll: Jointed at shoulders and hips, slender arms and
  legs, glass eyes, swivel neck, closed mouth, good wig, molded shoes or
  boots and stockings; dressed or undressed; all in good condition.

  4½–5½in (11.5–14.0cm) $600-650
Same as above with bare feet, 5–5½in (12.7–14.0cm) $700-750
Same as above with jointed elbows and knees, 5–5½in
  (12.7–14.0cm)   1250**
SFBJ model, 6–7in (15.2–17.8cm)   350**
J.V., 8in (20.3cm)   350**

**Not enough price samples to
compute a reliable range.

ABOVE LEFT: 5½in (14.0cm) French
with bare feet, all original. *H&J Foulke.*

ABOVE RIGHT: 5in (12.7cm) French
with blue boots. *Betty Harms Collection.*

LEFT: 6¾in (17.2cm) marked SFBJ,
gold stockings. *H&J Foulke.*

All—Bisque Dolls

(made in Japan)

MAKER: Various Japanese firms
DATE: Ca. 1915—on
MATERIAL: Bisque
SIZE: Various small sizes
MARK: "Made in Japan"

Baby Doll with bent limbs: Jointed shoulders and hips, molded and painted hair and eyes; not dressed; all in good condition.

Baby, White, 4in (10.2cm) $15-20   Black, 4in (10.2cm) $20
Betty Boop-type, 4—5in (10.2—12.7cm) $12
Baby with 2 faces $100-125
Child, 4—6in (10.2—15.2cm)   15-20
Comic Characters, 3—4in (7.6—
    10.2cm)   20—30*
Stiff Characters, 3—4in (7.6—10.2cm)
                4-6
Nodders, 4in (10.2cm)   15

*Depending upon rarity and desirability.

ABOVE: 4in (10.2cm) Nodder. *H&J Foulke*

LEFT: 5in (12.7cm) Black character. *H&J Foulke.*

5in (12.7cm) Baby with two faces. *H&J Foulke.*

All—Bisque Dolls
(Nippon)

MAKER: Various Japanese firms
DATE: Ca. 1915–on
MATERIAL: Bisque
SIZE: Various small sizes
MARK: "NIPPON"

All-Bisque Child Doll Marked "Nippon": Jointed at shoulders only, molded and painted hair and eyes, may have ribbed socks and one-strap shoes; some with molded clothes; some not dressed; all in good condition.

5in (12.7cm) $30-35
Baby Bud, 4½in
  (11.4cm)   65
Nodders, 3–4in
  (7.6–10.2cm)   25
Queue San, 4in
  (10.2cm)   65

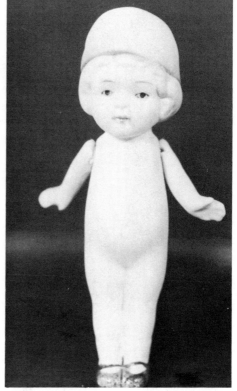

5½in (14.0cm) Girl with molded cap. *H&J Foulke.*

All Composition Doll

MAKER: Various American firms, such as Bester Doll Co., New Era Novelty Co., New Toy Mfg. Co., Superior Doll Mfg. Co., Colonial Toy Mfg. Co.

DATE: 1912—on

MATERIAL: Composition heads, ball-jointed composition bodies or bent-limb baby bodies

SIZE: Various

MARK: Various, according to company

All-Composition Character Baby: Composition with sleep eyes, open mouth with teeth, good wig, bent-limb baby body; appropriate clothes; all in good condition.   12—14in (30.5—35.6cm) $65-75; 20—22in (50.8—55.9cm) 100-125

All-Composition Child Doll: Composition with sleep eyes, open mouth, mohair wig, jointed composition body; appropriate clothes; all in good condition. 23—25in (58.4—63.5cm) $125-150

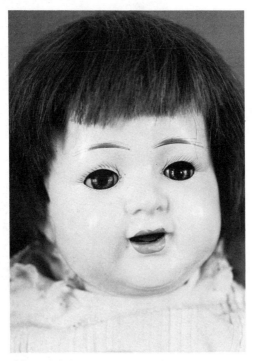

20in (50.8cm) all-composition Character Baby. *Joanna Ott Collection.*

Farnell's Alpha Toys

MAKER: J. K. Farnell Co., Ltd., Acton, London
DATE: 1930 s
MATERIAL: Felt and cloth
SIZE: Various
MARK: Cloth label on foot:

FARNELL'S ALPHA TOYS MADE IN ENGLAND

Alpha Toys Child: All-cloth with felt face, painted features, mohair wig; cloth body jointed at neck, shoulders and hips. Original clothes; all in good condition.

      Child, size 14in (35.6cm) $150-175
      Alpha Toys Coronation Doll of King
      George VI, size 16in (40.6cm)   200

15in (38.1cm) Girl in sailor outfit, all original. *H&J Foulke.*

16in (40.6cm) tall coronation dolls of King George VI in two different outfits. *H&J Foulke.*

American Character

MAKER: American Character Doll Co., New York City, N.Y., U.S.A.
DATE: 1919—on
MARK: Various for each doll

Sally: 1927. Composition head, arms and legs, cloth torso, molded and painted hair, tin sleep eyes, closed mouth. Original clothes; all in good condition.
MARK: PETITE   16—18in (40.6—45.7cm) $85-95
      SALLY   12in (30.5cm)   65-75

Puggy: 1931. All-composition chubby body jointed at neck, shoulders and hips. Molded and painted hair, painted eyes to side, pug nose, frowning face, closed mouth. Original clothes; all in good condition.
MARK: A PETITE DOLL

12in (30.5cm) $300-350

Tiny Tears: 1950. Hard-plastic head with sleep eyes and tear ducts, molded hair, drinks, wets, rubber body. Original clothes; all in good condition. (Later dolls had inset hair and vinyl body; still later dolls were all vinyl.) Various sizes.
MARK: Pat No. 2675644
      Ame—Character

Early one, 15—18in (38.1—45.7cm) $45-55

ABOVE: 9in (22.9cm) "Teeny Weeny Tiny Tears". *Beth Foulke Collection.*

BELOW: 23in (58.4cm) "Sweet Sue", dress not original. *Mary Lou Rubright Collection.*

Sweet Sue: 1953. Hard plastic and vinyl, some with walking mechanism, some fully jointed including elbows, knees and ankles; original clothes; all in excellent condition.
MARKS: Various, including: "A.C.", "Amer. Char. Doll", "American Character" in a circle.

18–24in (45.7–53.3cm) $75-100

Betsy McCall: 1957. All-hard plastic with vinyl arms, round face with sleep eyes, plastic lashes, rooted saran hair; legs jointed at knees. Original clothes; all in good condition.

8in (20.3cm) $40-50

MARK:

Whimsies: 1960. Stuffed vinyl body with molded vinyl head, painted features, smiling mouth, synthetic hair. Original clothes; all in good condition. Wide variety of characters.
MARK: WHIMSIE
AMER. DOLL & TOY CO.

19–21in (48.3–53.3cm)
$35-40

ABOVE: 19in (48.3cm) Whimsey with molded head. "Hedda Get Bedda" with 3 faces. *Mary Lou Rubright Collection.*

BELOW: 8in (20.3cm) "Betsy McCall", all original. *Mary Lou Rubright Collection.*

Arranbee

MAKER: Arranbee Doll Co., New York, ·
N.Y., U.S.A.
DATE: 1922–1960
MARK: "ARRANBEE" or "R & B"

Bottletot: 1926–on. All-composition
baby with bent arms and legs; molded
and painted hair, sleep eyes, open
mouth; celluloid hand with molded
bottle. Doll is unmarked; bottle is
marked Arranbee/Pat Aug. 10, 26.
Original clothes; all in good condition.
13in (33.0cm) $75-85**

**Not enough price samples to
compute a reliable range.

Storybook Dolls: 1930s. All-composition with swivel neck, jointed arms
and legs; molded and painted hair,
painted eyes; all original storybook
costumes; all in good condition.
In original box $85-95

Deanna Durbin type. 1938–on. Composition swivel shoulder head and limbs
on cloth torso, sleep eyes, closed
mouth, mohair or human hair wig.
Original clothes; all in good condition.
MARK: R & B ·
21in (53.3cm) $125-150

Debu' Teen: 1938–on. All-composition
or composition swivel shoulder head
and limbs on cloth torso, sleep eyes,
closed mouth, mohair or human hair
wig. Original clothes; all in good condition. Various sizes.
MARK: R & B
14in (35.6cm) $65-75 18in (45.7cm) 85-95

TOP: 19in (48.3cm) Deanna Durbin-type
girl, all original. *Maxine Salaman Collection*

MIDDLE: 15in (38.1cm) "Debu' Teen",
all original. *H&J Foulke.*

BOTTOM: 17in (43.2cm) "Nancy",
all original. *H&J Foulke.*

Sonja Henie type. 1939–on. All-composition with jointed neck, shoulders and hips, sleep eyes, closed mouth, mohair or human hair wig. Original skating clothes; all in good condition. Various sizes.

MARK: R & B   18–21in (45.7–53.3cm) $100-125*
                               *Same doll as Debu' Teen

Nancy: Up to 1940. All-composition or composition swivel shoulder head and limbs on cloth torso, sleep eyes and open mouth with teeth (smaller dolls have painted eyes and closed mouths); molded hair or original mohair or human hair wig. Original clothes; all in good condition. Sizes 12–20in (30.5–50.8cm).

MARK: ARRANBEE
On torso of 12in (30.5cm) size:
              NANCY

12in (30.5cm) $55-65
17–20in (43.2-50.8cm)   125-150

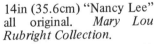

14in (35.6cm) "Nancy Lee"
all original. *Mary Lou Rubright Collection.*

Nancy Lee: 1940s. All-composition with jointed neck, shoulders and hips, sleep eyes, closed mouth, mohair or human hair wig. Original clothes; all in good condition. Various sizes. This face mold was also used for dolls which were given other names.

MARK: R & B

14in (35.6cm) $65-75

14in (35.6cm) "Nancy Lee Brother", all original. *H&J Foulke.*

Nanette: 1950s. All-hard plastic jointed at neck, shoulders and hips, synthetic wig, sleep eyes, closed mouth; original clothes; all in good condition. Various sizes. This face mold was also used for dolls which were given other names.
MARK: R & B

18–21in (45.7–53.3cm) $75-85

ABOVE LEFT: 18in (45.7cm) hard plastic "Nanette", all original. *Maxine Salaman Collection.*

ABOVE RIGHT: 13in (33.0cm) "Bottletot", all original.   *H&J Foulke.*

RIGHT: "Bo-Peep", all original in box. *H&J Foulke.*

Art Fabric Mills

MAKER: Art Fabric Mills, New York City, N.Y., U.S.A. (1899–1910);
 Selchow & Righter were sole distributors and in 1911 they were the
 successors (1911–1923)
DATE: 1899–1923
MATERIAL: Printed on cloth to be cut out, sewed and stuffed
SIZE: 6½–30in (16.5–76.2cm)
MARK: On foot: ART FABRIC MILLS
NEW YORK.
Pat. Feb. 13th 1900

Marked Art Fabric Mills Doll: Features and underclothes printed on
 cloth. Good condition (some soil acceptable). Undressed.

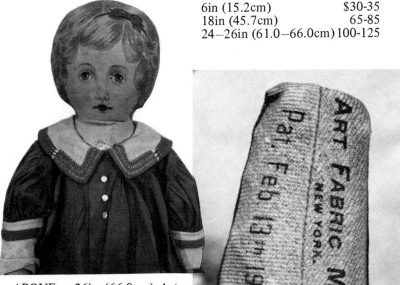

6in (15.2cm)	$30-35
18in (45.7cm)	65-85
24–26in (61.0–66.0cm)	100-125

ABOVE: 26in (66.0cm) Art
Fabric Mills Girl. *H&J Foulke.*

LEFT: Mark on foot.

Autoperipatetikos

(Walking Doll)

MAKERS: David S. Cohen & Joseph Lyon & Co. of New York, N.Y.;
Martin & Runyon of London, England and others.

DATE: 1862—Patented by Enoch Rice Morrison, N.Y., N.Y.

MATERIAL: Heads made of pale bisque, china, cloth or papier-mâché.
Under the skirt is the mechanism enclosed in a cardboard bell. The
base of this bell is a circle of wood with slits where the metal feet
protrude.

SIZE: 10in (25.4cm)

MARK: Found on underside of wooden circle.

Patented July 15th, 1862; also, in England.

Marked Autoperipatetikos: Head of china, bisque, cloth or papier-mâché,
leather arms, original clothes or nicely dressed. In working order.

Ordinary head
$600-700
Unusual head
$800-900

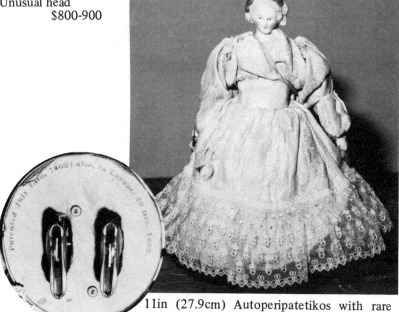

11in (27.9cm) Autoperipatetikos with rare
style head. *Grace Dyar*

Underside of doll showing mechanism and
mark.

B.F.

MAKER: Possibly Jumeau or Danel & Cie. as Bébé Française or Ferté as Bébé Ferté, Paris, France
DATE: Ca. 1880s–1890s
MATERIAL: Bisque head, composition body
SIZE: Various
MARK: "B. F." with size number

B. F. marked Bébé: Bisque head with closed mouth, paperweight eyes, pierced ears, good wig; jointed composition body; appropriate clothes; all in good condition.

20–24in (50.8–61.0cm) $2500-3000

26in (66.0cm) B 11 F. *Richard Wright.*

B.L.

MAKER: Possibly Jumeau for Louvre, a Paris store
DATE: Ca. 1880–1890
MATERIAL: Bisque head, composition body
SIZE: Various
MARK: "B. L." with size number

B. L. marked Bébé: Bisque head with closed mouth, paperweight eyes, pierced ears, good wig; jointed composition body; appropriate clothes; all in good condition.

20–24in (50.8–61.0cm) $2500-3000

28in (71.1cm) B. L.

Baby Bo Kaye

MAKER: Heads—Cameo Doll Co. (composition)
J.D. Kestner (bisque)
Bodies—K & K Toy Co.
DATE: 1925
MATERIAL: Bisque, composition or celluloid head with flange neck; composition or celluloid limbs, cloth body
SIZE: About 18in (45.7cm)
DESIGNER: J. L. Kallus
MARK: J. L. Kallus: Copr. Germany
1394/30

Baby Bo Kaye: Bisque head marked as above, molded hair, glass eyes, open mouth with two lower teeth. Body as above. Dressed. All in good condition.

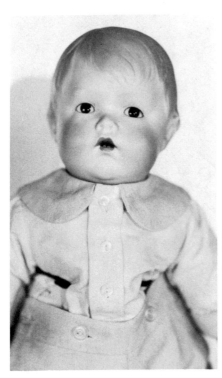

Bisque, 16—20in (40.6—
50.8cm) $1650
Celluloid   400**
All-Bisque, 5½in (14.0cm)
1200-1500**

**Not enough price samples to compute a reliable range

20in (50.8cm) Bisque-head "Baby Bo Kaye", all original. *Richard Wright Collection.*

MAKER: L. Amberg & Son, New York and Germany
DATE: 1924
MATERIAL: Bisque head, composition or kid jointed body
SIZE: 18−21in (45.7−53.3cm)
MARK: 19 © 24
      LA & S NY
      Germany
      −50−
      982/2

All-Bisque Baby Peggy: Smiling face, painted eyes, closed mouth, painted brown bobbed hair, jointed arms and legs, brown strap shoes and socks; undressed; all in good condition. Unmarked, but had a paper label on stomach.
      5½in (14.0cm) $225-250

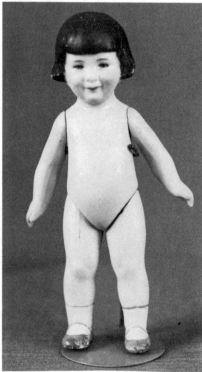

Baby Peggy: Bisque head with smiling face, closed mouth, brown sleep eyes, brown bobbed mohair wig; jointed body. Dressed or undressed. All in good condition.

18−21in (45.6−53.3cm)
      $2000**

**Not enough price samples to compute a reliable range.

5½in (14.0cm) all-bisque "Baby Peggy". *H&J Foulke.*

Baby Sandy

MAKER: Ralph Freundlich
DATE: 1939–1942
MATERIAL: All composition
SIZE: 7–26in (17.8–66.0cm)
MARK: On head: Baby Sandy
       On pin: The Wonder Baby
               Genuine Baby Sandy Doll

Marked Baby Sandy: All-composition with swivel head, jointed shoulders and hips. Chubby toddler body. Molded hair, smiling face. Larger sizes have sleep eyes, smaller ones painted eyes. Appropriate clothes. All in good condition.

8in (20.3cm)	$90-100
14in (35.6cm)	175-200

14in (35.6cm) "Baby Sandy", replaced dress. *Miriam Blankman Collection.*

Babyland Rag

MAKER: E. I. Horsman, New York City, N.Y., U.S.A.
DATE: 1904–1920
MATERIAL: All-cloth
SIZE: 12–30in (30.5–76.2cm)
MARK: Sometimes stamped on torso

Babyland Rag: Cloth face with hand-painted features; later with printed features; sometimes mohair wig, cloth body jointed at shoulders and hips. Original clothes. All in good condition.

13–15in (33.0–38.1cm) $90-110

14½in (36.9cm) tall Babyland Rag-type, all original. *Jan Foulke Collection.*

Bähr & Pröschild Characters

MAKER: Bähr & Pröschild, Ohrdruf, Thüringia, Germany
DATE: 1910—on
MATERIAL: Bisque head, composition bent-limb baby or toddler body
SIZE: Various
MARK:

with "Germany" and numbers 585, 604, 624, 678, 619

Marked B. P. Character: Bisque socket head, sleep eyes, open mouth, good wig, composition bent-limb baby body; dressed; all in good condition.

10—13in (25.4—33.0cm)	$300-350
15—16in (38.1—40.6cm)	400-450
24in (61.0cm)	650
Toddler, 14—15in (35.6—38.1cm)	500-550

21in (53.3cm) #619 Character Boy. *H&J Foulke.*

24in (61.0cm) #624 Character Baby. *H&J Foulke.*

Barbie^{T.M}

MAKER: Mattel, Inc.
DATE: 1959 to present
MATERIAL: Hard plastic and vinyl
SIZE: 11½–12in (29.2–30.5cm)
MARK: 1959–1962: Barbie TM/Pats. Pend./© MCMLVIII/by/ Mattel, Inc.
1963–1968: Midge TM/ © 1962/Barbie ®/©1958/by/Mattel, Inc.
1964–1966:© 1958/Mattel, Inc./U.S. Patented/U.S. Pat. Pend.
1966–1969:©1966/Mattel, Inc./U.S. Patented/U.S. Pat. Pend./ Made in Japan

---

First Barbie: 1959. Vinyl. White irises, pointed eyebrows, ponytail, black and white striped bathing suit, holes in feet to fit stand, gold hoop earrings. Mint condition. Made 3 months only.
11½in (29.2cm) boxed $500 up.
Doll only, no box or accessories $250-350

Second Barbie: 1959–1960. Vinyl. Same as above,·but no holes in feet, some wore pearl earrings. Mint condition. Made 3 months only.
11½in (29.2cm) boxed $500 up
Doll only, no box or accessories $250-350

Third Barbie: 1960. Vinyl. Same as above, but with blue irises and curved eyebrows. No holes in feet. Mint condition.
11½in (29.2cm) boxed $75-100

"Lilli" from West Germany, 1957. Forerunner of the Barbie doll and eagerly sought after by Barbie collectors. All original in mint condition with stand. $400–500 *H&J Foulke.*

ABOVE: Barbie #1, note the arched eyebrows, white irises and gold loop earrings. *Glenn Mandeville Collection*

RIGHT: Barbie #1 with box lid and package of accessories. *Glenn Mandeville Collection.*

Box end. *Glenn Mandeville Collection.*

Bathing Beauty

MAKER: Various German firms
DATE: 1920s
MATERIAL: All-bisque
SIZE: Up to about 7in (17.8cm) tall or long
MARK: Sometimes "Germany" and/or numbers

Bathing Beauty: All-bisque ladies, either nude or partially dressed in painted on clothing; in various sitting, lying or standing positions. Also may be dressed in bits of lace. Painted features and molded hair possibly with bathing cap (sometimes a bald head with a wig).

3—4in (7.6—10.1cm)	$50-75
5in (12.7cm)	85-95
8in (20.3cm)	225-250

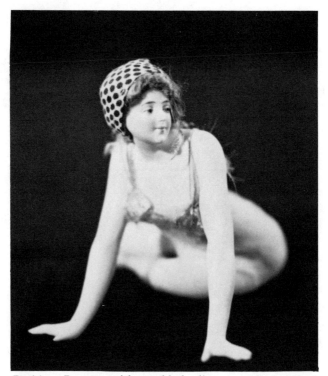

Bathing Beauty with molded slippers, wig, original clothes.

(So-called)

MAKER: Various French and German firms
DATE: 1875—on
MATERIAL: Bisque socket head, ball-jointed wood and composition
body with straight wrists
SIZE: Various
MARK: None, except sometimes numbers

Belton-type Child Doll: Bisque socket head, solid but flat on top with
two or three small holes, paperweight eyes, closed mouth, pierced
ears; wood and composition ball-jointed body with straight wrists;
dressed; all in good condition.

> 10–12in (25.4–30.5cm) $650-750*
> 14–16in (35.6–40.6cm)   850-950*
> 18–20in (45.7–50.8cm) 1150-1250*
> *Allow more for an especially fine and early face

11in (27.9cm) Belton-type with
skin wig, kid over wood and
composition arms. *Joanna Ott
Collection.*

19in (48.3cm) Belton-type. *Richard
Wright.*

Bergmann Child Doll

MAKER: C. M. Bergmann of Waltershausen, Thüringia, Germany; heads manufactured for this company by Armand Marseille, Simon & Halbig and perhaps others.
DATE: Various
MATERIAL: Bisque head, composition ball-jointed body
SIZE: Various
MARK:

C.M. BERGMANN
4/0

C. M. Bergmann
Waltershausen
Germany
1916
6½ a

Bergmann Child Doll: Ca. 1889—on. Marked bisque head, composition ball-jointed body, sleep or set eyes, open mouth, good wig, dressed. All in nice condition.

18—21in (45.7—53.3cm)
$250-300
23—25in (58.4—63.5cm)
300-350
30—31in (76.2—78.7cm)
475-500

Bergmann Character Baby: 1909—on. Marked bisque socket head, sleep eyes, open mouth, mohair wig, composition bent-limb baby body; dressed; all in good condition.

12in (30.5cm) $275-300**

**Not enough price samples to compute a reliable range

24in (61.0cm) C. M. Bergmann Child. *H&J Foulke.*

Betty Boop

MAKER: Cameo Doll Products Co.
DATE: 1932
MATERIAL: Composition head and torso; wood segmented arms and legs.
SIZE: 12½in (31.8cm)
MARK: "Betty Boop" label on body

Betty Boop: Composition swivel-head, painted and molded hair, large goo-goo eyes, tiny closed mouth. Composition torso with wood segmented arms and legs. Molded on bathing suit. All in good condition.

12in (30.5cm) $400-450

12in (30.4cm) "Betty Boop", all original and tagged. Rare form with composition legs. *Richard Wright Collection.*

Bisque Molded Hair
(Tinted Bisque)

MAKER: Various German firms
DATE: Last quarter 19th century
MATERIAL: Tinted bisque shoulder head; kid or cloth body
SIZE: Various
MARK: Sometimes numbers and/or Germany

Molded Hair Doll: Tinted bisque shoulder head with beautifully molded hair (usually blonde), painted eyes (sometimes glass), closed mouth, original kid or cloth body, appropriate clothes; all in good condition.

      15–17in (38.1–43.2cm) $200-250*
      20–24in (50.8–61.0cm)   350-450*
        *Allow extra for glass eyes

American School Boy (so-called): Bisque shoulder head, molded blonde hair (sometimes brown hair), glass eyes, kid or cloth body, good bisque or kid arms, closed mouth, nicely dressed; all in good condition. 12–14in (30.5–35.6cm) $300-350

LEFT: 12in (30.5cm) so-called "Highland Mary" with painted eyes. *Joanna Ott Collection.*

MIDDLE: 13in (33.0cm) so-called "American School Boy", glass eyes. *H&J Foulke.*

RIGHT: 15in (38.1cm) molded blonde hair with painted eyes. *H&J Foulke.*

Bisque Portrait Dolls

Admiral Dewey: 1898. Bisque head with portrait face, molded mustache and goatee, glass eyes; five-piece papier-mâché body; original uniform; all in good condition.
MARK: Sometimes <u>S</u> or <u>D</u> with a number.
8–9in (20.3–22.9cm) $600
Historical Gentleman
15in (38.1cm)   1500**

**Not enough price samples to compute a reliable range.

9in (22.9cm) "Admiral Dewey", all original.
Richard Wright.

Small "Uncle Sam". *Ann Lloyd.*

8½in (21.6cm) "Hexe".
Jan Naibert.

Uncle Sam: Ca. 1900. Bisque head portrait of an old man with mohair wig and goatee, glass eyes; composition body; original clothes; all in good condition.
MARK: Usually <u>S</u> and a number.
12in (30.5cm) $1500
Old Rip, 8–9in (20.3–22.9cm)
                          $600

Hexe: Ca. 1900. Bisque head portrait face witch, gray mohair wig, glass eyes; five-piece papier-mache body; appropriate clothes; all in good condition.
MARK: Hexe
12in (30.5cm) $1200-1500**

Black Dolls

Black Bisque Doll: Ca. 1880—on. Various French and German manufacturers from their regular molds or specially designed ones with Negroid features. Bisque socket head either painted dark or with dark coloring mixed in the slip; this runs from light brown to very dark; composition, or sometimes kid, body in a matching color; cloth bodies on some baby dolls; appropriate clothes; all in good condition.

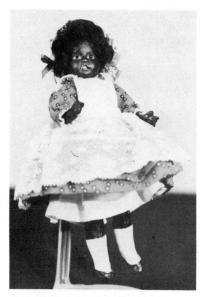

S&H 1358, 16—18in (40.6—45.7cm)	$2500**
S&H Child, 20—24in (50.8—61.0cm)	700-800
14—16in (35.6—40.6cm)	500-550
German, jointed body, 10—13in (25.4—33.0cm)	250-300
German, 5-pc. body, 8—9in (20.3—22.9cm)	175-200
A.M. #341, 10—12in long (25.4—30.5cm)	250-300
A.M. #351, 12—13in long (30.5—33.0cm)	325-350
16—18in long (40.6—45.7cm)	500-550
K★R #100, 16in (40.6cm)	1200**
Heubach Koppelsdorf 399, 8—10in (20.3—25.4cm)	300-350
Unis 60, 11—13in (27.9—33.0cm)	150-200

**Not enough price samples to compute a reliable range.

5½in (14.0cm) tiny German Character. *H&J Foulke.*

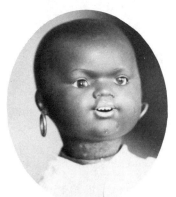

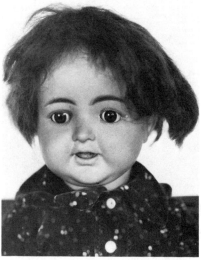

ABOVE: 18in (45.7cm) K★R 126 Baby. *Richard Wright.*

RIGHT: 14in (35.6cm) AM 362 Baby. *Jan Naibert.*

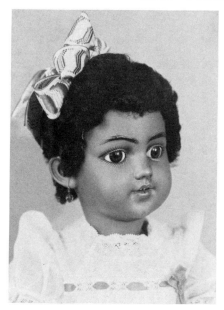

19in (48.3cm) S & H 1249. *Mary Lou Rubright Collection.*

12in (30.5cm) German girl incised 1000. *H&J Foulke.*

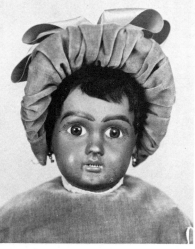

18in (45.7cm) S & H 1358. *Mary Lou Rubright Collection.*

18in (45.7cm) Steiner All Le Parisien. *Richard Wright.*

Papier-Mâché Black Doll: Ca. 1890. By various German manufacturers; papier-mâché character face, glass eyes, arms, and legs, cloth body; original or appropriate clothes; all in good condition.

10−12in (25.4−30.5cm)$135-150   10−12in (25.4−30.5cm)
                                                   sticks out tongue $225

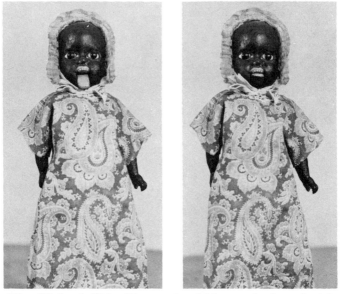

12in (30.5cm) Girl with mouth which opens when chest is pressed, all original. *H&J Foulke.*

Black Composition Doll: Ca. 1930. American-made bent-limb baby or mama-type body, jointed at hips, shoulders, and perhaps neck; molded hair, painted or sleep eyes; original or appropriate clothes. Some have three yarn tufts of hair on either side and on top of the head. All in good condition.

Baby, 10−12in (25.4−30.5cm)
                                        $40-50
Toddler, 15−17in (38.1−43.2cm)
                                        $65-85

8in (20.3cm) Black composition Baby. *H&J Foulke.*

Cloth Black Doll: Ca. 1910. American commercially made cloth doll with black face, painted or printed features, jointed arms and legs; original clothes; all in good condition.

20in (50.8cm) $125-150

24in (61.0cm) Black "Mammy". *H&J Foulke.*

14in (35.6cm) Black Babyland Rag-type doll, all original. *Jan Foulke Collection.*

Bonnie Babe
(Georgene Averill Baby)

MAKER: Heads by Alt, Beck & Gottschalck of Nauendorf, Thüringia, Germany. Cloth bodies by George Borgfeldt & Co. of New York, N.Y., U.S.A. Small socket heads by Gebruder Heubach, Licht, Thüringia, Germany.

DATE: 1926, renewed 1946

MATERIAL: Bisque heads, cloth bodies, composition arms and legs; all-bisque; bisque head, composition body

SIZE: Various

DESIGNER: Georgene Averill, U.S.A. (Madame Hendren)

MARK: *Copr. by Georgene Averill Germany*   1005/3652 plus another number, such as 1402 or 1368

Marked Bonnie Babe: Bisque head, cloth body, composition extremities, often of poor quality; molded hair, set or sleep eyes, open mouth with two teeth; dressed; all in good condition.

Length: 16–18in (40.6–45.7cm) $850-950
Celluloid head, 16in (40.6cm)   275-325

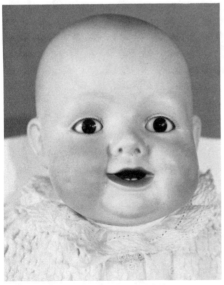

Georgene Averill, "Bonnie Babe".
Mary Lou Rubright Collection.

All-Bisque Bonnie Babe: Unmarked. Molded hair, open mouth with two lower teeth. Glass eyes, pink or blue molded slippers. Jointed at neck, shoulders and hips.
4½–5½in (11.5–14.0cm)
$750

All-Composition body: Bisque socket head, sleep eyes, open mouth with two lower teeth, mohair wig; fat papier-mâché type body; dressed; all in good condition. Marked 12386 or 1393 or possibly other numbers.
7–8in (17.8–20.3cm)
$1250**
**Not enough price samples to compute a reliable range.

Color photograph on page 6

Boudoir Dolls

MAKER: Various French, U.S. and Italian firms
DATE: Early 1920s into the early 1930s
MATERIAL: Heads of composition and other materials; bodies mostly
 cloth but also of composition and other substances.
SIZE: Many 24–36in (61.0–91.4cm); some smaller
MARK: Mostly unmarked

Boudoir Doll: Head of composition, cloth, or other material, painted
 features; composition or cloth stuffed body; unusually long extremities; usually high-heeled shoes; original clothes elaborately designed
 and trimmed. All in good condition.

24–28in (61.0–71.1cm)	$40-50
Smoking doll	150-175

26in (66.0cm) Boudoir Doll with cloth face.
H&J Foulke.

Brownies

MAKER: Arnold Print Works
DATE: 1892–1907
MATERIAL: All-cloth
SIZE: 8in (20.3cm)
DESIGNER: Palmer Cox
MARK: On rear of right foot:

_____ Copyrighted. 1892 _____
by PALMER COX

Brownie: Printed on cloth. Twelve different designs: Uncle Sam, Dude, Policeman, Irishman, Indian, Soldier, Sailor, German, Chinaman, John Bull, Highlander, Canadian. In good condition.

7in (17.8cm) $60-75

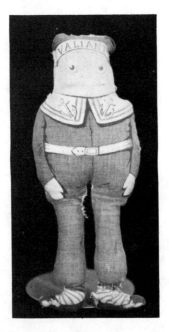

7½in (19.1cm) Brownie
"Valiant" 1892.   *H&J   Foulke.*

Bru Bébé

MAKER: Bru Jne. & Cie., Paris, France
DATE: Ca. 1878–1899
MATERIAL: Bisque swivel shoulder head, gusseted all-kid body with bisque hands or wood hands and legs; or bisque socket head on jointed composition body.
SIZE: 10in (25.4cm) and up
MARK: Incised Marks:

Paper label on body:

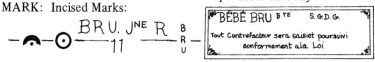

Marked Nursing Bru (Bébé Teteur): 1878–1898. Bisque head, shoulder plate and lower arms; kid body; upper arms and upper legs of metal covered with kid; lower legs of carved wood; or jointed composition body. Lovely glass eyes, attractive wig, open mouth with hole for nipple. Mechanism in head sucks up liquid, operates by turning key. Nicely clothed. All in good condition.

15in (38.1cm) Early-type	$6500
15in (38.1cm) Middle-period	4000
15in (38.1cm) S.F.B.J. type	2500

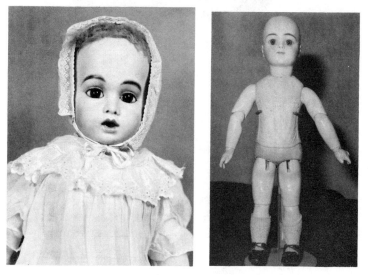

LEFT: 24in (61.0cm) Nursing Bru Jne, kid body. *Richard Wright.*

RIGHT: 15in (38.1cm) Bru Jne R, composition body with Bru label, marked shoes. *Crandall Collection.*

Marked Bru Bébé: Bisque head on body as above, beautiful wig, set blown glass eyes, closed mouth, pierced ears; lovely clothes. All in good condition.

Circle, Dot 19—22in (48.3—55.9cm) $8000up
Bru Jne, kid body 14—18in (35.6—45.7cm)   6500-8500
Bru Jne R, closed mouth, composition body
    19—22in (48.3—55.9cm)   4000-5000
Open mouth, kissing-walking, composition body
    23—24in (58.4—61.0cm)   2300-2500

14in (35.6cm) Bru Jne, kid body. *Mary Lou Rubright Collection.*

Brückner Rag Doll

MAKER: Albert Brückner, Jersey City, N.J., U.S.A.
DATE: 1901–on
MATERIAL: All-cloth with stiffened mask face
SIZE: About 13–15in (33.0–38.1cm)
MARK: On right front shoulder:

PAT'D. JULY 8ᵀᴴ 1901

Marked Brückner: Cloth head with printed features on stiffened mask face. Cloth body flexible at shoulders and hips. Appropriate clothes. All in good condition.

12in (30.5cm) White		$65-85
12in (30.5cm) Black		85-95
12in (30.5cm) Topsy Turvy		125-150

12in (30.5cm) Brückner Topsy Turvy doll, all original with label. *H&J Foulke.*

Buddy Lee

MAKER: Name of maker kept secret by H. D. Lee Co., Inc., Garment
  Manufacturers of Kansas City, Missouri, for whom dolls were made.
DATE: 1920–1962
MATERIAL: Composition from 1920 to 1948. Hard plastic from 1949
  until 1962.
SIZE: 13in (33.0cm) only
MARK: "BUDDY LEE" embossed across shoulders

Marked Buddy Lee: Early all-composition; molded, painted eyes and hair;
  jointed only at shoulders—legs apart; dressed in original Lee clothes.
  Eyes to side; all in good shape. Composition 13in (33.0cm) $125-150

Marked Buddy Lee: Later all-hard plastic doll. Mold changed slightly by
  slimming the legs, making the doll easier to dress and undress. This
  was done in 1949. Molded painted hair, painted eyes to side; jointed
  at shoulders; legs apart; dressed in Lee original clothes; all in nice condition.   Hard Plastic 13in (33.0cm) $90-100

13in (33.0cm) hard plastic
"Buddy   Lee",   original
"Phillips 66" outfit. *H&J
Foulke.*

Bye-lo Baby

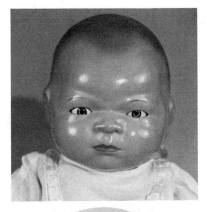

MAKER: Bisque heads—J. D. Kestner; Alt, Beck & Gottscholck; Kling & Co.; Hertel Schwab & Co.; all of Thüringia, Germany.
Composition heads—Cameo Doll Co., N.Y.
Celluloid heads—Karl Standfuss, Saxony, Germany
Wooden heads (unauthorized)— Schoenhut of Philadelphia
All Bisque Baby—J. D. Kestner
Cloth Bodies and Assembly— K&K Toy Co., N.Y.

DATE: 1922—on
SIZE: Bisque head—seven sizes 9—20in (22.9—50.8cm)
All-bisque—up to 8in (20.3 cm)
DESIGNER: Grace Storey Putnam, U.S.A.
DISTRIBUTOR: George Borgfeldt, N.Y.
MARKS: See various marks where indicated on pages 80 and 81.

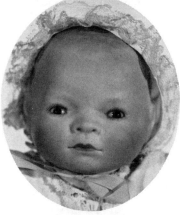

Composition Head Bye-lo Baby: Ca. 1924. Cloth body with curved legs, sleep eyes, composition hands, nice clothes, all in good condition.

Head circumference:
11—13in (27.9—33.0cm) $250-275

TOP: 15in (38.1cm) Cir. composition head Bye-lo, all original with label. *H&J Foulke.*

MIDDLE: 10in (25.4cm) Cir. bisque head Bye-lo. *H&J Foulke.*

BOTTOM: 13in (33.0cm) Cir. painted-bisque head Bye-lo. *H&J Foulke.*

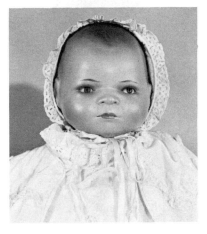

13in (33.0cm) Cir. wooden head Bye-lo. *Richard Wright.*

Bisque Head Bye-lo Baby: Ca. 1923. With bisque head, cloth body with curved legs (sometimes with straight legs), composition or celluloid hands; sleep eyes, dressed. (May have purple "Bye-lo Baby" stamp on front of body.)

MARK: © 1923 by

_____ Grace S. Putnam___

          MADE IN GERMANY

Head circumference:

8–10in (20.3–25.4cm)	$350-400
12–13in (30.5–33.0cm)	450-550
14–15in (35.6–38.1cm)	650-750
18in (45.7cm)	1250-1500
Rare Smiling Face	4000**
On composition body,	
12–13in (30.5–33.0cm)	900

**Not enough price samples to compute a reliable range

Painted Bisque Head Bye-lo Baby: Ca. late 1920s. Head has coating of flesh-colored paint, not baked in, washes and rubs off easily, sleep eyes; cloth body with composition hands; dressed, all in good condition.

Head circumference:
13in (33.0cm) $275-300

6½in (16.5cm) all-bisque Bye-lo with wig and glass eyes. *H&J Foulke.*

4½in (11.5cm) all-bisque Bye-lo with molded booties. *H&J Foulke.*

Schoenhut Bye-lo Baby: Ca. 1925. Wooden head with sleep eyes; cloth body; nice clothes; all in good condition. $1000 up

Marked All-Bisque Bye-lo Baby: 1925—on.
MARK: Dark green paper label on front torso often missing; incised on back 20-12 (or other stock and size number)

Copr. by
G.S. Putnam

6½in (16.5cm) all-bisque Bye-lo with glass eyes and swivel neck. *H&J Foulke.*

a. Solid head with molded hair and painted eyes, jointed shoulders and hips.

4in (10.2cm) $225-250
5in (12.7cm)   300-350
With booties, 4in (10.2cm) 300-325

b. Solid head with swivel neck, glass eyes, jointed shoulders and hips.

5—6in (12.7—15.2cm)   500-600

c. Head with wig, glass eyes, jointed shoulders and hips.

5—6in (12.7—15.2cm)   550-650

d. Action Bye-lo Baby, immobile in various positions, painted features.

3in (7.6cm)   300-350

Celluloid Head, 9in (22.9cm) cir.
                               275**
All-Celluloid, 5½in (14.0cm) 200**
**Not enough price samples to compute a reliable range.

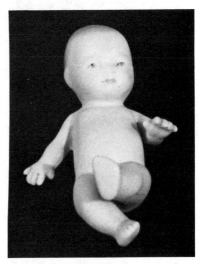

3½in (8.9cm) all-bisque Action Bye-lo. *H&J Foulke.*

C.O.D.

MAKER: Cuno & Otto Dressel of Sonneberg, Thüringia, Germany
DATE: Various
MATERIAL: Bisque head, jointed kid or cloth body or ball-jointed composition body
SIZE: Various
MARK: "C.O.D."
Germany

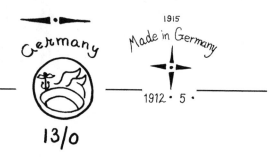

Child Doll: 1895—on. Marked bisque head, original jointed kid or composition body, good wig, glass eyes, open mouth; suitable clothes; all in good condition.
22—24in (55.9—61.0cm) $250-300

26in (66.0cm) C.O.D., composition body.
Mary Lou Rubright Collection.

Character Doll: 1909—on. Marked bisque socket head, ball-jointed composition body; painted eyes, mohair wig, closed mouth; suitable clothes; all in good condition.
14—16in (35.6—40.6cm)
$1500 up**

**Not enough price samples to compute a reliable range

17in (43.2cm) C.O.D. character girl with painted eyes. *Esther Schwartz Collection.*

Lady Doll: Ca. 1920s. Bisque socket head with young lady face, good wig, sleeping eyes, closed mouth; jointed composition body in adult form with molded bust, slim waist and long arms and legs, feet modeled to wear high-heeled shoes. Appropriate clothes. All in good condition. #1469

14in (35.6cm) $650-1200*

*Prices are not stable on this doll.

14in (35.6cm) COD/S&H 1469 lady doll, all original. *Esther Schwartz Collection.*

C.P.

MAKER: Catterfelder Puppenfabrik, Catterfeld, Thüringia, Germany
DATE: 1902—on
MATERIAL: Bisque head; composition body
SIZE: Various
MARK: C.P. or Catterfelder Puppenfabrik and Mold #201, 208, or 264

C.P. Child Doll: Ca. 1902—on. Bisque head, sleep eyes, open mouth with teeth, pierced ears, good wig; composition jointed body; dressed; all in good condition. #264   16—20in (40.6—50.8cm) $300-350

C.P. Character Baby: Ca. 1910—on. Bisque character face with wig or molded hair, painted or glass eyes; jointed baby body; dressed; all in good condition.   #263, 208   20—22in (50.8—55.9cm) $400-450*
28in (71.1cm)   750-800*
*Allow more for painted eyes and dome head.

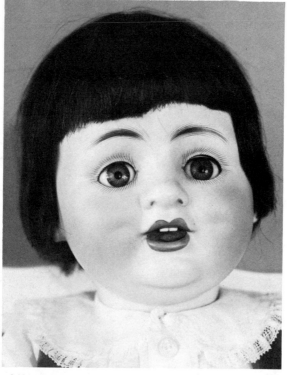

22in (55.9cm) C P 208/55 S Character Boy. *Mary Lou Rubright Collection.*

Campbell Kid

MAKER: E. I. Horsman Co., Inc., N.Y.; American Character Doll Co., N.Y.
DATE: 1910–on
MATERIAL: Composition head and arms, cloth body and legs; or all composition
SIZE: Usually 10–16in (25.4–40.6cm)
DESIGNER: Grace G. Drayton

Campbell Kid: 1910–1914. By Horsman. Marked composition head with flange neck, molded and painted bobbed hair, painted round eyes to side, watermelon mouth; original cloth body, composition arms, cloth legs and feet, original romper suit, all in nice condition.

MARK: **E.I.H. © 1910**
On head:

> The Campbell Kids
> Trademark by
> Joseph Campbell
> Mfg. by E. I. HORSMAN Co.

Cloth label on sleeve:

10–13in (25.4–33.0cm)
$90-100

12in (30.5cm) 1910 "Campbell Kid", all original. *Nancy Smith.*

Campbell Kid: 1923. By American Character, sometimes called "Dolly Dingle". All composition with swivel head, jointed shoulders and hips; molded and painted hair; eyes to side, watermelon mouth. Original clothes. All in good condition.
MARK: On back:
"A PETITE DOLL"
12in (30.5cm) $300-350

12½in (31.8cm) Petite "Campbell Kid", all original. *Maxine Salaman Collection.*

Campbell Kid: 1948. By Horsman. Unmarked all-composition, molded, painted hair, painted eyes to side, watermelon mouth. Painted white socks and black slippers. Original clothes. All in good condition.
12in (30.5cm) $200-225

12in (30.5cm) 1948 "Campbell Kid", all original with label. *H&J Foulke.*

Gene Carr Kids

MAKER: E. I. Horsman
DATE: 1916
MATERIAL: Composition heads, stuffed cloth body
SIZE: 14in (35.6cm)
DESIGNER: Bernard Lipfert from Gene Carr's cartoon characters
MARK: None

Gene Carr Character: Composition head with molded and painted hair, wide smiling mouth with teeth, eyes painted open or closed; cloth body with composition hands. Original or appropriate clothes; all in good condition. Names such as: "Snowball" (Black Boy); "Mike" and "Jane" (eyes open); "Blink" and Skinney" (eyes closed).

13in (33.0cm) $150

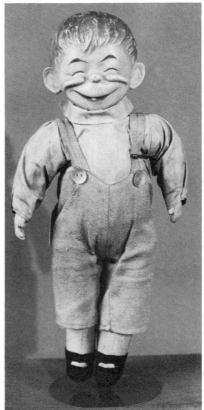

13in (33.0cm) "Blink". *H&J Foulke.*

Celluloid Dolls

MAKERS: Rheinische Gummi und Celluloid Fabrik Co. Mannheim-Neckarau, Bavaria, Germany and Buschow & Beck, Silesia and Saxony, Germany; also various other French and German companies

DATE: 1889–1940s

MATERIAL: All-celluloid or celluloid head with jointed kid, cloth, or composition body

SIZE: Various

MARK: Embossed turtle mark with or without the diamond frame; sometimes "SCHUTZ MARKE" and "Made in Germany". Also have been found with the marks of Kestner, Kammer & Rinehardt, Bruno Schmidt, and Kathe Kruse.

Rheinische Gummi

Buschow & Beck

18in (45.7cm) Celluloid Baby with inset eyes. *H&J Foulke.*

All-Celluloid Baby: Ca. 1910– on. Bent-limb baby, painted eyes, molded hair, jointed arms and/or legs, closed mouth, no clothes; all in good condition.

14–15in (35.6–38.1cm)
$45-55
glass eyes, 75-85

All-Celluloid Child Doll: Ca. 1910– on. Jointed at neck, shoulders, and hips; molded hair or wig, glass eyes (painted eyes on tiny dolls); dressed; all in good condition.

4–6in (10.2–15.2cm) $15-20
9–10in (22.9–25.4cm) 40-50
Glass eyes, 16–18in (40.6– 45.7cm) 100-125

7in (17.8cm) Celluloid Child with turtle mark. *H&J Foulke.*

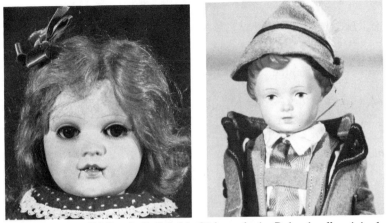

LEFT: 13in (33.0cm) Celluloid Girl made in Poland, all original. *H&J Foulke.*

RIGHT: 10in (25.4cm) Celluloid Boy with turtle mark, all original. *H&J Foulke.*

Celluloid shoulder head Child Doll: Ca. 1910—on. Painted or glass eyes, molded hair or wig, open or closed mouth; cloth or kid body, celluloid or composition arms, dressed; all in good condition.

12—14in (30.5—35.6cm)	$75-85
17—18in (43.2—45.7cm)	100-125
22in (55.9cm)	150

Celluloid socket head Child Doll: Ca. 1915—on. Glass eyes, sometimes flirty, wig, open mouth with teeth; ball-jointed or bent-limb composition body; dressed; all in good condition.

15—18in (38.1—45.7cm)
$150-175
23—25in (58.4—63.5cm)
225-275

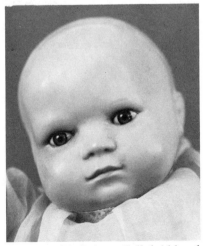

13in (33.0cm) long Celluloid-head hand Puppet, cloth body. *Joanna Ott Collection.*

Century Infant Doll

MAKER: Century Doll Co., New York, N.Y., U.S.A.; bisque heads by J. D. Kestner, Germany
DATE: Ca. 1925
MATERIAL: Bisque head, cloth body, composition arms (and legs)
SIZE: Various
MARK: "Century Doll Co." Sometimes ⟨K⟩ or Kestner "Germany"

Marked Century Infant: Bisque solid-dome head, molded and painted hair, sleep eyes, open/closed mouth; cloth body, composition hands or limbs, dressed, all in good condition.

Head circumference:
11in (27.9cm) $450-500
13in (33.0cm)   600-650

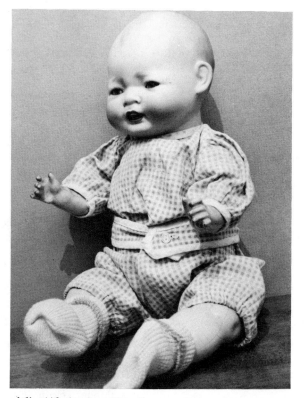

16in (40.6cm) smiling Century Baby. *H&J Foulke.*

Chad Valley

MAKER: Chad Valley Co. (formerly Johnson Bros., Ltd.), Birmingham,
  England
DATE: 1923—on
MATERIAL: All-cloth
SIZE: Various
MARK: Paper or cloth label

Chad Valley Doll: All-cloth, usually velvet body; jointed neck, shoulders
  and hips. Mohair wig, glass or painted eyes. Original clothes. All in
  good condition.

10—12in (25.4—30.5cm)
Characters, painted eyes $45-50
16—18in (40.6—45.7cm) Child,
  painted eyes   150-175
14—16in (35.6—40.6cm) Child,
  glass eyes   200-250
15in (38.1cm) Royal
  Children   450-475

14in (35.6cm) Chad
Valley Girl with coarse
fabric body, possibly a
war-time doll, all orig-
inal with tag. *H&J
Foulke.*

Chase Dolls

MAKER: Martha Jenks Chase, Pawtucket, Rhode Island, U.S.A.
DATE: 1893 to present
MATERIAL: Stockinet and cloth, painted in oils
SIZE: 9in (22.9cm) to life size
DESIGNER: Martha Jenks Chase
MARK: "Chase Stockinet Doll" on left leg or
under left arm, paper label on back
(usually gone)

PAWTUCKET, R.I.
MADE IN U.S.A.

Chase Doll: Head and limbs of stockinet, treated and painted with oils. Rough-stroked hair to provide texture. Cloth bodies jointed at shoulders, hips, elbows and knees; later ones only at shoulders and hips. Not in perfect condition.

Baby 16—20in (40.6—50.8cm) $300-350
Child, molded bobbed hair 12—15in (30.5—
    38.1cm)   400-450
Lady or Man, 15in (38.1cm)   675-725

Later Doll: Ca. 1930 or 1940. Entire doll of a latex-type material, molded and painted hair, painted features; jointed at shoulders and hips; boy and girl hairstyles; dressed; all in good condition.

14—16in (30.5—40.6cm) $135

ABOVE: 20in (50.8cm) Chase Boy. *Richard Wright Collection.*

RIGHT: 13in (33.0cm) Chase Baby. *H&J Foulke.*

(German)

MAKER: Often unknown
DATE: Various
MATERIAL: China head, cloth or kid body, china or leather arms
SIZE: Various
MARK: Often unmarked, sometimes marked with numbers and/or
"Germany"

Adelina Patti (so-called): Ca. 1870. Black-haired china shoulder head with high forehead, white center part with wings on each side, short overall curls, brushmarks at temple. Cloth body with leather arms or china arms and legs.
MARK: None

20—22in (50.8—55.9cm) $375-400

Bald (so-called Biedermeier): Ca. 1840. China shoulder head with bald head, some with black areas on top of head, blue painted eyes, proper wig; cloth body, bisque, china or leather arms; nicely dressed; all in good condition.
MARK: None

12—13in (30.5—33.0cm) $250-300
17—18in (43.2—45.7cm)   425-475

Bangs: Ca. 1880. Black or blonde-haired china shoulder head with bangs on forehead; cloth body with china arms and legs or kid body; dressed; all in good condition.
MARK: Some marked "Germany"

or Kling & Co.

22—24in (55.9—61.0cm)
$325-350

Blonde molded hair with bangs.
H&J Foulke

Brown Eyes: Ca. 1850. Black hair parted in center smooth to the head, pulled behind the ears; cloth body with leather arms; dressed; all in good condition.   14—15in (35.6—38.1cm) $350-400
MARK: none   20—22in (50.8—55.9cm)   550-600

Common or Low Brow: Late 1880s. Black or blonde wavy hair style on china shoulder head, blue painted eyes; old cloth or kid body with stub, leather, bisque or china limbs; appropriate clothes; all in good condition.

7—8in (17.8—20.3cm) $35-40
10—12in (25.4—30.5cm)   75-85
14—16in (35.6—40.6cm) 100-125
20—24in (50.8—61.0cm) 150-200

21in (53.3cm) common hairdo with pale blue eyes. *Joanna Ott Collection.*

Covered Wagon (so-called): 1840—1870. Black-haired china shoulder head with pink tint, hair parted in middle and close to head with vertical sausage curls; old cloth body with varied extremities; well dressed; all in good condition.
MARK: None

16—18in (40.6—45.7cm)$375-425

Curly Top (so-called): Ca. 1860. Black or blonde-haired shoulder head with distinctive large horizontal curls around forehead and face; old cloth body with leather arms or china arms and legs; nicely dressed; all in good condition.
MARK: None

16—20in (40.6—50.8cm)$400-450

15in (38.1cm) pink tint complexion with covered wagon hair style. *H&J Foulke.*

Dolley Madison (so-called): 1875—1895. Black-haired china shoulder head with molded ribbon bow in front and molded band on back of head; painted blue eyes; old cloth body with leather arms; nicely dressed; in good condition.
MARK: None
        17—21in (43.2—53.3cm) $325-350

Flat Top (so-called): Ca. 1850—1870. China shoulder head with black hair parted in middle, smooth on top with short curls, blue painted eyes; old cloth body, extremities of leather or china; appropriate clothes; all in good condition.
MARK: None
16—19in (40.6—48.3cm)
                $175-200
26—28in (66.0—71.1cm)
                250-300
29—31in (73.7—78.7cm)   350

Glass Eyes: Ca. 1850. Black-haired china shoulder head with hair parted in middle and styled very close to head, dark glass eyes. Cloth body with leather arms, appropriate clothes; all in good condition.
MARK: None
    24in (61.0cm) $1700

20in (50.8cm) flat top hair style. *Joanna Ott Collection.*

China with glass eyes. *Grace Dyar.*

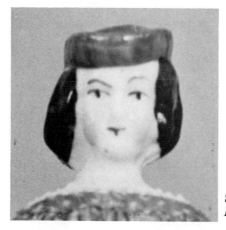

Hatted China Head: Ca. 1880.
Black hair, simply molded in
plain pouf style at nape of
neck, molded hat sitting mid-
way down forehead. Cloth
body, stone bisque limbs.
Dressed; all in good condition.

7—8in (17.8—20.3cm)
  As shown $175
  with poke bonnet   125

8in (20.3cm) hatted china.
H&J Foulke.

Man: Ca. 1850. Black-haired china shoulder head with short hair, brushmarks around face, blue painted eyes. Cloth body; appropriate
clothes; all in good condition.
MARK: None

16in (40.6cm) $500 up
Later, not so fine quality
   18—22in (45.7—55.9cm)
              $350-400

Small doll with short hair
style usually used for a man,
cloth body, wooden limbs, all
original. *H&J Foulke.*

Child, Motschmann-type with swivel neck: Ca. 1850. China head and flange neck with shoulder plate, midsection and lower limbs of china. Black painted hair, blue painted eyes. With or without clothes; all in good condition.

MARK: None

9in (22.9cm) $1450

8–10in (20.3–25.4cm) child with molded hair, swivel neck, cloth body, as shown   600**

**Not enough price samples to compute a reliable range.

ABOVE: 9½in (24.2cm) child with swivel neck, china limbs with bare feet. *H&J Foulke.*

RIGHT: 9in (22.9cm) child with swivel neck and Motschmann-type body. *Grace Dyar.*

Pierced Ears: Ca. 1860. China shoulder head with black hair styled with curls on forehead and pulled back to curls on lower back of head, blue painted eyes, pierced ears; original cloth body with leather arms or china arms and legs; appropriate clothes; all in good condition.

MARK: None

18–20in (45.7–50.8cm)$650 up*

*Depending upon rarity of hairdo

18in (45.7cm) china lady with pierced ears. *Grace Dyar.*

98   CHINA HEADS continued

Pet Name: Ca. 1905. China shoulder head, molded yoke with name in gold, black or blonde painted hair (one-third were blonde); painted blue eyes; old cloth body (some with alphabet or other figures printed on cotton material), china limbs; properly dressed; all in good condition. Used names such as: "Agnes", "Bertha", "Daisy", "Dorothy", "Edith", "Esther", "Ethel", "Florence", "Helen", "Mabel", "Marion" and "Pauline".

> 9in (22.9cm) $100-110
> 19—21in (48.3—53.3cm)   200-225

Snood: Ca. 1860. China shoulder head with black painted hair, slender features, painted blue eyes, molded eyelids, gold colored snood on hair; cloth body with leather arms or china limbs; appropriate clothes; all in good condition.
MARK: None

20—22in (50.8—55.9cm)
$500 up*

*Depending upon rarity of hair style.

17in (43.2cm) china lady with snood. *Grace Dyar.*

Spill Curl: Ca. 1870. China shoulder head with café-au-lait or black painted hair, massed curls on top spilling down back and sides onto shoulders, brushmarks around the forehead and temples, exposed ears; cloth body with china arms and legs; appropriate clothes; all in good condition.

MARK: None

18–20in (45.7–50.8cm)
$600-650

19in (48.3cm) china lady with "Spill curl" hair style. *Grace Dyar.*

Wood-Body China Head: Ca. 1840. Head with early hair style mounted on a peg-wooden body; usually with china lower limbs. Undressed; in good condition.

14in (35.6cm) $2200 up*

*Depending upon hair style

6in (15.2cm) china with pegged wood body. *H&J Foulke.*

China Head

(Japanese)

MAKER: Various Japanese firms
DATE: Ca. 1915—on
MATERIAL: China shoulder head and lower arms; cloth body
SIZE: Various
MARK: None or "Made in Japan"

Japanese China Head: Black curly hair in low brow style, painted eyes and features; cloth bodies of varying types with bisque lower arms.

14in (35.6cm) $65-75

14in (35.6cm) China Head Made in Japan. *H&J Foulke.*

Clear Dolls

MAKER: Emma Clear, Redondo Beach, CA., U.S.A.
DATE: 1940s—on
MATERIAL: Porcelain heads, glazed or unglazed, cloth bodies
SIZES: Various
MARK: In script "Clear" and date

Signed Clear doll: Shoulder head with molded hair and painted eyes, beautiful porcelain, exquisitely modeled, lovely decoration. Cloth bodies. Most models 18–22in (45.7–55.9cm) $225-275

15in (38.1cm) "Danny" by Emma Clear. *H&J Foulke.*

Cloth, Printed

MAKER: Various American companies, such as Cocheco Mfg Co, Lawrence & Co., and Arnold Print Works
DATE: 1896—on
MATERIAL: All-cloth
SIZE: 6—30in (15.2—76.2cm)
MARK: None on doll; mark could be found on fabric part which was discarded after cutting.

Cloth, Printed Doll: Face, hair, underclothes, shoes and socks printed on cloth. All in good condition. Dolls in underwear are sometimes found dressed in old underwear and frocks. Names such as: "Dolly Dear", "Merry Marie", etc.

Dolls with printed underwear:

6in (15.2cm)	$30-35
18in (45.7cm)	65-85
24—26in (61.0—66.0cm)	100-125

Boys and Girls with printed outer clothes, Ca. 1903:

18in (45.7cm)	$100-125
Santa, 1886	100-125
Darkey Doll, uncut	90-100
Aunt Jemima Family (four dolls)	175-200

ABOVE: Aunt Jemima Family. *Joseph Dent Collection.*

RIGHT: 4in (10.2cm) "The New Mail Baby" with original mailing label. *H&J Foulke.*

Clowns

MAKER: Various French and German firms
DATE: 1890—on
MATERIAL: Bisque or papier-mâché head, composition body
SIZE: Usually small
MARK: Various

Molded Bisque: Clown with molded bisque smiling face, painted or glass
eyes, molded hair or wig, clown paint on face, composition body,
clown costume.
12—14in (30.5—35.6cm) $600

Standard Bisque: Clown having standard bisque head painted with clown
make-up, composition body, glass eyes, open mouth, wig, clown
costume.
12—14in (30.5—35.6cm) $350-400

Jester, standard bisque face without clown make-up, clapping mechanism.
12in (30.5cm) $150-165

11½in (29.2cm) Jester with cymbals,
claps when stomach is pressed.

Dewees Cochran

MAKER: Dewees Cochran, Fenton, CA., USA
DATE: 1940–on
MATERIAL: Latex
SIZE: 9–18in (22.9–45.7cm)
DESIGNER: Dewees Cochran
MARK: Signed under arm or behind right ear

Dewees Cochran Doll: Latex with jointed neck, shoulders and hips, human hair wig, painted eyes, character face; dressed; all in good condition.

15–17in (38.1–43.2cm) Cindy (1947–1948) $600-650
Grow-up Dolls - - "Stormy", "Angel", "Bunnie", "J.J." and "Peter Ponsett" each at ages 5, 7, 11, 16, and 20 (1952–1956) $850-1000
American Children for Effanbee, See page 123
Look-Alike Dolls (6 different faces) $850-1000

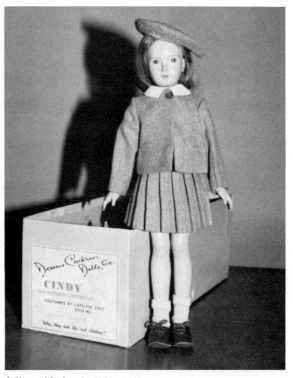

16in (40.6cm) "Cindy" with original box. *H&J Foulke.*

Composition, Miscellaneous

Kewpie-type Character Dolls: Ca. 1915—
on. Made by various American companies. Character face with large eyes
painted to the side; jointed arms; legs
together, usually on a base. Known by
names, such as "Cutie", "Sweetie",
etc. 12in (30.5cm) $50.

H&J Foulke.

H&J Foulke.

Composition Character Dolls:
Ca. 1915—on. Made by
various American companies. Composition head
with character face, painted features, molded hair,
hard cloth body, composition hands; appropriately
dressed; all in good condition.
14—16in (35.6—40.6cm)
$50—60
18—21in (45.7—53.3cm)
$65—75

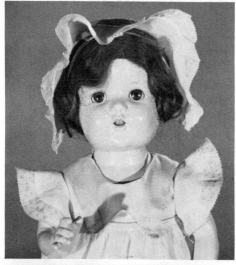

H&J Foulke.

Girl-type Mama Dolls: Ca. 1920—on. Made by various American companies. Composition head with sleep eyes, open mouth with teeth, lovely hair wig; composition shoulder plate, arms, and legs; cloth body; original clothes; all in good condition. Dolls of very good quality.
18—21in (45.7—53.3cm) $65—75
23—24in (58.4—61.0cm) $75—85

Character Doll: Ca. 1915—on. Maker Unknown. Entirely of a ceramic-type composition of fine quality; jointed at shoulders and hips; painted hair with a molded top knot; painted red stockings and black shoes; undressed.
10in (25.4cm) $125**

**Not enough price samples to compute a reliable range.

H&J Foulke.

Choir Boy: Ca. 1930–on. Made in Japan. All-composition with molded hair and painted features, book molded to hands, molded shoes and socks; choir robe; excellent condition. 10in (25.4cm) $50.

Ventriloquist Dolls: Ca. 1938–on. Various American companies in imitation of the Effanbee Charlie McCarthy doll. Composition head with movable jaw, arms, and legs; cloth body; original clothes; all in good condition. Known by names such as "Dummy Dan", "Gabby Joe". 15in (38.1cm) $50-60 In mint condition with original box $85-95

H&J Foulke.

H&J Foulke.

H&J Foulke.

Tonto and Lone Ranger: Ca. 1940? Dollcraft Novelty Company. Composition character face, hands, and feet, cloth body and limbs; original clothes; all in good condition.
21in (53.3cm) $250
In mint condition with original label and accessories. $350

Creche Figures

MAKER: Various European craftsman, primarily Italian
DATE: 18th and 19th centuries
MATERIAL: Wood and terra cotta on a wire frame
SIZE: Various
MARK: None

Creche Figures of various people in a Christmas scene: 18th and early 19th centuries. Gesso over wood head and limbs, fabric covered wire frame body; beautifully detailed features with carved hair and glass inset eyes, lovely hands; original or appropriate replacement clothes; all in good condition. 13—16in (33.0—40.6cm) $200-250

Mid 19th Century: Later doll with terra cotta head and limbs, painted eyes; fabric covered wire frame body; workmanship not as detailed; original or appropriate clothes; all in good condition.
12in (30.5cm) $125-150

8½in (21.5cm) Man and 12in (30.5cm) Lady Creche Figures, all original. *Joanna Ott Collection.*

D E P

MAKER: Maison Jumeau, Paris, France; (heads possibly by Simon Halbig)

DATE: Late 1890s

MATERIAL: Bisque socket head, French jointed composition body (sometimes marked Jumeau)

SIZE: About 12–33in (30.5–83.8cm)

MARK: DEP and size number (up to 16 or so); sometimes stamped in red "Tête Jumeau"

DEP: Bisque socket head, sleep eyes, painted lower lashes only, upper hair lashes (sometimes gone), open mouth, human hair wig, pierced ears. Jointed French composition body. Lovely clothes. All in good condition. 14–16in (35.6–40.6cm) $500-550
    19–23in (48.3–58.4cm)   650-700

16in (40.6cm) DEP. *H&J Foulke.*

Dean's Rag Book

MAKER: Dean's Rag Book Company, England
DATE: 1903—on
MATERIAL: Cloth
SIZE: Various
MARK: Cloth label, black stamp, or printed name

Printed on cloth: 1903—on. Various children, characters, and advertising dolls to cut out, sew, and stuff. In good condition.
  16—18in (40.6—45.7cm) $75-85
Felt-faced children: 1920s. Mask faces with molded and painted features, wigs, jointed arms and legs. Original clothes. In good condition.
  16in (40.6cm) $150-175
Velvet-faced: Late 1920s—on. Mask face with molded and painted features, wig, clothes sometimes an integral part of body.
  8—10in (20.3—25.4cm) Souvenir doll $45
  12in (30.5cm) girl $45-65*

*Allow extra for glass eyes.

14in (35.6cm) Dean's Rag Book Child, all original. *Jane Sheetz Collection. Photograph courtesy of Jane Sheetz.*

12in (30.5cm) Girl with velvet face. *H&J Foulke.*

Doll House Dolls

MAKER: Various German firms
DATE: Ca. 1890–1920
MATERIAL: Bisque shoulder head, cloth body, bisque arms and legs
SIZE: Various small sizes
MARK: Sometimes "Germany"

Doll House Doll: Man or lady 5½–7in (14.0–17.8cm), as above with painted eyes, molded hair, original clothes or suitably dressed; all in nice condition. $150*

> With glass eyes and wig $250-275
> With molded hair and painted eyes, ca. 1920 $100-125

> *Allow more for molded hats, grandfathers and unusual characters.

5in (12.7cm) Doll House Maid, all original. *H&J Foulke.*

Door of Hope

MAKER: Door of Hope Mission, China
DATE: 1917—on
MATERIAL: Wooden heads and hands, cloth bodies
SIZE: Various; usually under 13in (33.0cm)
MARK: Sometimes "Made in China" label

Door of Hope: Carved wooden head with painted and/or carved hair, carved features; cloth body; sometimes carved hands. Original handmade clothes, exact costuming for different classes of Chinese people. All in good condition.

11—13in (27.9—33.0cm) Adult $150-200
6—7in (15.2—17.8cm) Child   200

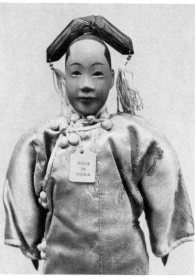

11in (27.9cm) Door of Hope Lady.
H&J Foulke.

12in (30.5cm) Door of Hope Man.
H&J Foulke.

Grace G. Drayton

MAKER: Various companies
DATE: 1909—on
MATERIAL: All-cloth, or composition and cloth combination, or all composition
SIZE: Various
MARK: Usually a cloth label or a stamp

Puppy Pippin: 1911, Horsman Co., N.Y. Composition head with puppy dog face, plush body with jointed legs; all in good condition. Cloth label.

About 8in (20.3cm) sitting $250**

Peek-a-Boo: 1913—1915, Horsman Co., N.Y. Composition head, arms, legs, and lower torso; cloth upper torso; character face with molded hair, painted eyes to side, and watermelon mouth; dressed in striped bathing suit, polka dot dress, or ribbons only; cloth label on outfit; all in good condition.

7½in (19.1cm) $85-95**

Chocolate Drop: 1923, Averill Manufacturing Co., N.Y. Brown cloth doll with movable arms and legs, painted features, three yarn pigtails; appropriate clothes; all in good condition. Stamped on front torso and paper label.

11in (27.9cm) $150**

Hug-Me-Tight: 1916, Colonial Toy Mfg, Co., N.Y. Mother Goose characters and others in one piece printed on cloth; all in good condition.

11in (27.9cm) $100**

Dolly Dingle: 1923, Averill Manufacturing Co., N.Y. Cloth doll with painted features and movable arms and legs; appropriate clothes; all in good condition. Stamped on front torso and paper label.

11in (27.9cm) $150**

**Not enough price samples to compute a reliable range.

Grace Drayton "Dolly Dingle". *Jan Foulke Collection.*

13in   (33.0cm) "Hug-Me-Tight." *Jan Foulke Collection.*

E.D. Bébé

MAKER: Unknown as yet but *possibly* by E. Denamur of Paris, France
DATE: Ca. 1885 into 1890s
MATERIAL: Bisque head, wood and composition jointed body
SIZE: Various
MARK: "E D", and sometimes a size number

Marked E. D. BÉBÉ: Bisque head, wood and composition jointed body,
good wig, pierced ears, beautiful blown glass eyes, nicely dressed, good
condition. Often found on a marked Jumeau body.

Closed mouth:
  21—23in   (53.3—58.4cm)
                         $2300-2600
Open mouth:
  18—21in   (45.7—53.3cm)
                         $900-1100

14in (35.6cm) E.D.
H&J Foulke.

MAKER: Fleischmann & Bloedel of Fürth, Bavaria and Paris, France
DATE: Founded in Bavaria in 1873. Also in Paris by 1890, then on into
S.F.B.J. in 1899
MATERIAL: Bisque head, composition jointed body
SIZE: Various
MARK: "EDEN BÉBÉ, PARIS"

Marked Eden Bébé: Bisque head, composition jointed body with un-
jointed wrists, beautiful wig, large set paperweight eyes, pierced ears,
lovely clothes, closed or open/closed mouth, all in nice condition.

Closed mouth:
20—22in (50.8—55.9cm)
$2200-2500
Open mouth:
18—21in (45.7—53.3cm)
$900-1100

ABOVE: 24in (61.0cm) Eden
Bébé, closed mouth. *Richard
Wright.*
LEFT: Eden Bébé, open
mouth. *Joanna Ott Collection.*

EFFanBEE

MAKER: EFFanBEE Doll Co., New York, N.Y., U.S.A.
DATE: 1912—on
MARKS: Various, but nearly always marked EFFanBEE on torso or head. Wore a metal heart-shaped bracelet; later a gold paper heart label.

Baby Dainty: 1912—1922. Composition shoulder head, painted molded hair, painted facial features (sometimes with tin sleep eyes), cloth stuffed body jointed at shoulders and hips, with curved arms and straight legs of composition; original or appropriate old clothes; all in good condition. Came with metal heart bracelet.

MARK: First Mold

Effanbee

Second Mold

EFFANBEE
BABY DAINTY

15in (38.1cm) $85-95

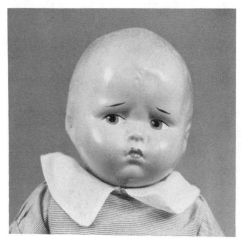

Baby Grumpy: 1912—1939. Composition shoulder head with frowning face, molded and painted hair, painted eyes, closed mouth, composition arms and legs, cloth body; original or appropriate old clothes; all in good condition. Came with metal heart bracelet.

MARK:

12in (30.5cm) $125

12in (30.5cm) "Baby Grumpy", all original. *H&J Foulke.*

Marilee: 1924. Composition shoulder head, arms and legs, cloth torso, sleep eyes, human hair wig, open mouth with teeth; original clothes; all in good condition. Various sizes. Came with metal heart bracelet.
MARK:

18in (45.7cm) $125

Bubbles: 1924—on. Composition head with blonde molded and painted hair, open mouth with teeth, sleep eyes, smiling face, cloth body, curved composition arms and legs; original or appropriate old clothes. All in good condition. Came with metal heart bracelet or necklace.
MARK:

19 © 24

EFFANBEE
DOLLS
WALK-TALK-SLEEP
MADE IN U.S.A.

EFFANBEE
BUBBLES
COPYR. 1924
MADE IN U.S.A.

16—20in (40.6—50.8cm) $100-125
24in (61.0cm)   150

Rosemary: 1925. Composition shoulder head, human hair wig, open mouth, tin sleep eyes; cloth torso, composition arms and legs; original or appropriate old clothes; all in good condition. Various sizes. Came with metal heart bracelet.
MARK:

EFFANBEE
ROSEMARY
WALK-TALK-SLEEP

18—22in (45.7—55.9cm)
$125-150

17in (43.2cm) "Rosemary", replaced dress. *Mary Lou Rubright Collection.*

Mae Starr: 1928. Composition shoulder head with open/closed mouth, sleep eyes, human hair wig, cloth body, composition limbs. Talking device in center of torso with records.

MARK:

MAE
STARR
DOLL

29in (73.7cm) $300-350

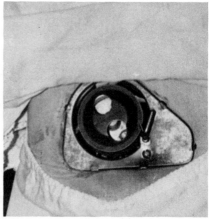

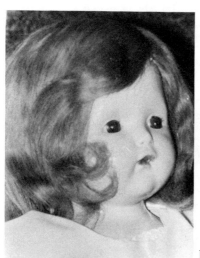

ABOVE: Talking device.

LEFT: 29in (73.7cm) Mae Starr. *Eileen   Wincklhofer   Collection. Photograph by Jerry Wincklhofer.*

Mary Ann and Mary Lee: 1928– on. Composition head on Lovums shoulder plate, composition arms and legs, cloth torso, open smiling mouth, sleep eyes, human hair wigs. Later version came on an all-composition body marked "Patsy–Ann" for Mary Ann and "Patsy-Joan" for Mary Lee. Came with metal heart bracelet. Appropriate clothes; in good condition.

MARK: ©

MARY-ANN

16in (40.6cm) Mary Lee $125-150
19in (48.3cm) Mary Ann   150

16in (40.6cm) "Mary Lee", replaced dress. *H&J Foulke.*

Lovums: 1928–1939. Composition swivel head on shoulder plate, arms and legs; pretty face, smiling open mouth with teeth, molded painted hair or wig, sleep eyes, cloth body; original or appropriate clothes; all in good condition. Various sizes. Came with metal heart bracelet. Note: The "Lovums" shoulder plate was used for many other dolls as well.

MARK: E F F AN B E E
LOVUMS
©
PAT. N⁰. I,283,558

16–20in (40.6–50.8cm) $100-125

Patsy Family: 1928–on. All-composition jointed at neck, shoulders and hips, molded hair (sometimes covered with wig), bent right arm on some members, painted or sleep eyes. Came with metal heart bracelet.

MARKS:

Bracelet

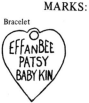

EFFANBEE
PATSY
BABY KIN

EFFANBEE
PATSY
DOLL

EFFANBEE
PATSY JR
DOLL

Patsy Family Prices

5½in (14.0cm) Wee Patsy
$175-195
8in (20.3cm) Baby Tinyette
100-110
8in (20.3cm) Patsy Babyette
125
9in (22.9cm) Patsyette
125-135
10in (25.4cm) Patsy Baby
125
11in (27.9cm) Patsy Jr.
125-135
11in (27.9cm) Patricia Kin
150-175
14in (35.6cm) Patsy
125-135
14in (35.6cm) Patricia
150

8in (20.3cm) "Patsy Babyette", all original with label. *H&J Foulke.*

16in (40.6cm) Patsy Joan
$175
19in (48.3cm) Patsy Ann
150-200
22in (55.9cm) Patsy Lou
250-275
26in (66.0cm) Patsy Ruth
350**
30in (76.2cm) Patsy Mae
400**

**Not enough price samples to compute a reliable range.

14in (35.6cm) 1946 "Patsy", all original in box. *H&J Foulke.*

26in (66.0cm) "Patsy Ruth", all original. *Maxine Salaman Collection.*

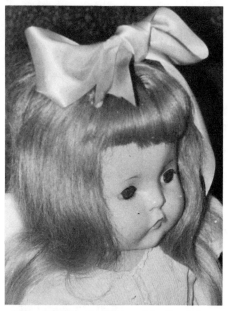

30in (76.2cm) "Patsy Mae". *Eileen Wincklhofer Collection. Photograph by Jerry Wincklhofer.*

Skippy: 1929. All-composition, jointed at neck, hips and shoulders. (Later a cloth torso, still later a cloth torso and upper legs with composition molded boots for lower legs.) Molded hair, painted eyes to side; original or appropriate clothes; all in good condition. Came with metal heart bracelet.

MARK: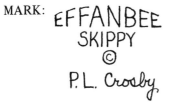

14in (35.6cm) $150-175
Mint with button   300

14in (35.6cm) "Skippy", all original. *Glenn Mandeville/Chip Barkel.*

W. C. Fields: 1930. Composition head, hands, and feet; cloth body; painted hair and eyes; strings at back of head to open mouth; original clothes; all in good condition.
MARK:
    W. C. FIELDS
AN EFFANBEE PRODUCT

17–20in (43.2–50.8cm)
                    $600**

*Not enough price samples to compute a reliable range.

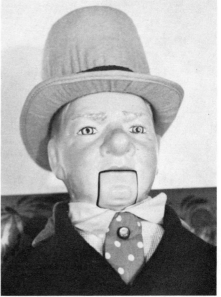

20in (50.8cm) "W.C. Fields", all original. *Richard Wright Collection.*

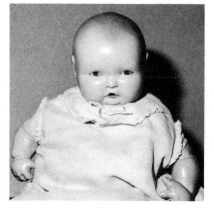

Lamkin: 1930s. Composition head, arms and legs with very deep and detailed molding. Cloth body, molded hair, sleep eyes, bow mouth. Original clothes; all in good condition.

MARK: On head:
          "LAMBKINS"
          (note spelling)
Paper heart tag:
          Lamkin

16in (40.6cm) $125-150*

16in (40.6cm) "Lamkin", all original. *Barbara Steiker.*

*Only in fair condition

Dy-Dee Baby: 1933—on. First dolls had hard rubber head with soft rubber body, open mouth for drinking, soft ears (after 1940), caracul wig or molded hair. Later dolls had hard plastic heads with rubber bodies. Still later dolls had hard plastic heads with vinyl bodies. Came with paper heart label. Various sizes from 9—20in (22.9—50.8cm)

                              MARK:
14—16in (35.6—40.6cm) $65—85

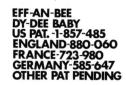

**EFF-AN-BEE
DY-DEE BABY
US PAT. -1-857-485
ENGLAND-880-060
FRANCE-723-980
GERMANY-585-647
OTHER PAT PENDING**

Anne Shirley: 1935—1940. All-composition jointed at neck, shoulders and hips; sleep eyes, closed mouth, human hair wig; original clothes; all in good condition. Various sizes. Came with metal heart bracelet. Anne Shirley body used on other dolls as well.
MARK: On back: EFFanBEE/ ANNE SHIRLEY.

15—18in (38.1—45.7cm) $125-150
20—21in (50.8—53.3cm)   200-225
27in (68.6cm)   350-400

21in (53.3cm) "Anne Shirley", all original bride outfit. *H&J Foulke.*

American Children: 1936–1939. Composition swivel head on composition body jointed at shoulders and hips. Four different faces designed by Dewees Cochran with either open or closed mouths, painted or sleep eyes, human hair wigs. Original clothes; all in good condition. Came with metal heart bracelet and paper heart label. Sizes 15in (38.1cm), 17in (43.2cm), 19in (48.3cm) and 21in (53.3cm).

MARK: On head: EFFANBEE/ AMERICAN/CHILDREN. On body: EFFANBEE/ANNE SHIRLEY.

15–21in (38.1–53.3cm) $750-950

19in (48.3cm) American Child, closed mouth version, all original. *H&J Foulke.*

17in (43.2cm) American Child Boy, painted eyes, all original. *H&J Foulke.*

17in (43.2cm) American Child, open-mouth version, all original. *H&J Foulke.*

Pennsylvania Dutch Dolls: 1936–1940s. Used "Baby Grumpy" shoulder head, cloth torso, composition arms and legs. Dressed in costumes to represent "Amish", "Mennonite", or "Brethren". Green wrist tag with black stamp indicated sect.

MARK:

(EFFanBEE Dolls WALK- TALK-SLEEP)

12–13in (30.5–33.0cm) $100

Charlie McCarthy: 1937. Composition head, hands and feet; cloth body; strings at back of head to operate mouth; painted hair and eyes; original clothes; all in good condition.
MARK: "EDGAR BERGEN'S CHARLIE McCARTHY, AN EFFanBEE PRODUCT"

17–20in (43.2–50.8cm) $200-250

(Photograph of Charlie McCarthy on page 128)

21in (53.3cm) Original Historical Doll, all original. 1760 Pre-Revolutionary model. *Rosemary Dent Collection.*

Historical Dolls: 1939. All-composition jointed at neck, shoulders and hips. Three each of 30 dolls portraying the history of American fashion 1492–1939. "American Children" heads used with painted eyes and elaborate human hair wigs. Elaborate original costumes using velvets, satins, silks, brocades, etc. All in good condition. Came with metal heart bracelet.

MARKS: On head: EFFANBEE
AMERICAN
CHILDREN
On body: EFFANBEE
ANNE SHIRLEY

21in (53.3cm) $1000

Historical Doll Replicas: 1939. All composition jointed at neck, shoulders and hips. Series of 30 dolls, popular copies of the original historical models (above) Painted eyes, human hair wigs. Original costumes all in cotton copies of those on the original models. Came with metal heart bracelet.
MARK: On torso: EFFanBEE
ANNE SHIRLEY
14in (35.6cm) $350-375

14in (35.6cm) Historical Doll Replica 1896 all original. *Rosemary Dent Collection.*

Suzette: 1939. All-composition jointed at neck, shoulders and hips, closed mouth, eyes painted to side, mohair wig; original clothes; all in good condition. Came with metal heart bracelet.

MARK:

SUZETTE
EFF an BEE
MADE IN
U.S.A.

11½in (29.2cm)
$100-110

Suzanne: 1940. All-composition jointed at neck, shoulders and hips, closed mouth, sleep eyes, mohair wig; original clothes; all in good condition. Came with metal heart bracelet.

MARK:

SUZANNE
EFFANBEE
MADE IN U.S.A

14in (35.6cm)
$125

Tommy Tucker: 1939–1949. Composition head with painted hair or mohair wig, closed mouth, chubby cheeks, flirting eyes; composition hands, stuffed body; original clothes; all in good condition. Also called "Mickey" and "Baby Bright Eyes". Came with paper heart tag.

Sizes   15–24in   (38.1–61.0cm)

MARK: On head: EFFANBEE U.S.A.

18in (45.7cm) $125-150

UPPER RIGHT: 11in (27.9cm) "Suzette" with molded hair, all original. *H&J Foulke.*

BOTTOM RIGHT: 16in (40.6cm) "Tommy Tucker", all original. *Glenn Mandeville/Chip Barkel.*

Portrait Dolls: 1940. All-composition, jointed at neck, shoulders, and hips, sleep eyes, mohair wigs. In costumes, such as ballerina, Bo-Peep, Gibson Girl, bride and groom, dancing couple. All original, in good condition.
MARK: None

11in (27.9cm) $150

ABOVE: 11in (27.9cm) Portrait Doll, ballerina. *H&J Foulke.*

LEFT: 11in (27.9cm) Portrait Doll, Gibson Girl. *H&J Foulke.*

Storybook-type: Ca. 1940. All-composition, jointed at shoulders and hips; appears to be the same doll as "Wee Patsy" with added mohair wig; molded shoes and socks, painted eyes; all original, in good condition.

6in (15.2cm) all original in box $125**

**Not enough price samples to compute a reliable range.

6in (15.2cm) Storybook-type doll, all original in box. *H&J Foulke.*

Little Lady: 1940–1949. All-composition jointed at neck, shoulders and hips, separated fingers, mohair or human hair wig, closed mouth, sleep eyes; original clothes; all in good condition. (During "War Years" some had yarn wigs and/or painted eyes.) Various sizes.

MARK: On back: EFFanBEE   Paper heart:
         U.S.A.   **"I am Little Lady"**

15–18in (38.1–45.7cm)
$125-150
27in (68.6cm) $350-400

RIGHT: 14in (35.6cm) "Little Lady", all original. *H&J Foulke.*

BELOW: 12in (30.5cm) "Sister", replaced clothes. *Nancy Smith.*

Brother and Sister: 1942. Composition swivel heads and hands, stuffed cloth body, arms and legs; painted eyes, yarn wigs. Original pink (sister) and blue (brother) outfits.
MARK: EFFANBEE

12in (30.5cm) Sister and 16in (40.6cm) Brother $100-125

Sweetie Pie: 1942. Composition head and limbs cloth torso, flirty eyes, closed mouth, caracul wig, original clothes, all in good condition. Available in 16in, 20in and 24in (40.6cm, 50.8cm and 61.0cm)
MARK: EFFANBEE © 1942   20–24in (50.8–61.0cm) $85-95

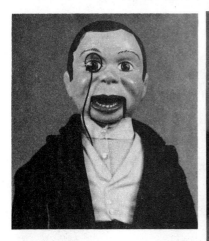

19in   (48.3cm)   "Charlie McCarthy", all original but missing hat. *H&J Foulke.*

17in (43.2cm) "Sweetie Pie", replaced clothes. *Joanna Ott Collection.*

Candy Kid: 1946. All-composition toddler, jointed at neck, shoulders and hips; molded hair, sleep eyes. Original clothes; all in good condition. Came with paper heart tag.
MARK: EFFanBEE   12in (30.5cm) $100-125

Honey: 1949–1955. All-hard plastic jointed at neck, shoulders and hips, sleep eyes, synthetic hair, mohair, or human hair; original clothes, all in good condition.
MARK: EFFANBEE

18in (45.7cm) $100-125

Limited Edition Dolls, Mint Condition:

1976 Patsy	$250
1978 Dewees Cochran	150
1979 Skippy	150

Joel Ellis

(Wooden Doll)

MAKER: Co-operative Manufacturing Co., Springfield, VT., U.S.A.
DATE: 1873
MATERIAL: Composition head, fully-jointed wooden body. Metal feet and wooden or metal hands.
SIZE: 12–18in (30.5–45.7cm)
MARK: None–unless black paper band around waist still exists with patent date printed on it.

Joel Ellis Wooden Doll: Composition head (over wood). Painted brown eyes, jointed wooden body (mortise-and-tenon), molded hair, metal hands and feet. Nicely dressed in old clothes. All in only fair condition.

12in (30.5cm)	$650
15in (38.1cm)	750

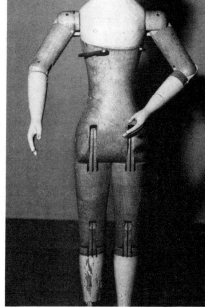

15in (38.1cm) Joel Ellis.
Grace Dyar.

F.G.

MAKER: A. Gaultier, Paris (1860); later F. Gaultier and Fils, St. Maurice, Charenton, Seine, Paris, France
DATE: Late 1860s—on
MATERIAL: Bisque head, kid or composition body
SIZE: Various
MARK: or F.G. on side of shoulder plate

Marked F. G. Fashion Lady: Late 1860s to 1930; bisque swivel head on bisque shoulder plate, original kid body, kid arms with wired fingers or bisque lower arms and hands; original or good French wig, lovely large stationary eyes, closed mouth, ears pierced; dressed; all in good condition.

12—14in (30.5—35.6cm)	$700-800
16—18in (40.6—45.7cm)	900-1250
21—23in (53.3—58.4cm)	1400-1650

Marked F. G. Bébé: 1879—1900 and probably later; bisque head, composition jointed body, good French wig, closed mouth, beautiful large set eyes, pierced ears, well dressed; all in nice condition.

Open mouth:
19—21in (48.3—53.3cm) 950

12—15in (30.5—38.1cm) 1200-1500
17—19in (43.2—48.3cm) 1750-1950
24in (61.0cm) 2400

Early kid body:
15—18in (38.1—45.7cm) $2100-2200

LEFT: 19in (48.3cm) F. G. in scroll. *Richard Wright.*
MIDDLE: 17in (43.2cm) F. G. in scroll. *H&J Foulke.*
RIGHT: 16in (40.6cm) early F. G. Fashion. *Mary Lou Rubright Collection.*

Famlee Doll

131

MAKER: Berwick Doll Co. and Change-O-Doll Co., New York, N.Y., U.S.A.

DATE: 1918–on

MATERIAL: Composition heads to screw onto cloth body, composition arms and legs

SIZE: 16 in. (40.6cm)

MARK: "PAT APR 12, 21" on screw cap

Famlee Doll: Three composition heads and one cloth body with threaded metal socket in top of body. Three sets of clothing. All in good condition. 16in (40.6cm) $175*

*Came in sets of up to 12 heads, so allow
extra for each additional head
18in (45.7cm) Boxed as pictured $350-400

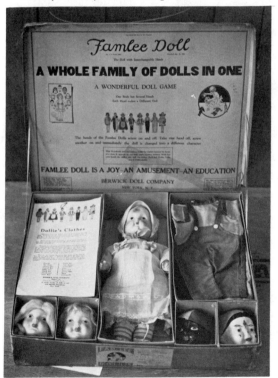

16in (40.6cm) Famlee doll in original box.
Maxine Salaman Collection.

French Bébé
(unmarked)

MAKER: Numerous French firms
DATE: Ca. 1860–1925
MATERIAL: Bisque head, jointed composition body
SIZE: Various
MARK: None, except perhaps numbers, Paris, or France

Unmarked French Bébé: Beautiful bisque head, swivel neck, set paperweight eyes, ears pierced, closed mouth, lovely wig, jointed French body, pretty costume, all in good condition.

17–18in (43.2–45.7cm) $1500-1800

Same as above except with open mouth:
20–22in (50.8–55.9cm) $900-1000

Character face: $850 up depending upon desirability of face.

10in (25.4cm) unmarked French Bébé, open mouth. *H&J Foulke.*

21½in (54.6cm) unmarked French Bébé. *Sheila Needle Collection. Photograph by Morton Needle.*

15in (38.1cm) unmarked French character girl. *H&J Foulke.*

French Fashion-Type
(Unmarked)

MAKER: Various French firms
DATE: Ca. 1860—1930
MATERIAL: Bisque shoulder head, jointed kid body
SIZE: Various
MARK: None, except possibly numbers or letters

French Fashion: Unmarked bisque shoulder head, swivel neck, kid body, kid arms--some with wired fingers, or old bisque arms; original or good wig; lovely blown glass eyes, closed mouth, earrings, original or other fine clothes, all in very good condition.

12—14in (30.5—35.6cm)	$700-800
16in (40.6cm)	900-1250
21—23in (53.3—58.4cm)	1400-1800
25in (63.5cm)	2000

16in (40.6cm) unmarked French Fashion-type. *Mary Lou Rubright Collection.*

French Fashion-Type
(Wood Body)

MAKER: Unknown
DATE: Ca. 1865—on
MATERIAL: Bisque head, fully-jointed wood body
SIZE: Various
MARK: Size numbers only

Wood Body Lady: Bisque swivel head on shoulder plate, paperweight eyes, closed mouth, pierced ears, good wig. Wood body, fully jointed at shoulders, elbows, wrists, hips and knees. Dressed. All in good condition.

16—18in (40.6—45.7cm) $2200-2500

Rare with ball-joint at waist and ankle joints

See page 336 for a photo of a French Fashion-type wood jointed body.

16in (40.6cm) French Fashion-type with wood jointed body. *Mary Lou Rubright Collection.*

Frozen Charlotte

MAKER: Various German firms
DATE: Ca. 1850s—early 1900s
MATERIAL: Glazed china
SIZE: 1—18in (2.5—45.7cm)
MARK: None, except for "Germany", or numbers or both

Frozen Charlotte: All-china doll, black, sometimes blonde molded hair parted down the middle, painted features. Hands extended, legs separated but not jointed. No clothes; perfect condition.

2—4in (5.1—10.2cm)	$25-50*
6in (15.2cm)	75*
13—15in (33.0—38.1cm)	300-350
16in (40.6cm)	400-450

*Allow extra for pink tone and especially fine decoration and modeling

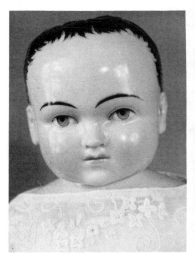

15in (38.1cm) Frozen Charlotte. *Mary Lou Rubright Collection.*

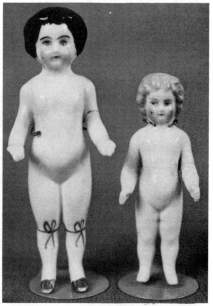

4½in (11.5cm) and 6in (15.2cm) Frozen Charlottes. *Joanna Ott Collection.*

Fulper Dolls

MAKER: Heads by Fulper Pottery Co. of Flemington, N.J., U.S.A.
Bodies by other companies, often Amberg or Horsman
DATE: 1918−1921
MATERIAL: Bisque heads; composition ball-jointed or jointed kid
bodies
SIZE: Various
MARK: "Fulper−Made in U.S.A." and others. Mark reproduced below.

Fulper Child Doll: Marked bisque head, good wig; kid jointed or composition ball-jointed body; set or sleep eyes, open mouth; suitably dressed.
All in nice condition. 15−18in (38.1−45.7cm) $350-400
               20−23in (50.8−58.4cm)   450-500
Fulper Baby or Toddler: Same as above, but with bent-limb or jointed
toddler body. 16−20in (40.6−50.8cm) $400-500

Fulper
Made in
USA
13

17 in (43.2cm) Fulper
Toddler Girl. *Esther
Schwartz Collection.*

20in (50.8cm) Fulper
Girl. *H&J Foulke.*

Georgene Novelties

MAKER: Georgene Novelties (Georgene Averill, Madame Hendren), N.Y., U.S.A.
DATE: 1930s
MATERIAL: All-cloth
SIZE: Various, but usually about 13in (33.0cm)
MARK: Usually a paper tag

Internationals and Children: Mask face with painted features, yarn hair, some with real eyelashes, cloth body with movable arms and legs. Attractive original clothes; all in excellent condition.

Foreign costume 12–14in (30.5–35.6cm) $30-35
24–26in (61.0–66.0cm)   75

Children 12–14in (30.5–35.6cm) $40-50

24in (61.0cm) Georgene Novelties Girl with yarn hair and inset eyelashes. *H&J Foulke.*

German Bisque Dolls
(Unmarked)

MAKER: Various German firms
DATE: 1880—on
MATERIAL: Bisque head, composition or kid body
SIZE: Various
MARK: Some numbered, some "Germany," some both

Child Doll with closed mouth: Ca. 1880—1890. Bisque shoulder head, kid or cloth body, gussetted at hips and knees, good bisque hands, nicely dressed; mohair wig; all in good condition.

Kid body:
14—16in (35.6—40.6cm)
$650-750*
20—24in (50.8—61.0cm)
900-1100*

*Allow extra for swivel neck, or unusual face.

Composition body:
15—16in (38.1—40.6cm)
$850-950
20—21in (50.8—53.3cm)
1100

Child Doll with open mouth: Late 1880s—1900. Fine, pale bisque head, ball-jointed composition body or kid body with bisque lower arms; good wig, open mouth, glass eyes; dressed; all in good condition.

16—18in (40.6—45.7cm)
$325-375

20—24in (50.8—61.0cm)   400-450
27—28in (68.6—71.1cm)   550-650

17in (43.2cm) Turned Shoulder Head, closed mouth. *Joanna Ott Collection.*

Name shoulder head Child: 1890 to World War I. Bisque shoulder head marked with doll's name, jointed kid or cloth body, bisque lower arms; well dressed, glass eyes, open mouth, good wig; all in good condition. Names include "Rosebud", "Lilly", "Daisy", "Alma", "Mabel", "Darling", "Ruth", 16–18in (40.6–45.7cm) $175-200
22–25in (55.9–63.5cm) 225-275

14in (35.6cm) Socket Head, composition body. *Joanna Ott Collection.*

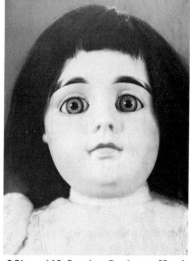

25in (63.5cm) Socket Head incised 630/13, paperweight eyes. *Joanna Ott Collection.*

Child Doll with open mouth: 1900–1940. Bisque head, ball-jointed composition, kid or cloth body with bisque lower arms; good wig, open mouth, glass sleep eyes, pretty clothes; all in good condition.

16–18in (40.6–45.7cm)
$200-225*
20–24in (50.8–61.0cm)
250-300*
27in (68.6cm)   400*

*Allow more for a doll with unusual face.

25in (63.5cm) Shoulder Head incised M. *Joanna Ott Collection.*

ABOVE: 14in (35.6cm) socket head incised 23.3X/DEP, paperweight eyes. *Joanna Ott Collection.*

RIGHT: 5in (12.7cm) tiny child, composition body. *H&J Foulke.*

Tiny (up to 10in or 25.4cm) child doll: Ca. 1900—1940. Bisque socket head of good quality, five-piece composition body of good quality with molded and painted shoes and stockings. Good wig, open mouth, set or sleep eyes. Cute clothes. All in good condition.

5—7in (12.7—17.8cm)	$110-125
8—10in (20.3—25.4cm)	150-175
Fully jointed body:	8—10in
(20.3—25.4cm)	225-250

ABOVE: 9in (22.9cm) character baby incised 405. *H&J Foulke.*

LEFT: 17in (43.2cm) character boy. *Richard Wright.*

Character Baby: 1910–on. Bisque head, good wig or solid dome with painted hair, sleep eyes, open mouth; composition bent-limb baby body; suitably dressed; all in good condition.

11–14in (27.9–35.6cm) $225-275*
18–20in (45.7–50.8cm)   350-400*

24in (61.0cm)   450*
*Allow more for open-closed mouth, closed mouth or unusual face

LEFT: 14in (35.6cm) Character Girl. *H&J Foulke.*

RIGHT: 19in (48.3cm) Character Girl incised 41.28. *H&J Foulke.*

MIDDLE: 14in (35.6cm) Character Boy incised 163/1. *Mary Lou Rubright Collection.*

15in (38.1cm) Character Girl incised 134. *Mary Lou Rubright Collection.*

Character Child: 1910—on. Bisque head with expressive character face. Good wig or solid dome head with painted hair; sleep or painted eyes; open or closed mouth; jointed composition body; dressed; all in good condition.

15—18in (38.1—45.7cm)
$750 up*

19—22in (48.3—55.9cm)
41.28 or 29 $400-450
15in (38.1cm) 134
1800-2000
14in (35.6cm) 163   950

*Depending upon individual face

Infant: 1924—on. Bisque head with molded and painted hair, glass sleep eyes; cloth body, celluloid or composition hands; dressed; all in good condition.

12—14in (30.5—35.6cm) long $275-325*

*More depending upon appeal and rarity of face.

RIGHT: 12in (30.5cm) Infant incised P+1002. *H&J Foulke.*

Smiling Infant. *Emma Wedmore Collection.*

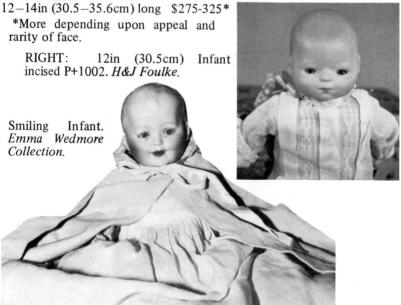

German Bisque "Dolly" Faces

Numerous companies produced the girl dolls with open mouths, sleep eyes, mohair wigs and ball-jointed composition or kid bodies between 1900–1930. These all run approximately the same price for a good-quality bisque head and appropriate body with nice clothes. Do not pay as much for the very late bisques and the cheaply-made bodies.

Trade Names

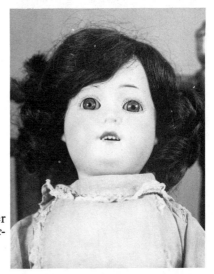

My Girlie
My Sweetheart
Viola
Princess
Duchess
Dollar Princess
Majestic
Darling
Pansy
Beauty
Columbia

19in (48.3cm) clover mark. *Joanna Ott Collection.*

Makers

G & S
MOA Welsch
P. Sch.
S & C
E. U. Steiner
G. B.
L H B
L H K
Gebrüder Knoch
Goebel

17in (43.2cm) Wm. Goebel. *Joanna Ott Collection.*

20–24in (50.8–61.0cm) $250-325
28in (71.1cm) 400

24in (61.0cm) "Dollar Princess".
Mary Lou Rubright Collection.

ABOVE: 22in (55.9cm)
"My Sweetheart". *Mary
Lou Rubright Collection.*

LEFT: 23in (58.4cm)
Gans & Seyfarth. *Joanna
Ott Collection.*

Gesland

MAKER: Heads: A. Gaultier, Paris; later F. Gaultier and Fils. Bodies:
E., F. & A. Gesland, Paris
DATE: Late 1860s—on
MATERIAL: Bisque head, stockinette stuffed body on wire frame.
Bisque or composition lower arms and legs.
SIZE: Various
MARK: Heads: **F. G**

Gesland Bodied Dolls: Fashion lady bisque swivel head, pierced ears,
closed mouth, paperweight eyes, good wig. Stockinette body with
bisque hands and legs. Dressed. All in good condition.

18—23in (45.7—58.4cm) $2500-3000

Bébé-type bisque swivel head: Pierced ears, closed mouth, paperweight
eyes, good wig. Stockinette body with composition lower arms and
legs. Dressed. All in good condition.

18—20in (45.7—50.8cm) $2500-2800

14in (35.6cm) Gesland body, F. G. head.
Richard Wright.

Giggles

MAKER: Cameo Doll Co., N.Y.
DATE: 1946
MATERIAL: All-composition
SIZE: 14in (35.6cm)
DESIGNER: Rose O'Neill
MARK: Paper wrist tag only

Giggles: Unmarked composition jointed at neck, shoulders, and hips; large painted eyes, closed mouth, molded hair with bun in back; original romper; all in very good condition.

14in (35.6cm) $300-350**
Mint with tag   400-450

**Not enough price samples to compute a reliable range.

14in (35.6cm) "Giggles", all original with tag. *H&J Foulke.*

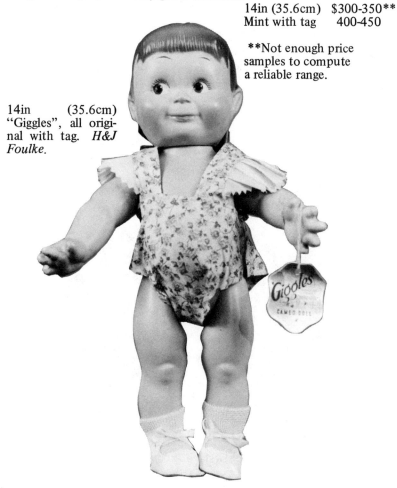

MAKER: Made in Germany for George Borgfeldt, New York, N.Y., U.S.A.

DATE: 1929

MATERIAL: Ceramic head, cloth torso, composition arms and legs

SIZE: 17−22in (43.2−55.9cm)

DESIGNER: Helen W. Jensen

MARK:

[sic] *Gladdie Copyriht By Helen W. Jensen*

Marked Gladdie: Ceramic head, molded and painted hair, glass eyes, open/closed mouth with molded teeth, laughing face, cloth torso, composition arms and legs; dressed; all in good condition.

17in (43.2cm) $800-900

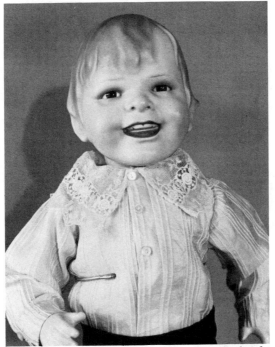

23in (58.4cm) "Gladdie". *Mary Lou Rubright Collection.*

Godey's Little Lady Dolls

MAKER: Ruth Gibbs, Flemington, N.J.
DATE: Ca. 1940s
MATERIAL: China head and limbs; cloth body
SIZE: Most 7in (17.8cm); a few 12in (30.5cm)
DESIGNER: Ruth Gibbs
MARK: Paper label inside skirt "Godey's Little Lady Dolls"

Ruth Gibbs Doll: China head with painted hair and features, pink cloth body with china limbs; original clothes, usually in an old-fashioned style.

7in (17.8cm) $30-35

ABOVE: 7in (17.8cm) "Godey's Little Lady Doll". *H&J Foulke.*

LEFT: Original box lid (part of).

Googly-Eyed Doll

MAKER: J. D. Kestner, Armand Marseille and other German and French firms

DATE: Ca. 1911—on.

MATERIAL: Bisque heads and composition or papier-mâché bodies or all bisque

SIZE: Usually small

MARK: Various

All-Bisque Googly: Jointed at shoulders and hips, molded shoes and socks, glass eyes, impish mouth, mohair wig. Undressed. In perfect condition.

4—5in (10.2—12.7cm) Glass eyes, stiff neck	$450
4—5in (10.2—12.7cm) Glass eyes, swivel neck	550-600
4—5in (10.2—12.7cm) Painted eyes, swivel neck	350-400
4—5in (10.2—12.7cm) Jointed elbows and knees	1250**

**Not enough price samples to compute a reliable range

5¾in (14.7cm) All-Bisque Googly with swivel neck. *H&J Foulke.*

6½in (16.5cm) A.M. 253 Googly. *H&J Foulke.*

17in (43.2cm) Googly with molded blonde hair, glass eyes, incised 163-6. *Richard Wright.*

13in (33.0cm) JDK 221. *Richard Wright Collection.*

Painted Eyes, Composition body: Marked bisque swivel head with painted eyes to side, molded hair, impish mouth; composition body jointed at shoulders and hips with molded and painted shoes and socks. Cute clothes. All in good condition.

7–8in (17.8–20.3cm) $325-350

Glass Eyes, Composition body: Marked bisque head; original composition body jointed at neck, shoulders and hips; molded and painted socks and shoes, googly eyes look to side, sleep or set; impish mouth closed, proper wig, cute clothes; all in nice condition.

JDK 221, 12–13in
(30.5–33.0cm) $4000-4500
#165, 173 13–15in
(33.0–38.1cm)   3600-4100
AM #323, 6½–7½in
(16.5–19.1cm)   550-650
9–10in (22.9–25.4cm)
                          750-850
AM #253 Watermelon
mouth, 6½–7½in
(16.5–19.1cm)   650
SFBJ #245, 8in
(20.3cm)   1650
13in (33.0cm)   3850

Composition Mask Face: 1912–1914. Made by various companies in 9½–14in (24.1–35.6cm) sizes; marked with paper label on clothing. Called "Hug Me Kiddies" as well as other trade names. Round composition mask face, round glass eyes looking to side, wig, watermelon mouth, felt body, original clothes; all in good condition.

14in (35.6cm) $650

16in (40.6cm) Googly incised 173/6. *Richard Wright Collection.*

12in (30.5cm) Mask Face Googly, all original. *H&J Foulke.*

7in (17.8cm) Gebruder Heubach "Elisabeth", all original. *Richard Wright Collection.*

Greiner

MAKER: Ludwig Greiner of Philadelphia, Penn., U.S.A.
DATE: 1858–1883
MATERIAL: Heads of papier-mâché; cloth bodies, homemade in most cases, but later some Lacmann bodies were used.
SIZE: Various, 13–over 35in (33.0–over 88.9cm)
MARK: Paper label on back shoulder:

GREINER'S
IMPROVED
———— PATENTHEADS ————
Pat. March 30TH'58

or

GREINER'S
PATENT DOLL HEADS
No7
Pat. Mar. 30'58. Ext.'72

Greiner: Blonde or black molded hair, painted features; homemade cloth body, leather arms, nice old clothes; entire doll in nice condition.

'58 Label, 20–23in (50.8–58.4cm) $450-550
'72 Label, 23–24in (58.4–61.0cm)   300-325

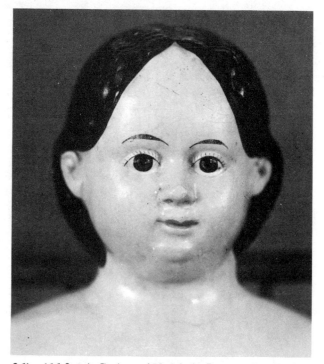

26in (66.0cm) Greiner, '58 label. *Joanna Ott Collection.*

H.A.

MAKER: Henri Alexander, Paris, France
DATE: 1889–1891; Tourrell 1892–1895; then merged with Jules Steiner
MATERIAL: Bisque head, jointed wood and composition body
SIZE: Various

MARK:

H. B. Bébé: 1889–1891. Bisque socket head with closed mouth, paperweight eyes, pierced ears, good wig; jointed composition and wood body; lovely clothes, all in good condition.

21in (53.3cm) $2500-2800**   **Not enough price samples to compute a reliable range.

17in (43.2cm) H. A. 7, marked Steiner body. *Crandall Collection.*

Half-Bisque Dolls

MAKER: Unknown
DATE: 1910
MATERIAL: Bisque with cloth upper legs and arms
SIZE: 4½—6½in (11.4—16.5cm)
MARK: "Germany"

Half-Bisque Dolls: Head and body to waist of one-piece bisque, molded hair, painted features, bisque hands, lower legs with white stockings and molded shoes with heels and bows, other parts of body are cloth. Appropriate clothes. All in good condition.

6½in (16.5cm) $150-200

6½in (16.5cm) Half-Bisque
Girl. *Mike White Collection.*

Heinrich Handwerck Child Doll ¹⁵⁵

MAKER: Heinrich Handwerck of Waltershausen, Thüringia, Germany
DATE: Ca. 1890—on
MATERIAL: Bisque head, composition ball-jointed body
SIZE: Various
MARK: "Germany—Handwerck" sometimes with "S & H" and numbers
such as 69, 79, 99, 109, 119, etc.

Hch 6/0 H.
germany

Marked Handwerck Child Doll: Bisque socket head, ball-jointed body,
open mouth, sleep or set eyes, original or good wig, pierced ears,
lovely old clothes; entire doll in good condition.
18—22in (45.7—55.9cm)
$300-350
24—26in (61.0—66.0cm)
400-500
28in (71.1cm)   600
36in (91.4cm)   1000
40—42in (101.6—106.0cm)
1500

Mold #109 17—19in
(43.2—48.3cm) $300-350
Mold #109 24—25in
(61.0—63.5cm)   450-500

24in (61.0cm) 109. *H&J Foulke.*

15in (38.1cm) Heinrich Handwerck. *H&J Foulke.*

Max Handwerck Child Doll

MAKER: Max Handwerck of Waltershausen, Thüringia, Germany
DATE: 1900—on
MATERIAL: Bisque socket head, ball-jointed composition body
SIZE: Various
MARK: "Max Handwerck" with numbers and sometimes "Germany";
also "Bébé Elite".

$$Max$$
$$HANDWERCK$$

$$Germany$$

Marked Max Handwerck Child Doll: Marked bisque socket head; original
or good wig, original ball-jointed body, pierced ears, set or sleep eyes,
open mouth; well dressed; all in good condition.

21—24in (53.3—61.0cm) $350-400   **Bébé Elite Character:**
                                          16in (40.6cm) $300-350

25in (63.5cm) Max Handwerck. *Mary Lou
Rubright Collection.*

Hansi

MAKER OR DISTRIBUTOR: P. J. Gallais & Co., Paris, France
DATE: 1917–1918
MATERIAL: Earthenware
SIZE: 7½in (19.1cm)
DESIGNER: Hansi
MARK: None on doll; paper wrist tag "Vive la France! Gretel"; on the other side "Hansi"

Yerri or Gretel: Earthenware head with painted eyes and hair, closed mouth; jointed five-piece earthenware body with painted shoes and socks; original. Alsasian costume. All in good condition.

     7½in (19.1cm) $225-250

7½in (19.1cm) "Gretel". *Becky Roberts.*

Happifats

MAKER: Registered by Borgfeldt in U.S. and Germany
DATE: 1913–1921
MATERIAL: All-composition, all-bisque or composition head and hands with stuffed body
SIZE: All bisque 3½–4½in (8.9–11.4cm); composition about 10in (25.4cm)
DESIGNER: Kate Jordan
MARK: ©

Happifats: All-bisque with jointed arms, painted features, molded clothes.
        German $200-225
        Nippon   125
        Composition   300 up**
          **Not enough price samples to compute a reliable range

4½in (11.5cm) German Happifats Girl. *Mary Lou Rubright Collection.*

Hatted or Bonnet Dolls
(Bisque)

MAKER: Various German firms
DATE: Ca. 1890–1920
MATERIAL: Bisque shoulder heads (usually stone bisque), cloth bodies, china or stone bisque extremities
SIZE: Usually 12in (30.4cm) and under
MARK: Some with numbers and/or "Germany"

Hatted or Bonnet Doll: Bisque head with painted molded hair and molded fancy bonnet with bows, ribbons, flowers, feathers, etc.; painted eyes and facial features; original cloth body with original arms and legs; good old clothes or newly dressed; all in good condition.

7–8in (17.3–20.3cm)	$125
13–15in (33.0–38.1cm)	225-275
All-bisque, 5–6in (12.7–15.2cm)	
common-type	$50-60
more unusual style	150-200

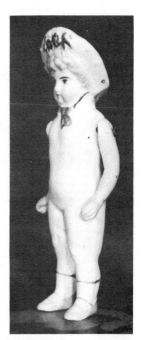

ABOVE: 4½in (11.5cm) white bisque doll with molded bonnet. *H&J Foulke.*

LEFT: 5½in (14cm) doll with molded bonnet. *H&J Foulke.*

HEbee-SHEbee Dolls

MAKER: Edward Imeson Horsman Co., New York, N.Y., (EIH), U.S.A.
   (All-bisque made in Germany)
DATE: 1925
MATERIAL: Composition; some all bisque
SIZE: Various
DESIGNER: Charles H. Twelvetrees
MARK: Sticker on foot

HEbee—SHEbee Doll: All-composition, jointed at shoulders and hips.
Painted eyes; molded white chemise and real ties in molded shoes.
Gummed label on foot. All in fair condition. Blue shoes indicate a
"HEbee"; pink ones a "SHEbee".

10—11in (25.4—27.9cm)	$300-325
Repainted	100-125

All-Bisque HEbee-SHEbee: Description as above.

German 4—5in (10.2—12.7cm)	$500-600
Nippon 4—5in (10.2—12.7cm)	175-200

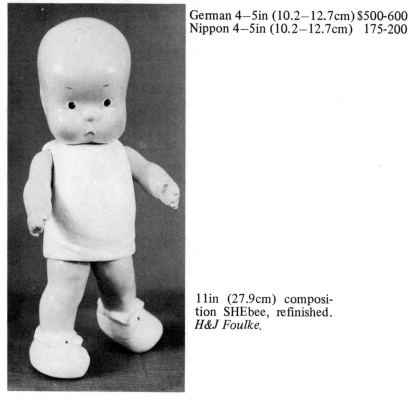

11in (27.9cm) composi-
tion SHEbee, refinished.
H&J Foulke.

Mme. Hendren
Character Dolls

MAKER: Averill Manufacturing Co., New York City, N.Y.
DATE: 1915—on
MATERIAL: Composition heads, cloth and composition bodies
SIZE: Various
MARK: Cloth tag attached to clothes

Tagged Mme. Hendren Character: Composition character face, usually with painted features, molded hair or wig (sometimes yarn). Hard stuffed cloth body with composition hands. Original clothes often of felt. Included Dutch children, Indians, Sailors, Cowboys, Blacks. All in good condition. 10—14in (25.4—35.6cm) $85-100

Mme. Hendren Child: Marked on head. Celluloid head with glass eyes; stuffed body with composition arms and legs. Original clothes. All in good condition 15in (38.1cm) $100-125
All composition 15in (38.1cm) 100-125
Dolly Reckord, 26in (66.0cm) 300-350
Mama Dolls, 16—18in (40.6—45.7cm) 75-100

ABOVE: 26in (66.0cm) Dolly Reckord, replaced dress. *Nancy Smith.*

LEFT: 12in (30.5cm) All-composition characters. *H&J Foulke.*

Gebrüder Heubach

MAKER: Gebrüder Heubach of Licht and Sonneberg, Thüringia, Germany
DATE: Dolls considered here mostly from 1910—on
MATERIAL: Bisque head, kid, cloth or jointed composition body or composition bent-limb body
SIZE: Various
MARK: "Gebrüder Heubach—Germany"

Heubach Character Child: Marked bisque head, character face, molded hair, intaglio eyes; jointed composition or kid body, closed or open/closed mouth, dressed; all in nice condition.

#8192, 17—20in (43.2—50.8cm)	$500-600
#6969, 6970, 7246, 15in (38.1cm)	1600-1800
#7604, laughing child, intaglio eyes, composition body, 13—15in (33.0—38.1cm)	450-500
#5636, laughing child, glass eyes, 16—18in (40.6—45.7cm)	1200-1400
#7977, Stuart baby, 10—12in (25.4—30.5cm)	1000-1200
glass eyes, 10in (25.4cm)	1500
#7788, Coquette, 12—14in (30.5—35.6cm)	600-650
17in (43.2cm)	750
#8774, "Whistling Jim",	850-950
#5777, "Dolly Dimple", 24in (61.0cm)	2000
#7622, pouty with molded hair, 14in (35.6cm)	700
18—20in (45.7—50.8cm)	900
Walker	500

Heubach Infants: Marked bisque head, molded hair or good wig, character face, composition bent-limb body; open or closed mouth, sleep or intaglio eyes, dressed; all in nice condition.

Pouty Babies 8—10in (20.3—25.4cm)

#7602 and others $250-325

"Whistling Jim" mold #8774. *Jan Foulke Collection.*

Pouties #6969 Girl and 6970 Boy. *Gail Hiatt Collection.*

12in (30.5cm) shoulder head #6736. *H&J Foulke.*

18in (45.7cm) shoulder head #9355 version of "Dolly Dimple", *Jilda Sallade Collection.*

ABOVE: 20in (50.8cm) incised "Santa". *Old Curiosity Shop.*

RIGHT: 16in (40.6cm) Laughing Boy, often mold #7604. *Old Curiosity Shop.*

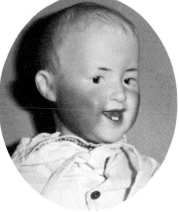

6½in (16.5cm) Pouty
Baby Twins. *H&J*
Foulke.

8½in (21.6cm) toddler,
often mold #5636.
Richard Wright.

MAKER: Ernst Heubach of Köppelsdorf, Thüringia, Germany
DATE: 1887—on
MATERIAL: Bisque head, kid, cloth or composition bodies
SIZE: Various
MARK:

Heubach-Köppelsdorf
250·15% ≙
Germany

Heubach Girl shoulder head, often mold number 275: Ca. 1887—on.
Bisque head, sleep eyes, open mouth, good wig; kid or cloth body
with bisque arms; dressed; all in good condition.

Shoulder head	17—19in (43.2—48.3cm)	$195-210
	12in (30.5cm)	130-135

Heubach Girl socket head, often mold number 250: Ca. 1887—on. Bisque head, good wig, sleep eyes, open mouth; jointed composition body, nice clothes; all in good condition.

8—9in (20.3—22.9cm)
$100-110
14—16in (35.6—40.6cm)
180-200
22—24in (55.9—61.0cm)
250-325

24in (61.0cm) Child
#250. *Mary Lou*
Rubright Collection.

10in   (25.4cm)   Baby
#267. *H&J Foulke.*

Character Baby: 1910–on. Often mold numbers 300, 320 and 342. Bisque head, good wig, sleep eyes, open mouth (sometimes also wobbly tongue and pierced nostrils); composition bent-limb baby or toddler body; dressed; all in good condition.

7in (17.8cm) $200
10–12in (25.4–30.5cm)
                    225-250
14–16in (35.6–40.6cm)
                    275-325
20–24in (50.8–61.0cm)
                    400-450
28in (71.1cm)   650-700

Character Children: 1910–on. Bisque shoulder head with molded hair, painted eyes, open/closed mouth; cloth body with composition lower arms. Came in several different styles.

#262 and other molded hair:
    12in (30.5cm) $300-400

7in   (17.8cm)   Baby
#300. *H&J Foulke.*

Infant: Ca. 1925. Mold number 349. Bisque head, sleep eyes, closed mouth, molded and painted hair; cloth body, composition or celluloid hands, appropriate clothes; all in good condition.

10–12in (25.4–30.5cm) $400**

#338 12in (30.5cm)   600**

    **Not enough price samples to compute a reliable range

7½in   (19.1cm)
Black Baby #399.
Louise Ceglia.

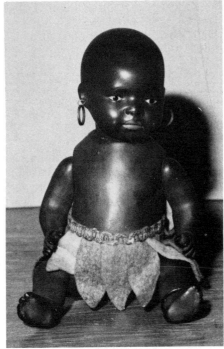

Black Baby: Ca. late 1920s. Mold number 399. Marked black bisque head, bent-limb or toddler black body, closed mouth, molded hair or black kinky wig, original grass skirt and brass jewelry, sleep eyes. All in good condition.

#399 Black:
    8−10in (20.3−25.4cm) $300-350

Gypsy: Ca. late 1920s. Mold number 452. Tan bisque head, matching toddler body, open mouth with teeth, mohair wig, brass earrings, sleep eyes; appropriate costume; all in good condition.

#452 Gypsy:
    10−12in (25.4−30.5cm) $300-350**

    **Not enough price samples to
compute a reliable range

Holz-Masse

(Composition)

MAKER: Cuno & Otto Dressel, Sonneburg, Thüringia, Germany
DATE: 1875—on
MATERIAL: Composition head, arms and legs; cloth body
SIZE: Various
MARK:

Marked Holz-Masse: Composition shoulder head, mohair wig, glass or painted eyes, sometimes pierced ears. Cloth body with composition arms and legs with molded boots. Old clothes. All in good condition.
18—21in (45.7—53.3cm) $250-275

20in (50.8cm) unmarked composition head of Holz-Masse type. *Joanna Ott Collection.*

Horsman

MAKER: E. I. Horsman Co., New York, N.Y., U.S.A.
DATE: 1901—on

Billiken: 1909. Composition head with peak of hair at top of head, watermelon mouth, slanted slits for eyes. Velvet or plush body. In fair condition only.
MARK: Cloth label on body; "Billiken" on right foot

12in (30.5cm) $175-200

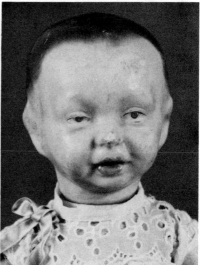

Baby Bumps: 1910. Composition head with molded hair and painted features, stuffed cloth body. Head looks like Kämmer and Reinhardt's "Baby" mold number 100.
MARK: None

14—15in (35.6—38.1cm) $100-125

LEFT: 13in (33.0cm) "Billiken" with paper label and stamp on foot. *Becky Roberts Collection.*

ABOVE: 16in (40.6cm) Baby Bumps-type head on jointed composition body. *H&J Foulke.*

Can't Break 'Em Characters: Ca. 1910. Heads and hands of "Can't Break 'Em" composition, hard stuffed cloth bodies with swivel joints at shoulders and hips; molded hair, painted eyes, character faces; appropriate clothes, all in good condition.
MARK: E.I.H. 1911

12in (30.5cm) $75-85

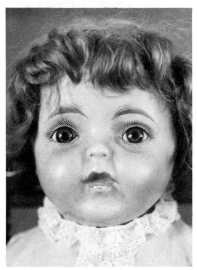

Campbell Kids: See pages 85 & 86.

Early Babies: Ca. 1915. Head of strong composition, hard stuffed cloth body, composition hands; good wig, glass eyes; appropriate clothes, all in good condition.
MARK: E.I.H. 1915
14in (35.6cm) $75

Rosebud: 1920s. Composition swivel head, smiling face with dimples, open mouth with teeth, tin sleep eyes, mohair wig; cloth torso, composition arms and legs; original clothes; all in good condition. Various sizes.
MARK: On head: ROSEBUD
18—22in (45.7—55.9cm) $65-85

LEFT: 12in (30.5cm) "Can't Break 'Em" character of 1911, probably "Fairy". *J&H Foulke.*

ABOVE: 17in (43.2cm) "Rosebud". *H&J Foulke.*

LEFT: 21in (53.3cm) early Horsman Baby with glass eyes. *Joanna Ott Collection.*

Tynie Baby: See page 323.

Baby Dimples: 1928. Composition head with smiling face, open mouth, tin sleep eyes, molded and painted hair; soft cloth body with composition arms and legs. Original or appropriate old clothes. All in good condition. Various sizes.
MARK: On head:

©
E.I.H. CO. INC.

16–20in (40.6–50.8cm) $100-125

Child Dolls: Ca. 1930s and 1940s. All composition with swivel neck, shoulders and hips; mohair wig, sleep eyes; original clothes, all in good condition.
MARK: HORSMAN
13–15in (33.0–38.1cm)
$45-55

15in (38.1cm) Horsman Art Doll, all original. *H&J Foulke.*

Mary Hoyer

MAKER: The Mary Hoyer Doll Mfg. Co., Reading, Penn., U.S.A.
DATE: Ca. 1925—on
MATERIAL: First all-composition; later all-hard plastic
SIZE: 14in and 18in (35.5 and 45.7cm)
MARK: Embossed on torso: The
Mary Hoyer
Doll

or in a circle:

ORIGINAL
Mary Hoyer
Doll

Marked Mary Hoyer: Material as above, swivel neck, jointed shoulders and hips. Sleep eyes with lashes, closed mouth, original wig. All in good condition. Original tagged factory clothes or garments made at home from Mary Hoyer patterns (many are crocheted).

Composition 14in (35.6cm)	$85
Hard plastic 14in (35.6cm)	85

LEFT: 14in (35.6cm) hard plastic Mary Hoyer, all original. *Mary Lou Rubright Collection.*

ABOVE: 14in (35.6cm) composition Mary Hoyer, painted eyes, all original, unmarked. These dolls were used during the years of World War II. *Virginia Slade Collection.*

A. Hülss

175

MAKER: Adolf Hülss of Walterhausen, Thüringia, Germany; heads by Simon & Halbig

DATE: 1915–1925

MATERIAL: Bisque socket heads, composition bodies (later heads of painted bisque)

SIZE: Various

MARK:

—*SIMON & HALBIG*————————————————————

Baby 10–12in (25.4–30.5cm) $250-300
Toddler 17–20in (43.2–50.8cm) 450-500*

*Allow extra for flirty eyes

21in (53.3cm) 156 Toddler, flirty eyes. *H&J Foulke.*

Hummel Dolls
(Rubber)

MAKER: Wm. Goebel, Porzellanfabrik, Germany
DATE: These dolls 1952–1964
MATERIAL: All rubber
SIZE: 11–12in (27.9–30.5cm)
DESIGNER: M. I. Hummel
MARK: Signed head, tagged clothes, also paper label

Hummel Doll: Rubber head, molded, painted hair, painted features; jointed neck, shoulders and hips. Original clothes. All in good condition.

12in (30.5cm) $100-125

Hummel dolls are now being made in vinyl. Do not pay old prices for new dolls.

12in (30.5cm) Hummel Boy, all original. *H&J Foulke.*

Ideal

MAKER: Ideal Novelty and Toy Co., Brooklyn, N.Y., U.S.A.
DATE: 1907–on
MARKS: Various, usually including "IDEAL"

Shirley Temple: 1935. For detailed information see pages 300–302.

Betsy Wetsy: 1937–on. Composition head with molded hair, sleep eyes, soft rubber body jointed at neck, shoulders and hips. Drinks, wets. Appropriate clothes; all in good condition. This doll went through many changes including hard plastic head on rubber body, later vinyl body; later completely vinyl. Various sizes.
MARK: IDEAL

12in (30.5cm) $35-40

Baby Snooks (Fanny Brice): 1938. Head, torso, hands and feet of composition; arms and legs made of flexible metal cable, molded hair, smiling mouth; original clothes; all in good condition.
MARK: On head: IDEAL
Round paper tag:
  "FLEXY–an Ideal Doll
Fanny Brice's Baby Snooks"

12in (30.5cm) $200

Deanna Durbin: 1938. All-composition jointed at neck, shoulders and hips, sleep eyes, smiling mouth with teeth, original human hair or mohair wig; original clothing; all in good condition. Various sizes.
MARK: Metal button with her picture: DEANNA DURBIN, IDEAL DOLL, U.S.A.

14in (35.6cm) $200-225
20–21in (50.8–53.3cm)350-400

21in (53.3cm) "Deanna Durbin", all original. *Maxine Salaman Collection.*

Judy Garland as Dorothy of the Wizard of Oz: 1939. All composition jointed at neck, shoulders and hips, dark human hair wig, dark sleep eyes, open mouth with teeth; original dress; all in good condition.

MARK: On head and body:
    IDEAL DOLL

16in (40.6cm) $850 up

12½in (31.8cm) "Mortimer Snerd", all original.

Mortimer Snerd: 1938–1939. Head, hands and feet of composition; arms and legs of flexible metal cable, torso of wire mesh; in original clothes; all in good condition.

MARK: Head embossed: "Ideal Doll"

13in (33.0cm) $200

16in (40.6cm) "Judy Garland", all original. *Glenn Mandeville/Chip Barkel.*

Snow White: 1939. All-composition jointed at neck, shoulders and hips, black mohair wig, lashed sleep eyes, open mouth; original dress with velvet bodice and cape, and rayon skirt with figures of seven dwarfs. In good condition.
MARK: On body: SHIRLEY TEMPLE/18
On dress: An Ideal Doll
18in (45.7cm) $300**

**Not enough price samples to compute a reliable range

Magic Skin Baby: 1940. Composition head with sleep eyes, closed mouth, stuffed latex rubber body, jointed shoulders and hips, molded hair. Later babies had hard plastic heads. Various sizes. Appropriate clothes, all in good condition.

MARK: On head: IDEAL

13—16in (33.0—40.6cm) $35-45

RIGHT: 16in (40.6cm) "Magic Skin Baby", all original. *Jan Foulke Collection.*

Pinocchio: 1940. Molded composition head with painted features, wooden segmented body; felt hat, red suit; all in good condition. MARK on front torso: PINOCCHIO/ Des. by Walt Disney/ Made by Ideal Novelty & Toy Co.

10½in (26.7cm) $125

Flexy Dolls: Ca. 1942. Head, hands and feet of composition; arms and legs of flexible metal cable, torso of wire mesh; in original clothes; all in good condition.

MARK: On head: "Ideal Doll"

12in (30.5cm) $85-95

12in (30.5cm) Flexy Girl, all original. *H&J Foulke.*

14in (35.6cm) "Toni", all original. *H&J Foulke.*

Toni and P–90 Family: 1948–on. Series of girl dolls. Most were completely of hard plastic with jointed neck, shoulders and hips, nylon wig, sleep eyes, closed mouth. Original clothes; all in excellent condition. Various sizes, but most are 14in (35.6cm). MARK: On head: IDEAL DOLL On body: IDEAL DOLL

          P–90

      Made in USA

Toni 14in (35.6cm)	$55-60
Mary Hartline 14in (35.6cm)	75
Betsy McCall 14in (35.6cm)	75
Harriett Hubbard Ayers 14in (35.6cm)	75
Miss Curity 14in (35.6cm)	75

RIGHT: 14in (35.6cm) "Miss Curity", all original. *Mary Lou Rubright Collection.*

LEFT: 14in (35.6cm) "Betsy McCall", all original. *H&J Foulke.*

Saucy Walker: 1951. All-hard plastic jointed at neck, shoulders and hips with walking mechanism, synthetic wig, flirty eyes, open mouth with tongue and teeth. Original clothes, all in good condition. Various sizes, usually 19–23in (48.3–58.4cm)
MARK: IDEAL DOLL
19–22in (48.3–55.9cm) $40-50

Peter and Patty Playpal: 1960. Vinyl heads with rooted hair, sleep eyes. Hard vinyl body jointed at shoulders and hips. Appropriate clothes. All in excellent condition.
MARK: Peter: IDEAL TOY CORP.
                    BE–35–38
            Patty: IDEAL DOLL
                    G–35

35–36in (88.9–91.4cm) $85

23in (58.4cm) "Saucy Walker". *Miriam Blankman Collection.*

10in (25.4cm) "Little Miss Revlon". *Mary Lou Rubright Collection.*

Miss Revlon: 1955. Vinyl head with rooted hair, sleep eyes, closed mouth, earrings, hard plastic body with jointed waist and knees, high-heeled feet; vinyl arms with polished nails. Original clothes; all in good condition.
MARK: On head and body: IDEAL DOLL

Miss Revlon, 17–19in (43.2–48.3cm) $40-45
Little Miss Revlon, 10½in (26.7cm) 30-35

Crissy and Family (Growing Hair Doll): 1968. Vinyl head with rooted hair and grow feature, painted or sleep eyes, smiling mouth; hard body jointed at waist, shoulders and hips. Original clothes, all in excellent condition. Various sizes.
MARK: Very lengthy but always includes IDEAL TOY CORPORATION.

Crissy, Velvet, Cinnamon	$10-12	Brandi, Dina	20
Mia, Kerry, Tressy	15	Cricket	25

15in (38.1cm) dolls from the "Crissy" family: "Mia", "Velvet", and "Dina", all original. *Beth Foulke Collection.*

Italian Hard Plastic

MAKER: Bonomi, Ottolini, Ratti, Furga, and other Italian firms
DATE: Late 1940s and 1950s
MATERIAL: Heavy hard plastic, sometimes painted, or plastic coated papier-mâché
SIZE: Various
MARK: Usually a wrist tag; company name on head

Italian Hard Plastic: Heavy, fine quality material jointed at shoulders and hips; human hair wig, sleep eyes, sometimes flirty, often a character face; original clothes; all in excellent condition.

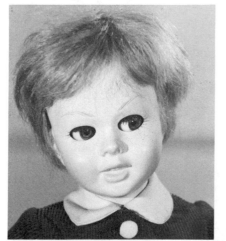

10–12in (25.4–30.5cm) $35-45
19–22in (48.3–55.9cm)
75-100*

*Allow extra for a very fancy costume.

15in (38.1cm) Girl by Bonomi, all original. *H&J Foulke.*

16in (40.6cm) Girl by Furga, all original. *H&J Foulke.*

Wrist Tag from above girl. *H&J Foulke.*

J.V. Child Doll

MAKER: J. Verlingue of Boulogne-sur-Mer, France
DATE: 1914—1921
MATERIAL: Bisque head, composition body
SIZE: Various
MARK:

PETITE FRANÇAISE
FRANCE
J V
⚓
3/0 D
LIANE

Marked J. V. Child: Bisque head, jointed papier-mâché body; good wig, glass eyes, open mouth, nicely dressed.

17—18in (43.2—45.7cm)
$350-400
19—21in (48.3—53.3cm)
450-550

19in (48.3cm) Liane. *Maxine Salaman Collection.*

Japanese Bisque
Caucasian Dolls

MAKER: Various Japanese firms; heads were imported by New York importers, such as Morimura Brothers, Yamato Importing Co., and others.

DATE: 1915—on

MATERIAL: Bisque head, composition body

SIZE: Various

MARK: Morimura Brothers

Various other marks with Japan or Nippon, such as J.W., F.Y., etc.

Character Baby: Bisque socket head, with glass or painted eyes, solid dome or wig, open mouth with teeth, dimples; composition bent-limb baby body, dressed. All in good condition.

10—12in (25.4—30.5cm)	$125-150
14in (35.6cm)	175
18—19in (45.7—48.3cm)	200-225

Child Doll: Bisque head, glass sleep eyes, open mouth, mohair wig; jointed composition or kid body, dressed. All in good condition.

22—24in (55.9—61.0cm)
$225-250
16—18in (40.6—45.7cm)
175-200

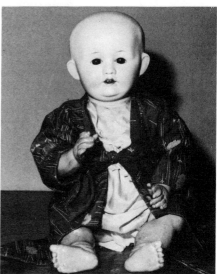

Character Baby with superimposed YI Japan for Yamato Importing Co. *Betty Ferrell Collection.*

Jullien Bébé

MAKER: Jullien, Jeune of Paris, France
DATE: 1875−1904 when they joined S.F.B.J.
MATERIAL: Bisque head, composition and wood body
SIZE: Various
MARK: "JULLIEN" with size number

JuLLiEN

———————————————————————— 1 ————————

Marked Jullien Bébé: Bisque head, jointed wood and composition body;
 lovely wig, paperweight eyes, closed mouth, pierced ears, pretty old
 clothes, all in good condition.

22−24in (55.9−61.0cm)	$2800-3000
Open mouth	
19−21in (48.3−53.3cm)	1100-1200

19in (48.3cm) "Jullien", closed mouth. *Richard Wright.*

Jumeau

MAKER: Maison Jumeau, Paris, France
DATE: Various
MATERIAL: Bisque head, kid or composition body
SIZE: Various
MARK: On body stamped in blue:

JUMEAU
MEDAILLE D'OR
PARIS

Various head marks (see individual dolls listed below).

Fashion Lady: Late 1860s—on. Usually marked with number only on head; blue stamp on body. Bisque swivel head on shoulder plate, paperweight eyes, pierced ears, closed mouth, good wig. All kid body or kid with bisque lower arms and legs. Appropriate clothes. All in good condition.

14—15in (35.6—38.1cm)	$1100-1200
19—21in (48.3—53.3cm)	1400-1600

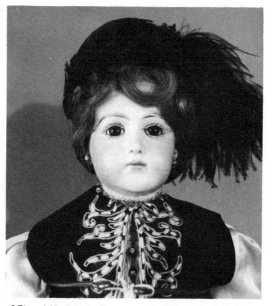

27in (68.6cm) Jumeau Fashion Lady, blue stamp on body. *Mary Lou Rubright Collection.*

30in (76.2cm) Long-Face Jumeau. *Crandall Collection.*   25in (63.5cm) Portrait Jumeau. *Richard Wright.*

Long-Face Bébé: Ca. 1870s. Usually marked with number only on head; blue stamp on body. Bisque socket head with beautiful wig, closed mouth, applied pierced ears, blown glass eyes; jointed composition body with straight wrists; lovely clothes; all in good condition.

26—29in (66.0—73.7cm) $8000 up

Portrait Bebé: Ca. 1870s. Usually marked with size number only on head; blue stamp on body. Bisque socket head with unusually large paperweight eyes, pierced ears, closed mouth, skin or other good wig; jointed composition body with straight wrists; nicely dressed. All in good condition.

17—19in (43.2—48.3cm) $3500-3800
22—24in (55.9—61.0cm)   4200-4500

23in (58.4cm) E.J. *Jan Foulke Collection.*

15in (38.1cm) Incised Jumeau. *H&J Foulke.*

E. J. Bébe: Ca. 1880. Head incised as below; blue stamp on body. Bisque socket head with closed mouth, paperweight eyes, pierced ears, good wig; jointed composition body with straight wrists; lovely clothes; all in good condition.

MARK: On head:

DÉPOSÉ
E. 7 J.

9in (22.9cm) rare size	$2500
14–16in (35.6–40.6cm)	2800-3000
18–19in (45.7–48.3cm)	3200-3500
23–25in (58.4–63.5cm)	4000-4500

Incised Jumeau Depose Bébé: Ca. 1880. Head incised as below; blue stamp on body. Bisque socket head with closed mouth, paperweight eyes, pierced ears, good wig; jointed composition body with straight wrists; lovely clothes; all in good condition.

MARK: on head JUMEAU
DEPOSE

18–19in (45.7–48.3cm) $3000

Tête Jumeau Bébé: 1879–1899, then through S.F.B.J. Red stamp on head as indicated below. Blue stamp or "Bébé Jumeau" oval sticker on body. Bisque head, original or good French wig, beautiful stationary eyes, closed mouth, pierced ears, jointed composition body with jointed or straight wrists; original or lovely clothes; all in good condition.

MARK: D É P O S É
          TETE JUMEAU
          B^{TE} SGDG
                6

14–16in (35.6–40.6cm)	$2000-2200
20–22in (50.8–55.9cm)	2500-2800
24–26in (61.0–66.0cm)	2900-3200
31in (78.7cm)	3900
Composition lady body, 20in (50.8cm)	4500**
Open mouth Bebe:	
14–16in (35.6–40.6cm)	900-1000
19–21in (48.3–53.3cm)	1150-1350
23–25in (58.4–63.5cm)	1500-1800
32in (81.3cm)	2200

**Not enough price samples to compute a reliable range.

13in (33.0cm) Tete Jumeau. *H&J Foulke.*

19in (48.3cm) Tete Jumeau, adult body. *Joanna Ott Collection.*

Jumeau Phonograph Doll: Ca. 1890s. Regular bisque Jumeau head, usually with open mouth, paperweight eyes, pierced ears, good wig. Jointed composition body with cavity in torso to accommodate a Lioret phonograph with wax cylinder, wound by key protruding from doll's back. Open mouth

    24in (61.0cm) closed mouth $3200 up**
    open mouth   2000**

1907 Jumeau Child: Ca. 1900. Sometimes red-stamped "Tête Jumeau". Bisque head, good quality wig, set or sleep eyes, open mouth, pierced ears; jointed composition body. Nicely dressed. All in good condition.

    19−21in (48.3−53.3cm) $1100-1200
    31−33in (78.7−83.3cm)   1800-2000

**Not enough price samples to compute a reliable range

BELOW: 26in (66.0cm) Jumeau with open mouth. *Joanna Ott Collection.*

ABOVE: 17in (43.2cm) Tête Jumeau with open mouth. *H&J Foulke.*

Jumeau Great Ladies: Ca. 1930s. Bisque socket head with adult features, closed mouth, fixed eyes; fancy mohair wig; five-piece composition body with painted black slippers, metal stand attached to foot. A series of ladies dressed in fancy costumes. All original, in excellent condition.
MARK: 221 on head
10–11in (25.4–27.9cm) $350**

Princess Elizabeth Jumeau: 1938 through S.F.B.J. Bisque socket head highly colored, with glass flirty eyes and closed mouth, good wig. Jointed composition body. Dressed. All in good condition.

MARK: 71 (UNIS FRANCE) 149
306
JUMEAU
1938
PARIS

19in (48.3cm) $800-900**

**Not enough price samples to compute a reliable range.

11in (27.9cm) Jumeau "Marie Antoinette". *H&J Foulke.*

Just Me Doll

MAKER: Armand Marseille of Köppelsdorf, Thüringia, Germany
DATE: Ca. 1925
MATERIAL: Bisque socket head, composition jointed body
SIZE: Various small sizes
MARK:

Just ME
Registered
Germany
A 3|0|5|0 M

Marked "Just Me": Bisque socket head, glass eyes to side, closed mouth, curly wig; composition body, dressed; all in good condition.

9–10in (22.9–25.4cm) $850-1000

Painted bisque socket head:

7–9in (17.8–22.9cm) $375-425

7½in (19.1cm) Painted Bisque "Just Me", all original. *H&J Foulke.*

Jutta Dolls

MAKER: Cuno and Otto Dressel, Sonneberg, Thüringia, Germany. Heads by Simon & Halbig and others.

DATE: 1906–1921

MATERIAL: Bisque head, composition body

SIZE: Various

MARK: "Jutta S & H", also numbers 1348 and 1349 for girl dolls; 1914 for character baby

Jutta
1914
8

1349
Jutta
S & H
11

Marked Jutta Character Baby: Bisque socket head, open mouth, sleep eyes, good wig; bent-limb composition baby body; dressed; all in good condition.

12–15in (30.5–38.1cm)	$300-350
20–22in (50.8–55.9cm)	450-475
24–26in (61.0–66.0cm)	550-650

Marked S & H Jutta Girl: Bisque socket head, open mouth, sleep eyes, pierced ears, good wig; ball-jointed composition body; dressed; all in good condition.

Child 19-22in (48.3–55.9cm)   400-425

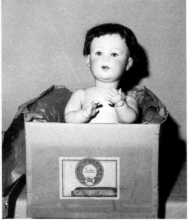

19in (49.3cm) Jutta character 1914 Toddler. *Mary Lou Rubright Collection.*

17in (43.2cm) Jutta 1914 baby showing jointed wrists and label on original box. *Esther Schwartz Collection.*

K&K 195

MAKER: K & K Toy Co., New York City, N.Y., U.S.A.
DATE: 1915–1925
MATERIAL: Bisque head, cloth and composition body
SIZE: Various
MARK: Used mold numbers 45, 56 and 60

K & K Character Child: Bisque head with sleep eyes, open mouth with teeth, mohair wig, cloth body with composition arms and legs. Appropriate clothes; all in good condition.

19–21in (48.3–53.3cm) $275-325

14in (35.6cm) K & K, all original in box. *Joyce Alderson Collection.*

K&W

MAKER: König & Wernicke, Waltershausen, Thüringia, Germany
DATE: 1912–on
MATERIAL: Bisque heads, composition bodies or all composition
SIZE: Various
MARK: "K & W" with mold numbers 98, 99 or 1070; Made in Germany"
(with size number)

K & W Character: Bisque head with open mouth, sleep eyes, good wig; composition baby or toddler body; appropriate clothes; all in good condition.

18–20in (45.7–50.8cm) $375-425

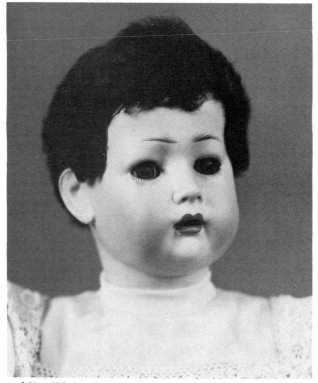

15in (38.1cm) K & W Toddler 1070. *Joanna Ott Collection.*

Kamkins

MAKER: Louise R. Kampes Studios, Atlantic City, N.J., U.S.A.
DATE: Ca. 1920
MATERIAL: Molded mask face, cloth stuffed torso and limbs
SIZE: Various, about 16–19in (40.6–48.3cm)
MARK: Red paper heart on left side of chest:

Also sometimes stamped with black
on foot or back of head:

KAMKINS

A DOLLY MADE TO LOVE
PATENTED BY L.R. KAMPES
ATLANTIC CITY, N.J.

KAMKINS
A DOLLY MADE TO LOVE
PATENTED
FROM
L.R. KAMPES
ATLANTIC CITY
N.J.

Marked "Kamkins": Molded mask face with painted features, wig, cloth
body and limbs, dressed, all in good condition.

19–20in (48.3–50.8cm) $375-425

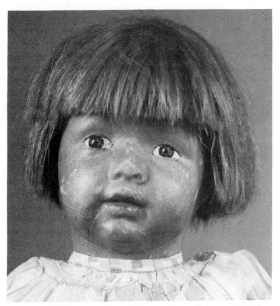

19in (48.3cm) Kamkins, all original. *H&J Foulke.*

Kämmer & Reinhardt

MAKER: Kammer & Reinhardt of Waltershausen, Thüringia, Germany; heads often by Simon & Halbig

DATE: 1895–on

MATERIAL: Bisque socket head, composition body; later papier-mâché, rubber or celluloid heads, composition bodies

SIZE: 5½in (14.0cm) on up

MARK: In 1895 began using K(star)R, sometimes with "S & H", often "Germany". Mold number for bisque socket head begins with a 1; for papier-mâché, 9; for celluloid, 7.

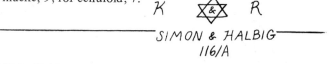

SIMON & HALBIG
116/A

Child Doll: 1895–1930s. Often mold number 403. Bisque head, original or good wig, sleep eyes, open mouth, pierced ears, dressed, ball-jointed composition body; all in good condition.

15–17in (38.1–43.2cm)	$300-350*	
21–24in (53.3–61.0cm)	400-450*	*Allow extra for flirty eyes
28in (71.1cm)	550-600*	
40–42in (101.6–106.7cm)	1650-1950	

Kaiser Baby #100: 1909. Solid-dome bisque head, original composition bent-limb body, intaglio eyes, dressed, open/closed mouth, all in good condition.

10–11in (25.4–27.9cm)	$400-450
13–15in (33.0–38.1cm)	500-600
20in (50.8cm)	800

Character Babies: 1909–on, usually mold number 126, less often mold numbers 121, 122 and 128. Bisque head, original or good wig, sleep eyes, open mouth, composition bent-limb body, nicely dressed; may have voice box or spring tongue; all in good condition.

#126 Baby

10–11in (25.4–27.9cm)	$300
15–17in (38.1–43.2cm)	400-425
20–22in (50.8–55.9cm)	450-500
25in (63.5cm)	550-600
33in (83.8cm)	1250

#126 Toddler

6½–8in (16.5–20.3cm)	325-350
12–15in (30.5–38.1cm)	425-500
20–22in (50.8–55.9cm)	600-650

#121, 122, 128 Baby

13–14in (33.0–35.6cm)	400-450
20–22in (50.8–55.9cm)	550-600

#121, 122 Toddler

16–18in (40.6–45.7cm)	650-700

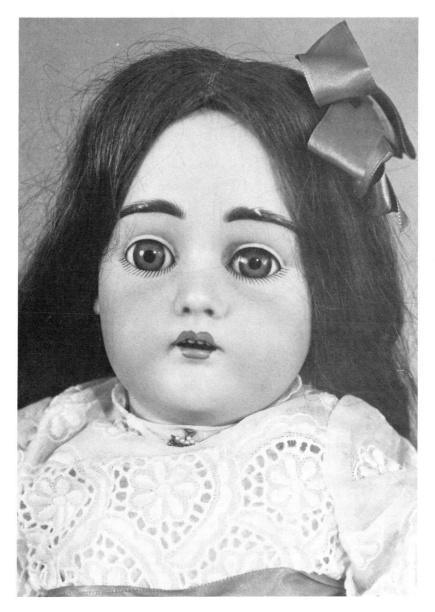

28in (71.1cm) Child doll, incised K.R. *H&J Foulke*

Character Children: 1910—on. Bisque socket head, good wig, painted or glass eyes, closed mouth, composition ball-jointed body, nicely dressed; all in good condition.

#101	8—10in (20.3—25.4cm)	$900-1000
	16in (40.6cm)	1600-1800
#114	8in (20.3cm)	1000
	14in (35.6cm)	2000-2100
	19in (48.3cm), glass eyes	3750**
#115 or 115A,	15—16in (38.1—40.6cm)	2000
#116 or 116A,	15—16in (38.1—40.6cm)	1500-1700
#118A	25in (63.5cm)	1350**
#109	22in (55.9cm)	5000-5500
#117 or 117A,	13—15in (33.0—38.1cm)	1800-2000
	21in (53.3cm)	2500-2800
#117n (flirty eyes),	18—21in (45.7—53.3cm)	900-1000
#102, 107, 112,	16—18in (40.6—45.7cm)	7000 up**
#127 Toddler,	15in (38.1cm)	750-850
	19in (48.3cm)	1000-1100

   **Not enough price samples to compute a reliable price range

Tiny Child Doll: Post World War I. Bisque head, mohair wig, sleep eyes, open mouth. Five-piece composition body with molded and painted shoes and socks.
   6—9in (15.2—22.9cm) $175-225

Infant: 1924—on. Bisque head, molded and painted hair, glass eyes, open mouth; pink cloth body, composition hands; nicely dressed; all in good condition.
   14in (35.6cm) $1000**

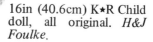

   **Not enough price samles to compute a reliable range.

16in (40.6cm) K★R Child doll, all original. *H&J Foulke.*

RIGHT: 6in (15.2cm) K★R Child walking doll, all original. *H&J Foulke.*

BELOW: Very rare K★R 102 Character Boy. *Old Curiosity Shop.*

ABOVE: 7in (17.8cm) K★R Child, unusual with closed mouth. *H&J Foulke.*

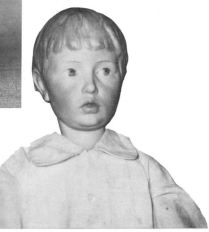

LEFT: 11in (27.9cm) K★R #100 Baby. *H&J Foulke.*

ABOVE: 15in (38.1cm) K★R 115A. *Becky Roberts.*

LEFT: 22in (55.9cm) K★R 109. *Richard Wright.*

RIGHT: 13in (33.0cm) K★R
101 Character Girl. *Rosemary
Dent Collection.*

BELOW: 16in (40.6cm) K★R
114 Character Girl. *Rosemary
Dent Collection.*

11½in (29.2cm) Character Girl
incised only 125, possibly one of
the missing K★R numbers. *Esther
Schwartz Collection.*

15in (38.1cm) K★R
115A, molded hair.
Richard Wright Collection.

14in (35.6cm) K★R
117A. *H&J Foulke.*

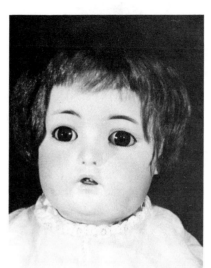 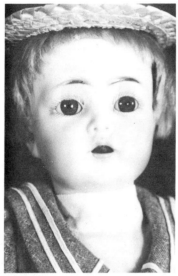

RIGHT: 14in (35.6cm) K★R 117n. *H&J Foulke.*

LEFT: 14in (35.6cm) K★R 118A. *H&J Foulke.*

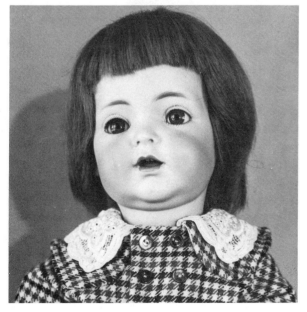

24in (61.0cm) K★R 121 Toddler. *Mary Lou Rubright Collection.*

23in (58.4cm) K★R 122 Baby. *H&J Foulke.*

25in (63.5cm) K★R 126 Toddler with flirty eyes. *H&J Foulke.*

14in (35.6cm) K★R Infant, very rare, all original. *Richard Wright.*

6½in (16.5cm) K★R 126
Toddler. *H&J Foulke.*

25in (63.5cm) K★R 128
Toddler. *Mary Lou
Rubright Collection.*

K★R 127 Toddler. *H&J Foulke.*

ABOVE: 19in (48.3cm) K★R 926 Toddler, all composition, all original. *H&J Foulke.*

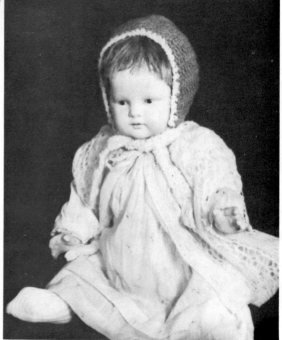

12in (30.5cm) K★R Baby, rubber head, painted eyes, mohair wig, composition body. *H&J Foulke.*

Kestner

MAKER: J. D. Kestner, Jr., Waltershausen, Thüringia, Germany
DATE: Ca. 1880—on
MATERIAL: Bisque heads, kid or composition bodies; bodies on tiny
dolls are jointed at the knee, but not the elbow
SIZE: Various
MARK: Socket Head—Numbers such as 171, 146, 164, 192 (pierced
ears), 195 (see Mark A)
Shoulder Head—Numbers such as 154, 159 (see Mark A)
Both—A5, B6, C7 and Made in Germany
Composition Body—See Mark B   Mark C:
Kid Body—Sometimes Mark C

Mark A: *made in*   Mark B: Excelsior
— D *Germany. 8.* ——————— D.R.P. N₀ 70686 ——————
   162.   Germany

Child doll, closed mouth, marked with size number only: Ca. 1880.
Bisque head, closed mouth, paperweight or sleep eyes, good wig, composition ball-jointed body with straight wrists. Well dressed; all in
good condition.

14—16in (35.6—40.6cm)
$800-1000
20—22in (50.8—55.9cm)
1200-1400

X and pouty faces:
12—15in (30.5—38.1cm)
$1000-1200

X1:
16—18in (40.6—45.7cm)
$1500-1650

Closed mouth shoulder head doll:
Ca. 1880. Same as child doll
above but on kid body with
bisque arms.

14—16in (35.6—40.6cm)
$650-750
20—22in (50.8—55.9cm)
850-950

#698 and similar turned heads:
16—20in (40.6—50.8cm)
$650-850

17in (43.2cm) pouty Kestner,
unmarked. *Joanna Ott Collection.*

14in (35.6cm) closed mouth Kestner, unmarked. *Joanna Ott Collection.*

25in (63.5cm) Kestner 154 shoulder head. *Joanna Ott Collection.*

Child doll, open mouth: Late 1880s to late 1930s. Mold numbers such as 171, 146, 164, 168, 195. Bisque socket head on ball-jointed body; sleep eyes, open mouth, good wig; dressed; all in good condition. MARK:

made in
D *Germany. 8.*
162.

Early with compo body, straight wrist:

18—22in (45.7—55.9cm) $400-500

Child #171, 146, 167, etc.

7—8in (17.8—20.3cm $200-225

12—14in (30.5—35.6cm)   250-300

16—19in (40.6—48.3cm)   300-350

24—26in (61.0—66.0cm)   450-550

36in (91.4cm)   1000-1200

#192, 15—16in (38.1—40.6cm)
                           $350-375

24in (61.0cm)   550

8—9in (20.3—22.9cm)   225-250

Bisque shoulder head on jointed kid body; Mold number such as 154, 159. Sleep eyes, open mouth, good wig; dressed; all in good condition. Prices as above. Allow extra for swivel neck.

#154,

16—18in (40.6—45.7cm) $300-350
21—25in (53.3—63.5cm)   350-450

Character Baby and Toddler: 1910–on. Mold numbers such as 151, 152, 142, 211, 257, 226, 260. Bisque head, molded and/or painted hair or good wig; bent-limb body, open mouth, sleep eyes or set, well dressed; nice condition.

MARK: *made in* 10
F. Germany.
211
J. D. K.

#150, 142, 151 and solid-dome
10–12in (25.4–30.5cm) $250-300
17–21in (43.2–53.3cm) 400-450
23in (58.4cm) 550

#152
10–12in (25.4–30.5cm) 250-300
16–18in (40.6–45.7cm) 350-400
20–22in (50.8–55.9cm) 425-465

#211, 226
13–15in (33.0–38.1cm) 325-375
19–20in (48.3–50.8cm) 475-500

Hilda, 237, 245, 1070
10–12in (25.4–30.5cm)1100-1200
14–16in (35.6–40.6cm)1400-1600
19–21in (48.3–53.3cm)1900-2100
24in (61.0cm) 2400

#239
17in (43.2cm) 500

#247
12in (30.5cm) 500
17in (43.2cm) 750

#257 Baby
12–15in (30.5–38.1cm) 325-375
16–18in (40.6–45.7cm) 400-450
25–26in (63.5–66.0cm) 650-750

17½in (44.5cm) Kestner 152, jointed body, all original. *H&J Foulke.*

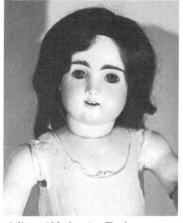

16in (40.6cm) Early open mouth Kestner with two upper teeth. *Sue Bear Collection.*

18in (45.7cm) JDK 226 Character Baby. *H&J Foulke.*

21in (53.3cm) Kestner, no mold number, jointed body, all original. *H&J Foulke.*

13in (33.0cm) JDK Character Baby, no mold number. *H&J Foulke.*

15in (38.1cm) 152
Character.   *H&J
Foulke.*

7in (17.8cm) Kestner
143 Character Child.
H&J Foulke.

19in (48.3cm) JDK 241 Girl.
Esther Schwartz Collection.

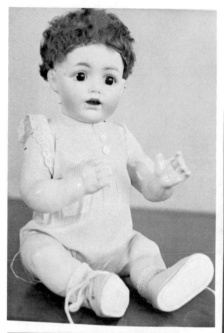

LEFT: 13in (33.0cm) JDK 257 Character Baby. *H&J Foulke.*

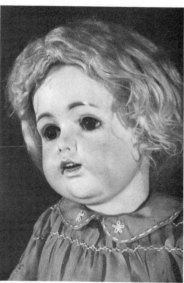

ABOVE: 24in (61.0cm) JDK 260 Toddler. *H&J Foulke.*

LEFT: 13in (33.0cm) JDK 211 Character Baby. *H&J Foulke.*

Character Child: 1910—on. Mold numbers such as 183, 185, etc. Bisque head character face, painted or glass eyes, closed or open/closed mouth, plaster pate, wig. Good jointed composition body. Dressed. All in good condition.

#260 or 257 Child or Toddler
8in (20.3cm)	$350-400
13—16in (33.0—40.6cm)	400-450
22—24in (55.9—61.0cm)	650-700

#143
7—8in (17.8—20.3cm)	325
13—15in (33.0—38.1cm)	350-400
19—20in (48.3—50.8cm)	550-600

#180, 184, 185, 178
11—14in (27.9—35.6cm)	1250-1450*
18in (45.7cm)	1800*

  *Allow more for glass eyes

#241
25in (63.5cm)	2000-2500**

#249
24in (61.0cm)	600-650**

11½in (29.2cm) Boxed Set:
One body, four heads $3500

**Not enough price samples to compute a reliable range.

11½in (29.2cm) Kestner Boy #184. *Rosemary Dent Collection.*

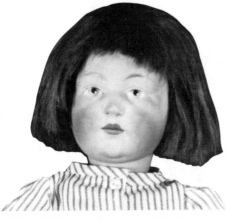

19in (48.3cm) Kestner 187 Character Boy. *Richard Wright.*

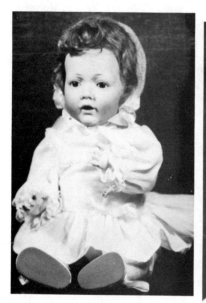

14in (35.6cm) JDK Hilda 245.
H&J Foulke.

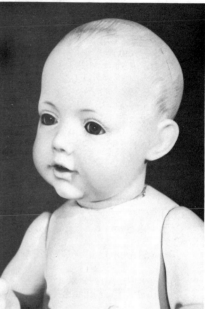

16in (40.6cm) JDK Hilda 1070.
H&J Foulke.

11in (27.9cm) JDK Hilda 237.
H&J Foulke.

Gibson Girl: Ca. 1910. Sometimes mold number 172; sometimes marked "Gibson Girl" on body. Bisque shoulder head with *closed* mouth, uplifted chin, glass eyes, good wig. Kid body with bisque lower arms. Beautifully dressed. All in good condition.

10in (25.4cm)	$1000
21in (53.3cm)	2650

#162 Lady, composition body

17–20in (43.2–50.8cm) $750-850

21in (53.3cm) Kestner Gibson Girl. *Mary Lou Rubright Collection.*

Kewpie

MAKER: Various
DATE: 1913—on
SIZE: 2in (5.1cm) on up
DESIGNER: Rose O'Neill, U.S.A. U.S. Agent: George Borgfeldt & Co.,
N.Y., U.S.A.
MARK: Red and gold paper heart or shield on chest and round label on
back

All-Bisque: Made by J. D. Kestner and other German firms. Often have
imperfections in making. Sometimes signed on foot "O'Nei∫ .
Standing, legs together, arms jointed, blue wings,
painted features, eyes to side.

Bisque		
	2—2½in (5.1—6.4cm)	$55-65
	4—5in (10.2—12.7cm)	85-95
	7in (17.8cm)	150-175
	8—9in (20.3—22.9cm)	250-300
	Jointed hips 4in (10.2cm)	400
	Black Hottentot, 5in (12.7cm)	300

Action Kewpies (sometimes stamped © .)

The Governor 3½in (8.9cm)	$350
Huggers 3½in (8.9cm)	125
Traveler 3½—4½in (8.9—11.5cm)	
	250-300
Guitar Player 3½in (8.9cm)	275

**Bisque head on chubby jointed
toddler body, glass eyes:** (Also,
sometimes on a cloth body.)
Made by J. D. Kestner.
12in (30.5cm) $4000 up**

**Not enough price samples to
compute a reliable range

5¾in (14.7cm) standing
Kewpie, all bisque. *H&J
Foulke.*

Celluloid: Made by Karl Standfuss, Deuben near Dresden, Saxony, Germany. Straight standing, arms jointed, blue wings. Very good condition.

2in (5.1cm)	$25
5in (12.7cm)	35-40
8in (20.3cm)	85

All Composition: Made by Cameo Doll Co., Rex Doll Co., and Mutual Doll Co., all of New York, U.S.A. All composition jointed at neck, shoulders and hips.

11–13in (27.9–33.0cm)	
	$100-125
Black	200**

ABOVE LEFT: 4in (10.2cm) Kewpie "Governor". all bisque. *Mary Lou Rubright Collection.*

ABOVE RIGHT: 3½in (8.9cm) Kewpie "Traveler", all bisque. *Mary Lou Rubright Collection.*

RIGHT: Rare Kewpie "Doodle Dog." *Becky Roberts Collection.*

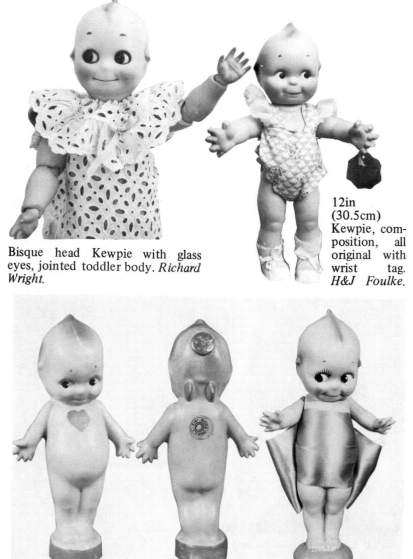

Bisque head Kewpie with glass eyes, jointed toddler body. *Richard Wright.*

12in (30.5cm) Kewpie, composition, all original with wrist tag. *H&J Foulke.*

LEFT: Kewpie composition talcum powder container, label front and back. *H&J Foulke.*
MIDDLE: Back view of talcum Kewpie.
RIGHT: 12in (30.5cm) composition Kewpie with 1913 label. *H&J Foulke.*

All Cloth: Made by Richard G. Kreuger, Inc., N.Y., Pat. number 1785800. Mask face with fat-shaped cloth body, including tiny wings and peak on head. Cloth label sewn in side seam.
12–14in (30.5–35.6cm) $65-85

8in (20.3cm) hard plastic Kewpie. *H&J Foulke.* $40-45

10in (25.4cm) Cuddle Kewpie. *Jan Foulke Collection.*

Kley & Hahn

MAKER: Kley & Hahn of Ohrdruf, Thüringia, Germany
DATE: 1895—on
MATERIAL: Bisque head, composition body
SIZE: Various
MARK:

>K&H<
Germany

K H
Walküre

Character Baby: Mold numbers such as 167 and 176. Bisque head, good wig, sleep eyes, open mouth. Bent-limb baby body. Nicely dressed. All in good condition.

ABOVE: 28in (71.1cm) Kley & Hahn Walkure Child. *H&J Foulke.*

16in (40.6cm) Kley & Hahn Character Boy. *Esther Schwartz.*

#167, 176
11—12in (27.9—30.5cm)	$300-325
14—17in (35.6—43.2cm)	350-400
22—25in (55.9—63.5cm)	500-600

#531, 525, ptd eyes, dome head
14—17in (35.6—43.2cm)	400-450

Character Child: Bisque head, wig, glass or painted eyes, closed mouth; jointed composition child or toddler body; fully dressed; all in good condition. Mold #520, 526, 546   21in (53.3cm) $2500-3000

Child Doll: Mold #250 or Walkure mark. Bisque head, open mouth, wig, glass eyes; jointed composition child body; fully dressed; all in good condition.

20–21in (50.8–53.3cm)
$275-300
24–26in (61.0–66.0cm)
400-450
28in (71.1cm)   550
30in (76.2cm)   600-650

21in (53.3cm) Kley & Hahn character girl #546. *Richard Wright Collection.*

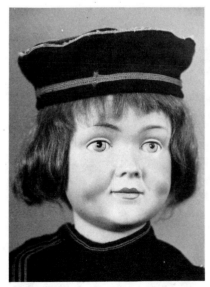

21in (53.3cm) Kley & Hahn character boy #520. *Joanna Ott Collection.*

Kling Bisque Head

MAKER: Kling & Co., Ohrdruf, Thüringia, Germany
DATE: 1880–on
MATERIAL: Bisque shoulder head, cloth body, bisque lower limbs
SIZE: Various
MARK:

Bisque shoulder head: Ca. 1880. Usually with molded hair, painted eyes (sometimes glass), closed mouth; cloth body with bisque lower limbs. Dressed. All in good condition.

Molded hair, 15–18in (38.1–45.7cm) $200-250

Bisque socket head: Ca. 1890s. On ball-jointed composition body, sleep eyes, good wig, open mouth. Nice clothes, all in good condition.

Socket head, 18–21in (45.7–53.3cm) $275-300**

**Not enough price samples to compute a reliable range

15in (38.1cm) Kling shoulder head #377, cloth body, all original. *H&J Foulke.*

Krauss

MAKER: Gebrüder Krauss of Eisfeld, Thüringia, Germany
DATE: Ca. 1907
MATERIAL: Bisque head, ball-jointed composition body
SIZE: Various
MARK: Numbers such as 165 and "Germany"

Marked Krauss Doll: Bisque head, ball-jointed body, sleep eyes, open
mouth, good mohair wig, dressed, all in good condition.

    —18—21in (45.7—53.3cm) $225-250—
    22—24in (55.9—61.0cm)   275-325

23in (58.4cm) Gebruder
Krauss. *Sheila Needle
Collection.*

Käthe Kruse

MAKER: Käthe Kruse, Berlin, Germany
DATE: 1910—on
MATERIAL: Molded muslin head (hand-painted), jointed cloth body. Later of hard plastic material.
SIZE: Various
MARK: On cloth: "Käthe Kruse" on sole of foot, sometimes also "Germany" and a number *Käthe Kruse* 81971 *Made in Germany*

Hard plastic on back: Turtle mark and "Käthe Kruse"

Cloth Käthe Kruse: Molded muslin head, hand-painted. Jointed at shoulders and hips, suitably dressed, in good condition.

Early cloth 16—17in (40.6—43.2cm) $550-625
All original, mint   800
1923 model with wig; all original   500-550

U.S. Zone Germany, mint, all original   400-425

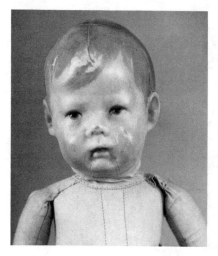

ABOVE: Early Käthe Kruse child. *H&J Foulke.*

RIGHT: U. S. Zone Germany. Käthe Kruse girl, all original. *H&J Foulke.*

Hard Plastic Käthe Kruse: Wig and moving eyes (also molded hair and painted eyes), jointed neck, shoulders and hips. Original clothes. All in good condition.

14—16in (35.6—40.6cm) $275

RIGHT: Ca. 1923 Käthe Kruse boy, all original. *H&J Foulke.*

LEFT: Hard plastic Käthe Kruse boy, all original. *H&J Foulke.*

Lanternier Child

MAKER: A. Lanternier & Cie. of Limoges, France
DATE: Ca. 1891—ca. 1925
MATERIAL: Bisque head, papier-mâché body
SIZE: Various
MARK: Anchor with "Limoges A. L.—France" or "Fabrication Française
A.L. & Cie. Limoges", sometimes "Cherie", "Favorite", "La
Georgienne", "Lorraine"

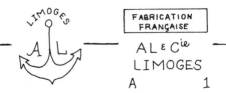

Marked Lanternier Child: Bisque head, papier-mâché jointed body, good
or original wig, large stationary eyes, open mouth, pierced ears, pretty
clothes; all in good condition.

15—17in (38.1—43.2cm)	$450
20—23in (50.8—58.4cm)	550-600

Marked Toto: Bisque character face with smiling face, open/closed mouth
with molded teeth, glass eyes, pierced ears, good wig, jointed French
composition body; dressed; marked "Toto, AL & C, Limoges"; all in
good condition.

15—16in (38.1—40.6cm) $750

15in (38.1cm) Lanternier
Child. *Mary Goolsby.*

Leather Dolls

MAKER: Unknown French maker
DATE: Ca. 1920
MATERIAL: All-leather
SIZE: Small
MARK: None on doll; may have "Made in France" label

Leather doll: Baby or child doll with molded and painted hair, painted features, jointed shoulders and hips; original clothes; excellent condition.

4–5in (10.2–12.7cm) $400

6in (15.2cm) all leather Boy, all original. *Jan Foulke Collection.*

Lenci

MAKER: Enrico & Signora Scavini, Italy
DATE: 1920–on
MATERIAL: Pressed felt head with
    painted features, jointed felt bodies
SIZE: 5–45in (12.7–114.3cm)

Lenci di E. SCAVINI
TURIN (Italy)
Made in ITALY
N. 159G
Pat. Sept. 8, 1921 Pat. N. 142433
Bre SGDG. X 87395. Brevetta 501.198

MARK: "LENCI" on cloth and various paper tags; sometimes stamped
    on bottom of foot

Lenci: All-felt (sometimes cloth torso) with swivel
    head, jointed shoulders and hips. Painted
    features, eyes usually side-glancing. Original
    clothes, often of felt or organdy. In very good
    condition.
Miniatures & Mascottes, 8–9in (20.3–22.9cm) $125-175
Children #300, 109, 149, 159
    16–22in (40.6–55.9cm) $500-750
"Lucia" face, 14in (35.6cm) $350-400
Ladies and long-limbed novelty dolls, 24–28in
    (61.0–71.1cm) $350-450
Glass eyes, 20in (50.8cm) $850**

**Not enough price samples to compute a reliable range

Lenci Child #300 face,
all original. *H&J Foulke.*

Lenci Child #149 face, all
original. *H&J Foulke.*

RIGHT: 16in (40.6cm) Lenci school boy and school girl, all original. *Beth Foulke Collection.*

BELOW: Lenci child #1500 face, all original. *H&J Foulke.*

14in (35.6cm) Girl with "Lucia" face, all original. *H&J Foulke.*

14in (35.6cm) "Lucia", all original. *Beth Foulke Collection.*

ABOVE: 17in (43.2cm) girl with "Laura" face, all original. *Beth Foulke Collection.*

LEFT: 8in (20.3cm) Lenci farm girl, all original. *H&J Foulke.*

14in (35.6cm) Lenci lady doll, all original. *Beth Foulke Collection.*

27in (68.6cm) Lenci clown, all original. *Alma Wolfe Collection.*

Lenci-Type

MAKER: Various Italian, French and English firms such as Marguerin, Alma, etc.
DATE: 1920–1940
MATERIAL: Felt and cloth
SIZE: 6in (15.2cm) up
MARK: Various paper labels

Felt or Cloth Doll: Painted features, mohair wig, original clothes or costume.

> **Child dolls**
> > 16–18in (40.6–45.7cm) up to $250 depending upon quality
>
> **Foreign costume**
> > 7½–8½in (19.1–21.6cm) $20-30

18in (45.7cm) Lenci-type girl with felt face, cloth body, all original. *H&J Foulke.*

8in (20.3cm) Lenci-type pair, felt faces, all original. *H&J Foulke.*

MAKER: Liberty & Co. of London, England
DATE: 1906–on
MATERIAL: All-fabric
SIZE: Various
MARK: Cloth label or paper tag "Liberty of London"

British Coronation Dolls: 1939. All-cloth with painted and needle sculpted faces; original clothes; excellent condition. The Royal Family and Coronation Participants,

5½–9½in (14.0–24.2cm) $45-55

Other English Historical and Ceremonial Characters: All-cloth with painted and needle sculpted faces; original clothes; excellent condition.

9in (22.9cm) $45-65

9½in (24.2cm) Liberty of London Coronation Doll of King George VI. *H&J Foulke.*

Limbach

MAKER: Limbach Porzellanfabrik, Limbach, Thuringia, Germany
DATE: Factory started in 1772; date for beginning of doll production
not established
MATERIAL: Bisque head, composition body
SIZE: Various
MARK: Sometimes with "Wally"

MADE IN GERMANY

Limbach Child Doll: Ca. 1890. Bisque head, glass eyes, open mouth
with teeth, good wig; composition jointed body; dressed; all in good
condition. 22—24in (55.9—61.0cm) $250-325

Limbach Character Baby: Ca. 1910. Bisque head with molded hair, glass
or painted eyes, open/closed mouth; composition baby body; dressed;
all in good condition. 12in (30.5cm) Mold #8682 $800**
 **Not enough price samples to compute a reliable range.

LEFT: 12in (30.5cm) Limbach
8682 character, French jointed
composition body. *Richard
Wright Collection.*

ABOVE: 24in (61.0cm) Lim-
bach "Wally". *Mary Lou Rubright Collection.*

Little Annie Rooney

MAKER: Cameo Doll Co., N.Y. - - composition; German manufacturer - - all bisque
DATE: 1925—on
MATERIAL: All-composition or all-bisque
SIZE: All-bisque 4in (10.2cm); composition 16in (40.6cm)
DESIGNER: Jack Collins and Joseph Kallus
MARK: Composition - - none; All bisque

Germany.

LITTLE ANNIE ROONEY
REG. U.S. PAT. OFF
CORP. BY JACK COLLINS

All-Bisque Little Annie Rooney: Molded clothes, jointed arms, painted features, yarn hair, red felt hat; excellent condition.
4in (10.2cm) $150-175
Composition Little Annie Rooney: All-composition jointed at neck, shoulders, and hips, legs as black stockings, feet with molded shoes; painted round eyes, watermelon mouth, braided wig; original clothes; all in good condition. 16in (40.6cm) $600**

**Not enough price samples to compute a reliable range.

4in (10.2cm) all-bisque "Little Annie Rooney". *Jan Foulke Collection.*

General Douglas MacArthur

MAKER: Freundlich Novelty Corp. of New York, N.Y., U.S.A.
DATE: Ca. early 1940s
MATERIAL: All-composition, molded hat, jointed at shoulders and hips
SIZE: 18in (45.7cm)
MARK: Tag with "General MacArthur" and manufacturer's name and
address, etc.

General MacArthur: All-composition, molded hat, painted features. One
arm made to salute if desired. Original khaki uniform with tags;
jointed at shoulders and hips; all in good condition.

18in (45.7cm) $150-175

Armed Services Dolls
Men and Women with
molded caps, 15in
(38.1cm) $75-85

18in (45.7cm) General
MacArthur, all original. *H&J
Foulke.*

Margie and Joy

MAKER: Cameo Doll Co., New York, N.Y., U.S.A.
DATE: Margie, 1929; Joy, 1932
MATERIAL: Composition, segmented wood body
SIZE: 9½–10in (24.1–25.4cm)
DESIGNER: J. L. Kallus
MARK: Red Triangle label on chest: MARGIE
Des. & Copyright
by Jos. Kallus
Round label on chest: JOY
Des. & Copy't
J. L. Kallus

Margie: Composition head with smiling face; molded hair, painted eyes, closed mouth with painted teeth. Segmented wood body. All in good condition. Undressed. 10in (25.4cm) $125-150

Joy: Composition head with smiling face, molded curls with loop for a bow; wood segmented body; undressed. 10in (25.4cm) tall. $175-200

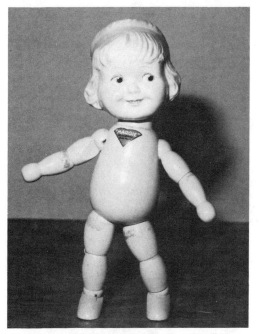

10in (25.4cm) "Margie". *Gordon Hitchings.*

Marottes
(Whirling Musical Doll)

MAKER: Various German and French firms
DATE: 1890–1921
MATERIAL: Bisque head on wooden stick
SIZE: Usually small
MARK: Various

Marotte: Bisque head with glass eyes, good wig, mounted on a wooden stick, plays a musical tune when twirled, fancy hat; all in working condition.

French head, closed mouth   16in (40.6cm)
$800-1000
German head, 11–13in (27.9–33.0cm)
275-325

AM 390 Marotte. *Louise Ceglia*

Mascotte

MAKER: May Freres Cie, 1890–1897; Jules Nicholas Steiner, 1898–on.
  Paris, France
DATE: 1890–1902
MATERIAL: Bisque head, composition and wood jointed body
SIZE: Various
MARK: BÉBÉ MASCOTTE
  PARIS

Bébé Mascotte: Bisque socket head, paperweight eyes, pierced ears, closed mouth, good wig; jointed composition and wood body; appropriate clothes; all in good condition.

20–24in (50.8–61.0cm)
$2400-2800

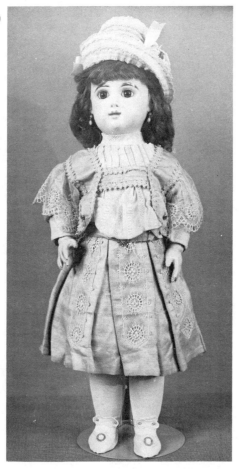

20in (50.8cm) Mascotte.
Joanna Ott Collection.

Mason & Taylor
(Wooden Doll)

MAKER: D. M. Smith & Co., Springfield, VT., U.S.A.
DATE: 1881–1893
MATERIAL: Composition heads, wood body, arms and legs. Hands and feet made of pewter or lead. Older type had spoon hands and wooden feet.
SIZE: 12in (30.5cm)
MARK: None unless black paper band carrying patent dates is still around waist

---

Marked Mason and Taylor Doll: Composition head, wood body, legs and arms; hands and feet usually of metal, fully jointed, dressed; all in fair condition.

12in (30.5cm) $450-550

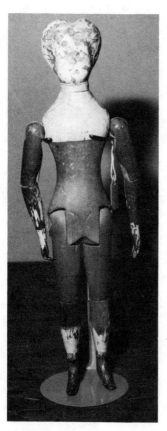

12in (30.5cm) Mason & Taylor. *Grace Dyar.*

Metal Baby

MAKER: Various U.S. Companies
DATE: Ca. 1920–on
MATERIAL: All-metal, or metal head with composition baby body
SIZE: Various
MARK: Various

Metal Baby: All-metal (with bent limbs) jointed at shoulders and hips with metal springs; molded and painted hair and facial features; painted eyes; closed mouth. Appropriate clothes. All in good condition.

12–14in (30.5–35.6cm) $50-75

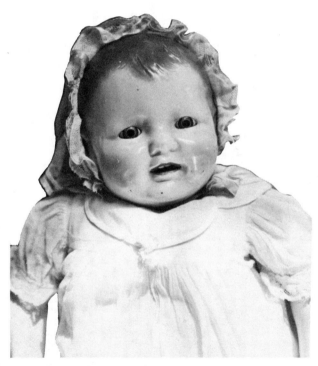

Large Metal Head Baby. *Louise Ceglia.*

Metal Heads

MAKER: Buschow & Beck, Germany (Minerva); Karl Standfuss, Germany (Juno); Alfred Heller, Germany (Diana)
DATE: Ca. 1894—on
MATERIAL: Metal shoulder head, kid or cloth body
SIZE: Various
MARK:

Marked Metal Head: Metal shoulder head on cloth or kid body, bisque or composition hands, dressed; good condition, not repainted.

With molded hair, painted eyes:
    16—20in (40.6—50.8cm) $55-75
With molded hair, glass eyes:
    17—19in (43.2—48.3cm)   75-85
With wig and glass eyes:
    20—22in (50.8—55.9cm)   85-95

18in (45.7cm) and 22in (55.9cm) Minerva tin head dolls with painted eyes and commercial cloth bodies; 17in (43.2cm) Minerva tin head with wig and glass eyes; 12in (30.5cm) brass head with glass eyes and Kidolene body. *Joanna Ott Collection.*

Metal, Swiss

MAKER: A. Bucherer, Amriswil, Switzerland
DATE: 1921
MATERIAL: Composition head, hands, and feet; metal ball-jointed body
SIZE: 8in (20.3cm) average
MARK: MADE IN
                    SWITZERLAND
————————————— PATENTS —————————————
                    APPLIED FOR

Bucherer Doll: Composition character head often with molded hat;
    metal ball-jointed body; original clothes, often felt; all in good condi-
    tion.
        Comic characters, Mutt, Jeff, Maggie, Jiggs, etc. $200 up
        Regular People, lady, man, fireman, etc. $100-125

7–8in (17.8–20.3cm)
Mutt and Jeff Comic
Characters. *Howard
Foulke Collection.*

Mibs

MAKER: Louis Amberg & Son, New York, N.Y., U.S.A.
DATE: Ca. 1921
MATERIAL: All-bisque, composition shoulder head, arms and legs; cloth body
SIZE: Composition: 16in (40.6cm); all bisque: 3–6in (7.6–15.2cm)
DESIGNER: Helen Drucker
MARK: All bisque:

©
LA&S 1921
Germany
or paper label on chest: "Please
Love Me
I'm
MIBS"

Composition: (paper label)
"Amberg Dolls
Please Love Me
I'm Mibs"

Composition Mibs: Composition shoulder head with molded and painted blonde hair, painted blue eyes, closed mouth, wistful expression; cloth body with composition arms and legs; appropriate old clothes; all in good condition.
16in (40.6cm) $300-350**

All-Bisque Mibs: Molded and painted features, jointed at shoulders and sometimes hips, painted shoes and socks, undressed; all in good condition.
3in (7.6cm) $175-200
**Not enough price samples to compute   4¾in (12.2cm)   225-250
a reliable range

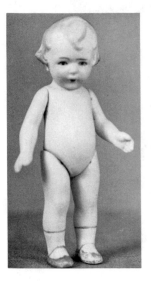

ABOVE: 17in (43.2cm) composition "Mibs", replaced dress. *Beth Foulke Collection.*

LEFT: 4¾in (12.2cm) all-bisque "Mibs". *Beth Foulke Collection.*

Molded-Hair Papier-Mâché

(So-called Milliner's Model)

MAKER: Unknown German firms
DATE: Ca. 1820s into the 1850s
MATERIAL: Papier-mâché shoulder heads, stiff slender kid bodies, wooden extremities
SIZE: Various
MARK: None

Molded-Hair Papier-Mâché: Unretouched shoulder head, various molded hairdos, original kid body, wooden arms and legs, painted features, eyes blue, black or brown. Original or very old handmade clothing; entire doll in fair condition.

8–10in (20.3–25.4cm)	$200 up*
16–22in (40.6–55.9cm)	400 up*
26–28in (66.0–71.1cm)	600 up*

*Depending upon condition and rarity of hairdo
Males 20–24in (50.8–61.0cm)
750-850*
*Allow extra for glass eyes

15in (38.1cm) Molded-Hair Papier-Mâché Milliner's Model. *Joanna Ott Collection.*

Molly-'es

MAKER: International Doll Co., Philadelphia, Pa., U.S.A.
DATE: 1920 s–on
MATERIAL: All-cloth or all-composition; later hard plastic and vinyl
SIZE: Various
DESIGNER: Mollye Goldman
MARK: Usually a paper tag, dolls unmarked except for vinyl

Babies: All-composition jointed at neck, shoulders and hips, molded hair or wigs, sleep eyes. Beautiful original outfits. All in good condition. 15–18in (38.1–45.7cm) $65-75

Internationals: All-cloth with mask faces, painted features, mohair wigs (sometimes yarn), variety of costumes. All original clothes; in excellent condition. 13in (33.0cm) $40-45

Sabu: All-brown composition. Very elaborate costume based on the character in *The Thief of Bagdad.* Original clothes; all in good condition. $250**

Young Ladies: All-composition jointed at neck, shoulders and hips, lovely wig, sleep eyes. Beautiful original clothes. All in good condition. 21in (53.3cm) $250-300**

**Not enough price samples to compute a reliable price range

10in (25.4cm) Molly–'es Dutch Twins with glass eyes. *H&J Foulke.*

15in (38.1cm) Molly–'es all cloth International doll. *H&J Foulke.*

Monica

MAKER: Monica Doll Studios, Hollywood, CA., U.S.A.
DATE: 1941–1951
MATERIAL: All-composition
SIZE: 15in (38.1cm), 17in (43.2cm), 20in (50.8cm), 22in (55.9cm),
    24in (61.0cm); later 11in (27.9cm)
MARK: None

Monica: Composition swivel head, human hair rooted in scalp, painted
    eyes with eye shadow, closed mouth, composition body with adult-
    type legs and arms, fingers with painted nails. Dressed. In good condi-
    tion (nearly all have crazing on faces).

All sizes $225-250

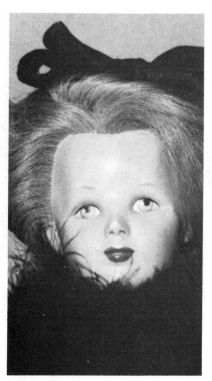

21in (53.3cm) "Monica". *Miriam
Blankman Collection.*

Mon Trésor

MAKER: Henri Rostal, Paris, France
DATE: 1914
MATERIAL: Bisque head, ball-jointed composition body
SIZE: Various
MARK: "Mon Trésor"

Marked "Mon Trésor": Bisque socket head, sleep eyes, open mouth with teeth, good wig, pierced ears, ball-jointed composition body, dressed; all in good condition.

      22−24in (55.9−61.0cm) $600-650**
        **Not enough price samples to compute a reliable range

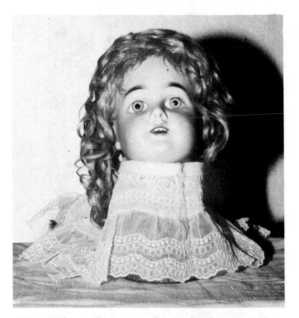

Mon Trésor, Germany. *Emma Wedmore Collection.*

Motschmann

MAKER: Ch. Motschmann, Sonneberg, Thüringia, Germany
DATE: 1857—1860s
MATERIAL: Papier-mâché, composition and cloth
SIZE: 8in (20.3cm) to about 28in (71.1cm)
MARK: On cloth upper leg:

Marked Motschmann or unmarked Motschmann-type Baby: Wax over
composition head with painted hair or wig, glass eyes, closed mouth or
open with bamboo teeth. Composition lower torso, arms and legs
jointed at ankles and wrists. Cloth midsection and upper arms and legs
called floating joints.

> 12—15in (30.5—38.1cm) $225-250
> 24—26in (61.0—66.0cm)   375-425

For photograph see *Collector's Encyclopedia of Dolls* by the Colemans,
page 456.

Multi-Faced Doll

MAKER: Perhaps Carl Bergner of Sonneberg, Thüringia, Germany
DATE: 1899
MATERIAL: Bisque head with three faces, cloth torso, composition arms and cap
SIZE: Smaller, such as 11in (27.9cm) and 13in (33.0cm)
MARK: "C. B." on back shoulder

Marked "C. B." Multi-face: Bisque head with three different faces (usually sleeping, laughing and crying). Dressed. All in good condition.

$1500*   *Doll with black face will
be much higher.

14in (35.6cm) two-faced doll showing white side, incised DEP 202. *Mary Lou Rubright Collection.*

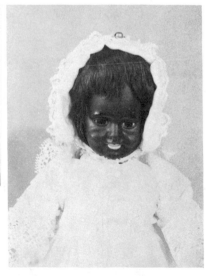

14in (35.6cm) two-faced doll showing black side. *Mary Lou Rubright Collection.*

Munich Art Dolls

MAKER: Marion Kaulitz
DATE: 1908–1912
MATERIAL: All-composition, fully jointed bodies
SIZE: Various
DESIGNER: Paul Vogelsanger, and others
MARK: Sometimes signed on doll's neck

Munich Art Dolls: Molded composition character heads, with handpainted features; fully jointed composition bodies; dressed; all in good condition. 19in (48.3cm) $400-500**

  **Not enough price samples to compute a reliable range.

3 dolls of the Munich Art type, all original. *Nancy Schwartz Blaisure Collection.*

Nancy Ann Storybook

MAKER: Nancy Ann Storybook Dolls Co., South San Francisco, CA., U.S.A.

DATE: Mid 1930s

MATERIAL: Painted bisque; later, plastic

SIZE: About 5½in (14.0cm)

MARK: On back: Story
                         Book
                         Doll
                         U.S.A.

      Painted Bisque before the first mark.

      Hard Plastic: STORYBOOK
                                  DOLLS
                                  U.S.A.
                                  TRADEMARK
                                  REG.

    Also a wrist tag identifying particular model

Marked Storybook Doll: Painted bisque, one-piece body, head and legs, jointed arms, mohair wig, painted eyes, original clothes. Good condition.

                  Painted Bisque $25
                  Hard Plastic   15

3in (7.6cm) hard plastic Storybook baby, all original with wrist tag. *H&J Foulke.*

6in (15.2cm) hard plastic "Graduation". *Beth Foulke Collection.*

New Born Babe

(Amberg Baby)

MAKER: Louis Amberg & Son, New York, N.Y., U.S.A.
DATE: 1914; reissued in 1924
MATERIAL: Bisque head, cloth body
SIZE: Various
DESIGNER: Jeno Juszko
MARK: " © L. A. & S. 1914, G 45520 Germany#4", also "Heads copy-
righted by LOUIS AMBERG and SON"

New Born Babe: Marked bisque head, cloth body, celluloid, rubber or
composition hands; painted bald head, sleep eyes, closed mouth, nicely dressed; all in good condition.

Length:
    8–10in (20.3–25.4cm) $250-300
    12–13in (30.5–33.0cm)   425-450
    15–18in (38.1-45.7cm)   550-600

8in (20.3cm) "New Born
Babe". *H&J Foulke.*

Oriental Dolls

Japanese Traditional Girl Doll: 1850—on. Papier-mâché swivel head on shoulder plate, hips, lower legs and feet (early ones have jointed wrists and ankles); cloth midsection, cloth (floating) upper arms and legs; pierced ears and nostrils; hair wig; dark glass eyes; original or appropriate clothes; all in good condition.

Early 20th Century 12—15in (30.5—38.1cm) $60-75
1930s 10—12in (25.4—30.5cm)   35

Japanese Traditional Baby Doll: Ca. 1926—on. Papier-mâché with bent arms and legs; hair wig; dark glass eyes; original or appropriate clothes; all in good condition.

10—12in (25.4—30.5cm) $40-45

Chinese Traditional Doll: Early 1900s. Papier-mâché head and hands painted pink, large ears, nicely painted eyes, black hair wig, cloth body and legs; original Chinese pajama-type outfit. Stamped "Made in China" on foot. All in excellent condition. 12in (30.5cm) $30-35

10in (25.4cm) Japanese Traditional Doll, Ca. 1900. *H&J Foulke.*

12in (30.5cm) Chinese papier-mâché, all original. *H&J Foulke.*

Oriental Bisque Dolls: Ca. 1900—on. Made by German firms such as Simon & Halbig, Armand Marseille, J.D. Kestner, and others. Bisque head tinted yellow; matching ball-jointed or baby body.

S&H 1329 Girl 15—16in (38.1—40.6cm) $1200*
A.M. 353 Baby 8—10in (20.3—25.4cm)   450-550
J.D.K. 243 Baby 13—14in (33.0—35.6cm)   1600-1800
All-bisque, swivel neck 4—5in (10.2—12.7cm)   400-450

*Allow more for mold #1129 and 1199.

Oriental Composition Dolls: Ca. 1930. Unknown maker, possibly American. All-composition baby, jointed at shoulders and hips, painted facial features; original costume of colorful taffeta with braid trim; sometimes with black yarn hair; feet painted black or white for shoes.

10—12in (25.4—30.5cm) $50-60

ABOVE LEFT: 15in (38.1cm) German bisque Oriental Girl #220. *Mary Lou Rubright Collection.*

ABOVE RIGHT: 14in (35.6cm) JDK 243 Oriental Baby, all original. *Richard Wright Collection.*

RIGHT: 10in (25.4cm) Oriental all-composition Baby, all original. *H&J Foulke.*

Orsini

MAKER: Unknown, but all-bisque dolls were possibly by J.D. Kestner
DATE: 1916—on
MATERIAL: Bisque head with cloth and/or composition body or all-bisque
SIZE: Various
DESIGNER: Jeanne Orsini
MARK: Character heads: All-bisque:

All-bisque:

JIO © 1920
JIO © 1919

All-Bisque Character: Jointed at shoulders and hips, character face, sleep eyes, wig, painted shoes and stockings over the knee. Paper label on front: "ViVi", MiMi", DiDi", and "ZiZi", 5in (12.7cm) or 7in (17.8cm) tall.

    MiMi or DiDi 5in (12.7cm) $1150-1250
Character Baby: Bisque head with smiling face, glass eyes, open or open/closed mouth, wig or molded hair; composition and/or cloth body; dressed and in excellent condition. Sometimes in painted bisque. 18in (45.7cm) $1500-1600**
    **Not enough price samples to compute a reliable range.

ABOVE: 5in (12.7cm) Orsini "DiDi".
H&J Foulke.

LEFT: 5in (12.7cm) Orsini "MiMi".
H&J Foulke.

P.D. Bébé

259

MAKER: Probably Petit & Dumontier, Paris
DATE: 1878–1890
MATERIAL: Bisque head, composition body
SIZE: Various
MARK: "P. D." with size number

P. D. Bébé: Bisque head with paperweight eyes; closed mouth, pierced ears, good wig; jointed composition body (some have metal hands), appropriate clothes; all in good condition.

18–20in (45.7–50.8cm) $2500**
**Not enough price samples to compute
a reliable range

16½in (41.9cm) P 2 D. *Emma Wedmore Collection.*

P.M.

MAKER: Otto Reinecke of Hof-Moschendorf, Bavaria, Germany
DATE: 1909—on
MATERIAL: Bisque head, bent-limb composition body
SIZE: Various
MARK: "P M" also **ℝ** and numbers such as 23 and 914,
also Germany. (PM for Porzellan-
fabrik Moschendorf) **P M**

On back of head: "Trebor" **914.**

────────────────────── **Germany** ──────────────────────
1

Marked Reinecke Baby: Bisque socket head, sleep eyes, open mouth, good wig, five-piece composition bent-limb baby body. Dressed, all in nice condition.

Character Baby	Trebor child
10—12in (25.4—30.5cm) $225-250	16—19in (40.6—48.3cm)
14—16in (35.6—40.6cm) 275-325	$275-325**
21—24in (53.3—61.0cm) 400-450	

**Not enough price samples to compute a reliable range

10in (25.4cm) P.M. 914 Character Baby.
Barbara Foster.

Painted Bisque

(Tiny Dolls)

MAKER: Various German firms
DATE: Ca. 1930
MATERIAL: All-bisque with a layer of flesh colored paint
SIZE: Under 6in (15.2cm)
MARK: Various

Painted Bisque Tinies: All-bisque jointed at shoulders and hips, molded hair, painted features, molded and painted shoes and socks. Dressed or undressed.

Child		
	3½–4½in (8.9–11.4cm)	$15-20
	7–8in (17.8–20.3cm)	30-40
Baby		
	2½–3½in (6.4–8.9cm)	15-20

4in (10.2cm) painted bisque pair. *H&J Foulke.*

Papier-Mâché

(French-Type)

MAKER: Unknown
DATE: Ca. 1825–1860
MATERIAL: Papier-mâché shoulder head, pink kid body
SIZE: Various
MARK: None

French-type Papier-Mâché: Shoulder head with painted black pate, brush
marks around face, nailed on wig (often missing), open mouth with
bamboo teeth, pierced nose, set-in glass eyes; pink kid body with stiff
arms and legs; appropriate old clothes. All in good condition, showing
some wear.

12–15in (30.5–38.1cm)	$350-375*
22–24in (55.9–61.0cm)	650-750*
28–33in (71.1–83.8cm)	850-1000*

*Allow more for the closed-mouth
narrow-faced version.

23in (58.4cm) French-type
papier-mâché, glass eyes. *Elizabeth McIntyre.*

Papier-Mâché

(German)

MAKER: Various firms
DATE: Ca. 1865
MATERIAL: Papier-mâché shoulder head; cloth body, sometimes leather arms
SIZE: Various
MARK: Usually unmarked, some early ones marked

△ A.W. Ser : a/3

German Papier-Mâché: Ca. 1875–1900. Shoulder head with molded and painted black or blonde hair, painted eyes, closed mouth; cloth body sometimes with leather arms; old or appropriate clothes. All in good condition, showing some wear.

14–16in (35.6–40.6cm) $125-150
With wig and glass eyes,
20–24in (50.8–61.0cm)   150-200

German Papier-Mâché: Ca. 1920–on. Papier-mâché head and hands or arms; hard stuffed cloth body, painted eyes, good hair wig; original child clothes; all in good condition. 12–14in (30.5–35.6cm) $50-60

12in (30.5cm) German papier-mâché, ca. 1930, all original. *H&J Foulke.*

21in (53.3cm) German papier-mâché with "Unbreakable Heads" label. *Joanna Ott Collection.*

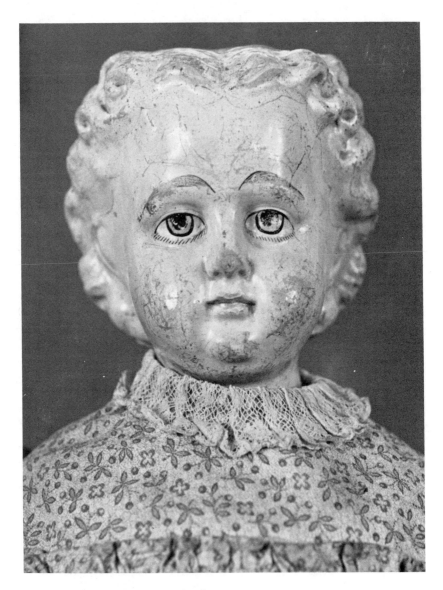

Much loved German papier-mâché with blonde hair. *Joanna Ott Collection.*

Parian-Type

(Untinted Bisque)

MAKER: Various German firms
DATE: Ca. 1860s through 1870s
MATERIAL: Untinted bisque shoulder head; cloth or kid body; leather, wood, china or combination extremities
SIZE: Various
MARK: None

Unmarked Parian: Pale or untinted shoulder head, sometimes with molded blouse; pierced ears, closed mouth, beautifully molded hairdo, painted eyes, cloth body, lovely clothes; entire doll in fine condition.

        14—17in (35.6—43.2cm) $250-300*
        20—22in (50.8—55.9cm)   350-400*

        Fancy hairdo and elaborately decorated blouse $600 up
          *Allow more for glass eyes, swivel neck,
        unusual hair style, flowers in hair

ABOVE: 21in (53.3cm) rare parian-type lady with molded flowers and necklace. *Grace Dyar.*

RIGHT: 16in (40.6cm) Parian-type boy with glass eyes, all original. *Grace Dyar.*

Paris Bébé

MAKER: Danel & Cie., Paris, France, (later possibly
    Jumeau)
DATE: 1889–1895
MATERIAL: Bisque socket head, jointed composition
    body
SIZE: Various
MARK: On head:

On body:

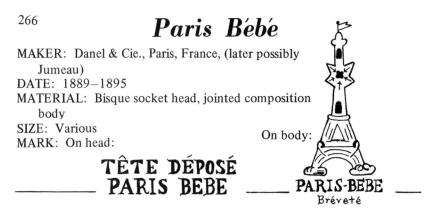

TÊTE DÉPOSÉ
PARIS BEBE

PARIS-BEBE
Bréveté

Marked Paris Bébé: Bisque socket head, paperweight eyes, pierced ears, closed mouth, good wig, composition jointed body, dressed; all in good condition.

21–25in (53.3–63.5cm) $2600-3000

25in (63.5cm) Paris Bebe. *Richard Wright.*

Parsons-Jackson Baby

MAKER: Parsons—Jackson Co. of Cleveland, Ohio, U.S.A.
DATE: 1910—1919
MATERIAL: Biskoline (similar to celluloid) jointed with steel springs
SIZE: Various
MARKS: Embossed figure of small stork on back of head and/or on
back or shoulders sometimes with "TRADEMARK
PARSONS—JACKSON, CO.
CLEVELAND, OHIO"

On head: On body:

PARSONS-JACKSON CO.
CLEVELAND, OHIO.

Marked Parsons—Jackson Baby: Socket head and bent-limb baby body of
Biskoline; molded-painted hair, painted eyes, spring joint construc-
tion. Nicely dressed; all in good condition.

12in (30.5cm) $125-135

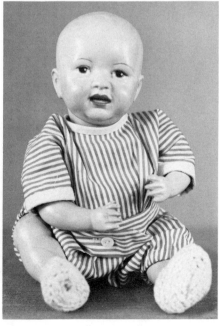

11in (27.9cm) Parsons-
Jackson baby. *H&J
Foulke.*

Peg-Wooden or Dutch Dolls

²⁶⁸

MAKER: Craftsmen of the Grödner Tal, Austria and Sonneberg, Thüringia, Germany
DATE: Late 18th–20th century
MATERIAL: All-wood, ball-jointed (larger ones) or pegged
SIZE: Various
MARK: None

Late 18th and Early 19th Century: Delicately carved head, varnished, carved and painted hair and features, sometimes with a yellow tuck comb in hair, painted spit curls, sometimes earrings; mortise and tenon peg joints; old clothes; all in good condition.
14–17in (35.6–43.2cm) $3000
Early to Mid 19th Century: Wooden head with painted hair, carving not so elaborate as previously, sometimes earrings, spit curls. Dressed; all in good condition.

3–5in (7.6–12.7cm)	$150-175
12–13in (30.5–33.0cm)	650-750
19–21in (48.3–53.3cm)	900-1000

Late 19th
10–12in (25.4–30.5cm)
$100-125
Early 20th
10–12in (25.4–30.5cm)
$40-50

19, 10, 11 and 7in (48.3, 25.4, 27.9 and 17.8cm) Peg wooden dolls. *Joanna Ott Collection.*

Phénix Bébé

MAKER: Henri Alexandre, Paris, France; Tourrel; Jules Steiner; Jules Mettais
DATE: 1889–1900
MATERIAL: Bisque head, jointed composition body (sometimes one-piece arms and legs)
SIZE: Various
DESIGNER: Henri Alexandre

PHÉNIX

MARK:

(BÉBÉ PHÉNIX)   PHÉNIX–BABY   ★ 95

Marked Bébé Phénix: Beautiful bisque head, French jointed body, closed mouth, pierced ears, lovely old wig, bulbous set eyes, well dressed; all in good condition.

Closed mouth
16–18in (40.6–45.7cm) $2000-2200
23–26in (58.4–66.0cm)   2500-2800
Open mouth
17–19in (43.2–48.3cm)   1000-1100

For photograph of a Phenix Bébé, see color photograph on title page.

Philadelphia Baby

MAKER: J. B. Sheppard & Co., Philadephia, Penn., U.S.A.
DATE: Ca. 1900
MATERIAL: All-cloth
SIZE: 18–22in (45.7–55.9cm)
MARK: None

Philadelphia Baby: All-cloth with treated shoulder-type head, lower arms and legs. Painted hair, well-molded facial features, ears. Stocking body. Fair condition only, showing much wear.

21in (53.3cm) $750

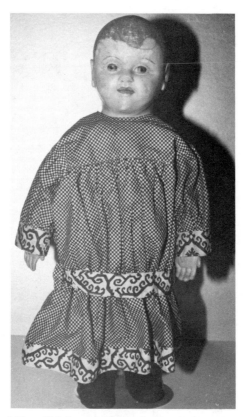

21in (53.3cm) Philadelphia Baby, face touched up. *H&J Foulke.*

Piano Baby

MAKER: Gebrüder Heubach, Kestner and other makers
DATE: 1880−on
MATERIAL: All-bisque
SIZE: Usually under 12in (30.5cm), some larger
MARK: Many unsigned; some with maker's particular mark

Piano Baby: All-bisque immobile with molded clothes and painted features, made in various sitting and lying positions.

3−4in (7.6−10.2cm)	$40-50*
7−8in (17.8−20.3cm)	100-125*
11−12in (27.9−30.5cm)	200-225*
4in (10.2cm) wigged	150-175

    *More depending upon quality
and uniqueness.

4½in (11.5cm) rare black Piano Baby, incised
Mackemull Collection.

Pincushion Dolls

MAKER: Various German firms
DATE: 1900—on
MATERIAL: China
SIZE: Up to about 7in (17.8cm)
MARK: "Germany" and numbers

Pincushions: China half figures with molded hair and painted features, usually with molded clothes, hats, lovely modeling and painting.

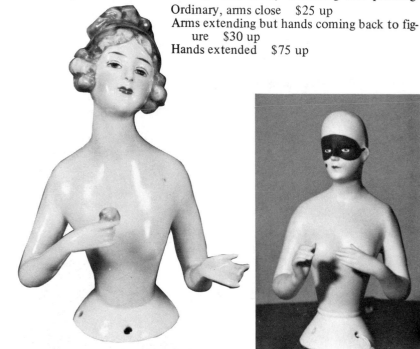

Ordinary, arms close $25 up
Arms extending but hands coming back to figure $30 up
Hands extended $75 up

5½in (14.0cm) Lady marked Germany. *Sheila Needle Collection. Photo by Morton Needle.*

5in (12.7cm) Rare lady with molded black mask, Goebel mark. *Doll Royalle.*

4in (10.2cm) Dressel and Kister lady reading a love letter. *H&J Foulke.*

4in (10.2cm) "Carmen" incised Germany 14303. *H&J Foulke.*

Poir Dolls

MAKER: Eugenie Poir, France; also Gre-Poir
DATE: 1920s
MATERIAL: All-cloth
SIZE: Various
MARK: None on doll; paper label on clothes

All Cloth Poir: All-cloth movable arms and legs, painted facial features, mohair wig, original clothes, all in good condition.

16in (40.6cm) $160-185

16in (40.6cm) Eugenie Poir doll with original square label. *Jane Sheetz Collection. Photograph courtesy of Jane Sheetz.*

Pre-Greiner
(So-called)

MAKER: Unknown U.S. firm
DATE: First half of 1800 s
MATERIAL: Papier-mâché shoulder head; stuffed cloth body, mostly homemade, wood, leather or cloth extremities
SIZE: Various
MARK: None

Unmarked Pre-Greiner: Papier-mâché shoulder head; painted black hair, center part; vertical curls in back, pupil-less black glass eyes. Cloth stuffed body, leather extremities, dressed in good old or original clothes; all in good condition.

21—23in (53.3—58.4cm)	$700-800*
28—30in (71.1—76.2cm)	900-1000*
With painted eyes	
18—21in (45.7—53.3cm)	$500-550

*Allow extra for flirty eyes

20 and 21in (50.8 and 53.3cm) Pre-Greiner dolls with painted eyes. *Joanna Ott Collection.*

Queen Anne-Type

MAKER: English Craftsmen
DATE: Late 17th–mid 19th century
MATERIAL: All-wood or wooden head and torso with leather or cloth limbs
SIZE: Various
MARK: None

18th Century: Carved wooden face, pupil-less glass eyes (sometimes painted), dotted eyebrows and eyelashes, flax or hair wig, jointed wooden body; old clothes, all in good condition.

15–20in (38.1–50.8cm) $3000 up

Late 18th to Early 19th Century: Wooden head, gessoed, dotted eyelashes and eyebrows, glass eyes (later sometimes blue), pointed torso; old clothes; all in good condition.

14–16in (35.6–40.6cm) $1200-1500**
**Not enough price samples to compute a reliable range

10in (25.4cm) Queen-Anne type with painted eyes. *Joan Kindler.*

R.A.

MAKER: Th. Recknagel of Alexandrinenthal, Thüringia, Germany
DATE: Various
MATERIAL: Bisque head, composition or wood-jointed body
SIZE: Various, usually smaller
MARK: R. A. with numbers, sometimes "Germany"

R. A. Child: Ca. 1890s–World War I. Marked bisque head, jointed composition or wooden body, set or sleep eyes, open mouth, good wig; some dolls with molded painted shoes and socks; all in good condition.

9–10in (22.9–25.4cm)	$100-125
13–14in (33.0–35.6cm)	150-160

R. A. Character Baby: 1909–World War I. Bisque socket head; composition bent-limb baby or straight-leg curved-arm toddler body; sleep or set eyes. Nicely dressed; all in good condition.

9–12in (22.9–30.5cm) $150-200

R. A. Character Baby as above but with painted eyes and molded cap.
Bonnet Baby
8–11in (20.3–27.9cm) $500-600

9in (22.9cm) R. A. baby incised 28/1, molded white cap with blue pom pom. *H&J Foulke.*

9in (22.9cm) R. A. baby incised 22/1, molded white cap with blue ribbon trim. *H&J Foulke.*

R.D. Bébé

MAKER: Rabery and Delphieu of Paris, France
DATE: 1856 (founded)–1899–then with S. F. B. J.
MATERIAL: Bisque head, composition body
SIZE: Various
MARK: "R. D." (from 1890)
    On back of head: R ⅝ D
    Body mark:

BÉBÉ RABERY
Sᶜ ———
——— (Please note last two lines illegible)

Marked R. D. Bébé: Bisque head, jointed composition body, lovely wig, paperweight eyes, closed mouth, beautifully dressed; entire doll in nice condition.

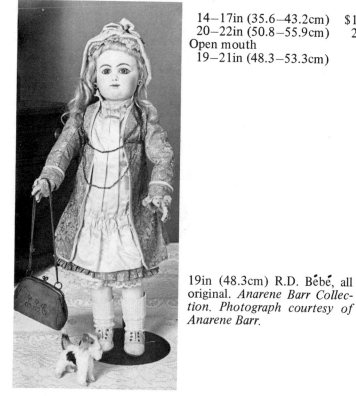

14–17in (35.6–43.2cm)	$1400-1800
20–22in (50.8–55.9cm)	2000-2300
Open mouth	
19–21in (48.3–53.3cm)	900-1000

19in (48.3cm) R.D. Bébé, all original. *Anarene Barr Collection. Photograph courtesy of Anarene Barr.*

Raggedy Ann and Andy

MAKER: Various
DATE: 1915 to present
MATERIAL: All-cloth
SIZE: 4½–39in (11.5–99cm)
CREATOR: Johnny B. Gruelle
MARK: As indicated below

Early Raggedy Ann and Andy: All-cloth with movable arms and legs; button eyes, painted features, brown yarn hair; legs or striped fabric for hose and black for shoes; original clothes; all in fair condition.
MARK: PATENTED SEPT. 7, 1915
(black stamp on front torso)

  15–17in (38.1–43.2cm) $90-100 each

Molly-'es Raggedy Ann and Andy: 1935–1938, manufactured by Molly-'es Doll Outfitters. Same as above, but with red hair and printed features; original clothes; all in good condition.
MARK: Raggedy Ann and Raggedy Andy Dolls
   Manufactured by Molly'es Doll Outfitters
(printed writing in black on front torso)

  18in (45.7cm) $65-75 each

Georgene Raggedy Ann and Andy: 1938–1963, manufactured by Georgene Novelties. Same as above, but with red hair and printed features; original clothes; all in good condition.
MARK: Cloth label sewn in side seam of body.
  15–18in (38.1–45.7cm)
    $30-35 each

Knickerbocker Toy Co. Raggedy Ann and Andy: 1963 to present. Available in toy stores

Molly-'es Raggedy Ann and Andy. *Jan Foulke Collection.*

Revalo

MAKER: Gebrüder Ohlhaver, Thüringia, Germany
DATE: 1921—on
MATERIAL: Bisque socket head, ball-jointed composition body
SIZE: Various
MARK:

Revalo
Germany
3

Character Baby or Toddler: Bisque socket head, sleep eyes, hair eye-lashes, painted lower lashes, open mouth, good wig; ball-jointed toddler or baby bent-limb body; dressed; all in good condition.
15in (38.1cm) Toddler $350-400

Character Doll: Bisque head with molded hair, painted eyes, open/closed mouth. Composition body. Dressed. All in good condition.

Coquette, 10—12in (25.4—30.5cm) $500—600
Molded hair child, 14in (35.6cm) $650

Child Doll: Bisque socket head, sleep eyes, hair eyelashes, painted lower lashes, open mouth, good wig; ball-jointed composition body; dressed; all in good condition.
14—17in (35.6—43.2cm) $350-375
22—23in (55.9—58.4cm) 425-475

ABOVE: 14½in (36.9cm) Revalo 22-2 Toddler. *H&J Foulke.*

RIGHT: 15in (38.1cm) Revalo Child doll. *Esther Schwartz.*

Grace Corry Rockwell

MAKER: Unknown
DATE: 1920s
MATERIAL: Bisque head; cloth and composition body
SIZE: About 20in (50.8cm)
MARK:

**Copr. by
Grace C. Rockwell
Germany**

Grace Corry Child: Composition smiling face, painted eyes, closed mouth, molded hair, sometimes with wig; cloth and composition body; appropriate clothes; all in good condition. Some dolls with tagged Madame Hendren clothing have heads by Grace Corry. See *3rd Blue Book of Dolls and Values,* page 153.

14in (35.6cm) $200-250

Grace Corry Rockwell Child: Bisque head with sleep eyes, closed mouth, molded hair or wig; cloth and composition body; appropriate clothes; all in good condition. 20in (50.8cm) $2500**

**Not enough price samples to compute a
reliable range

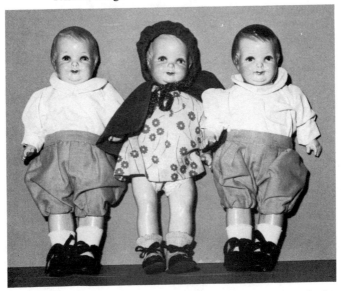

Dolls by Grace Corry with composition heads and limbs; the center doll is all original. *Esther Schwartz Collection.*

Rohmer Fashion

MAKER: Mademoiselle Marie Rohmer, Paris, France
DATE: 1866–1880
MATERIAL: China or bisque shoulder head, jointed kid body
SIZE: Various
MARK:

Rohmer Fashion: China or bisque swivel shoulder head; jointed kid body, set glass eyes, bisque or china arms, kid or china legs, closed mouth, some ears pierced, lovely wig, fine costuming; entire doll in good contion. $3500 up

15in (38.1cm) Signed Rohmer china head
and arms. *Richard Wright Collection.*

Roullet & Decamps

MAKER: J. Roullet & E. Decamps, Paris, France
DATE: Ca. 1895
MATERIAL: Usually bisque head, mechanical body
SIZE: Various
MARK: L'Intrépide Bébé
      R.D.

R. D. Mechanical Doll: Bisque head, closed mouth, paperweight eyes, good wig; appropriate clothes; mechanical key wind walking body; all in good condition.

26in (66.0cm) $2800-3200

Roullet & Decamps, Bébé L'Intrepide, key wind walker. *Richard Wright.*

S & Co.

MAKER: S & Co.
DATE: Ca. 1910—on
MATERIAL: Bisque socket head, composition baby body
SIZE: Various
MARK: Stamped in green

GESCHUTZ S & Co GERMANY

Incised "Lori": Solid-dome head, painted hair, sleep eyes, closed mouth; composition baby body with bent limbs; dressed; all in good condition.

9—11in (22.9—27.9cm)	$800-900
20—22in (50.8—55.9cm)	1800-2000

Mold #232 (open-mouth "Lori"): Same as above, but with open mouth.
21in (53.3cm) $900-1000

DIP: Bisque socket head, sleep eyes, closed mouth, wig; composition baby body with bent limbs; dressed; all in good condition.

9—10in (22.9—25.4cm)	$500
16in (40.6cm)	800

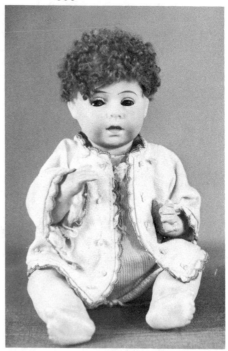

10in (25.4cm) Character toddler incised FO, intaglio eyes. *Richard Wright.*

9in (22.9cm) Character incised DIP. *H&J Foulke.*

MAKER: Sociéte Française de Fabrication de Bébés & Jouets, Paris, France
DATE: Various
MATERIAL: Bisque head, composition body
SIZE: Various
MARK:

S. F. B. ✓
236
PARIS

Child Doll: 1899–on. Marked bisque head, jointed composition body, pierced ears, sleep eyes, open mouth, good French wig, nicely dressed, all in good condition.

#301

7in (17.8cm)	$150-200*
12—14in (30.5—35.6cm)	400-450*
18—20in (45.7—50.8cm)	700-750*
23—25in (58.4—63.5cm)	800-850*
28—30in (71.1—76.2cm)	950-1100*
32—34in (81.3—86.4cm)	1300-1500*

#60

14—16in (35.6—40.6cm)	400-450
20—22in (50.8—55.9cm)	550-600
12in (30.5cm) Costume doll, 5 pc body	
	225-250

#230

24in (61.0cm)	1200

*Allow more for Jumeau look and fine quality.

22in (55.9cm) SFBJ 301 red stamp Tete Jumeau, lady body. *Richard Wright.*

10in (25.4cm) SFBJ 301 child, all original. *H&J Foulke.*

Walking & Kiss-Throwing: 1905—on. Marked bisque head, composition body with straight legs, walking mechanism at top, hand raises to throw a kiss, head moves from side to side, eyes flirt, glass eyes, good wig, open mouth, pierced ears, nicely dressed; all in working order.

22—24in (55.9—61.0cm) $1100-1200

Character Dolls: 1910—on. Marked bisque head, sleep eyes, wig; molded, sometimes flocked hair on mold numbers 237, 226, 227 and 235; composition body. Nicely dressed. All in good condition.

#236
12—15in (30.5—38.1cm)$750-850
19—21in (48.3—53.3cm)
                1000-1200
#237, 226, 235, 227
15—17in (38.1—43.2cm)
                1500-1650
#251
15—18in (38.1—45.7cm)
                1200-1500

#247
18—20in (45.7—50.8cm)
                2000-2300
#252
24in (61.0cm) Toddler   7000

#238
16in (40.6cm)   2000-2200

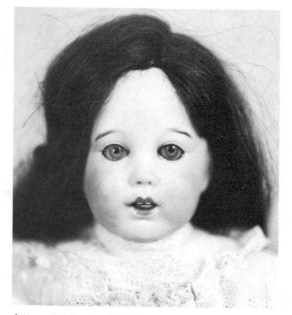

14in (35.6cm) SFBJ 251 Toddler. *Richard Wright.*

RIGHT: 18in (45.7cm) SFBJ
234 character baby, rare number.
Richard Wright Collection.

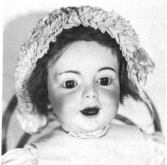

ABOVE: 8in (20.3cm) **SFBJ**
252 Pouty Baby. *Richard Wright
Collection.*

RIGHT: 13½in (34.3cm) SFBJ
226 Character Boy. *Mary Lou
Rubright Collection.*

18in (45.7cm) SFBJ 238 Character Girl. *Mary Lou Rubright Collection.*

15in (38.1cm) SFBJ 247 Toddler. *Mary Lou Rubright Collection.*

S & Q

MAKER: Possibly Schuelzmeister & Quendt, Boilstadt, Thüringia, Germany
DATE: Ca. 1920–1925
MATERIAL: Bisque head, composition body
SIZE: Various
DISTRIBUTOR: John Bing Co., N.Y.
MARK:

301

Germany

S & Q Character Baby: Mold number 201. Bisque head with sleep eyes, open mouth with tongue and teeth, slightly smiling, mohair wig; composition baby body; nicely dressed; all in good condition.

18–22in (45.7–55.9cm) $375-425

S & Q Child Doll: Mold number 301. Bisque head with sleep eyes, open mouth with teeth, mohair wig, jointed composition body, nicely dressed.

23–26in (58.4–66.0cm) $275-325

16in (40.6cm) S&Q 201 Baby. *Emma Wedmore Collection.*

Santa Claus

MAKER: Various
DATE: 1920 s—on
MATERIAL: Composition and cloth
SIZE: Various
MARK: None

Santa Claus Doll: All composition jointed at neck and shoulders with molded black boots; molded whiskers, hair and cap; painted eyes. Original Santa Claus suit; all in good condition.

19in (48.3cm) $250

20in (50.8cm) Santa Claus. *Mary Lou Rubright Collection.*

Bruno Schmidt

MAKER: Bruno Schmidt of Waltershausen, Thüringia, Germany
DATE: 1900—on
MATERIAL: Bisque head, composition body
SIZE: Various
MARK:

and numbers

Marked B. S. W. Character Baby: Bisque head, open mouth, sleep eyes, good wig, composition bent-limb baby body; dressed; all in good condition.

12—15in (30.5—38.1cm)	$300-350
18—22in (45.7—55.9cm)	400-450

Marked B. S. W. Child Doll: Bisque head, open mouth, sleep eyes, good wig, jointed composition child body, dressed; all in good condition.

24in (61.0cm)	$400-450
32in (81.3cm)	750

B. S. W. Tommy Tucker Character (molded and painted hair):

Tommy Tucker #2048

17—19in (43.2—48.3cm)	$700-750
22—24in (55.9—61.0cm)	900-1000

Wendy #2033

18in (45.7cm)	$4000 up**

**Not enough price samples to compute a reliable range

ABOVE: 34in (86.4cm) Bruno Schmidt Child doll. *Mary Lou Rubright Collection.*

LEFT: 10in (25.4cm) Bruno Schmidt "Tommy Tucker". *Mary Lou Rubright Collection.*

Franz Schmidt

MAKER: Franz Schmidt & Co. of Georgenthal near Waltershausen, Thüringia, Germany
DATE: Ca. 1911
MATERIAL: Bisque socket head, jointed bent-limb or toddler body of composition
SIZE: Various
MARK: "F. S. & CO.
      Made in Germany"
Numbers such as 1295, 1272. Deponiert included.

1295
F. S. & Co.
Made in
Germany
30

Marked F. Schmidt Doll: Bisque character head, may have open nostrils, sleep eyes, open mouth, good wig; jointed bent-limb body; suitably dressed, all in good condition.

#1272, 17in (43.2cm) $425-475*
   *Allow extra for toddler body
#1295, 19–24in (48.3–61.0cm)   475-550*
   *Allow extra for flirty eyes

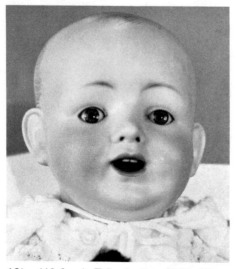

19in (48.3cm) F.S. & Co. 1272 Character. *Mary Lou Rubright Collection.*

Schmitt Bébé

MAKER: Schmitt & Fils, Paris, France
DATE: Ca. 1879–1891
MATERIAL: Bisque socket head, composition jointed body
SIZE: Various
MARK: On both head and body:

Marked Schmitt Bébé: Bisque socket head with closed mouth, large paperweight eyes, skin or good wig, pierced ears; Schmitt-jointed composition body. Appropriate clothes. All in good condition.

15–18in (38.1–45.7cm) $3500-4500

14in (35.6cm) Schmitt. Crandall Collection.

Schoenau & Hoffmeister

MAKER: Schoenau & Hoffmeister of Burggrub, Bavaria, Germany
DATE: Various
MATERIAL: Bisque head, composition body
SIZE: Various
MARK: "Porzellanfabrik Burggrub" or 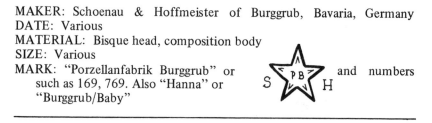 and numbers
such as 169, 769. Also "Hanna" or
"Burggrub/Baby"

Oriental: Ca. 1900. Mold number 4900. Bisque socket head tinted yellow, open mouth, black glass eyes, black mohair wig, yellow composition ball-jointed body (five-piece body on small sizes). Japanese outfit. All in good condition.

    8in (20.3cm) $300-350
    12–15in (30.5–38.1cm)   750-850

Child Doll: 1901–on. Mold numbers such as 1909, 5500, 5800, 5700. Bisque head, ball-jointed body, open mouth, sleep eyes, original or good wig, original or good clothes; all in nice condition.

    18–20in (45.7–50.8cm) $225-275
    23–27in (58.4–68.6cm)   325-400

ABOVE: 13in (33.0cm) Hanna toddler. *Joanna Ott Collection.*

LEFT: 8in (20.3cm) 1909 child. *H&J Foulke.*

Character Baby: 1910 on. Mold numbers 169, 769 or "Hanna", "Burggrub Baby" or "Porzellanfabrik Burggrub". Bisque socket head, open mouth, good wig, sleep eyes, composition bent-limb baby body; all in good condition.

10–12in (25.4–30.5cm)	$225-250
16–18in (40.6–45.7cm)	300-350
24–25in (61.0–63.5cm)	450

Princess Elizabeth: Late 1930s. Bisque head with glass sleep eyes, smiling mouth with teeth, good wig; chubby five-piece composition body; appropriate clothes; all in good condition. Marked Porzellanfabrik Burggrub/Princess Elizabeth.

16in (40.6cm)	$2000-2200
21in (53.3cm)	2600-2800

Black Hanna: Ca. 1910–on. Bisque socket head tinted light or dark brown, open mouth, black eyes, black mohair wig. Black composition body, grass skirt. All in good condition.

7in (17.8cm) $125-150

Pouty Baby, 12in (30.5cm) $600-650**

**Not enough price samples to compute a reliable range.

22in (55.9cm) "Princess Elizabeth". *Mary Lou Rubright Collection.*

13in (33.0cm) rare baby or toddler, cloth torso, composition arms and legs. *Mary Lou Rubright Collection.*

Schoenhut

MAKER: Albert Schoenhut & Co., Philadelphia, Penn., U.S.A.
DATE: Various
MATERIAL: Wood, spring-jointed, holes in bottom of feet to fit metal stand
SIZE: Various models 11—21in (27.9—53.3cm)
DESIGNER: Early: Adolph Graziana and Mr. Leslie
Later: Harry E. Schoenhut
MARK: Paper label: Incised:

SCHOENHUT DOLL
PAT. JAN. 17, '11, U.S.A.
& FOREIGN COUNTRIES

Character: 1911—1930. Wooden head and spring-jointed wooden body, marked head and/or body, original or appropriate wig, brown or blue intaglio eyes, open/closed mouth with painted teeth or closed mouth; original or suitable clothing, nothing repainted; all in good condition.
16—19in (40.6—48.3cm)

Pouty $500*
Smiling   650*

*More depending upon rarity of face.

16in (40.6cm) Pouty Schoenhut.
H&J Foulke.

Character with molded hair: Ca. 1911–1930. Wooden head with molded hair, comb marks, possibly a ribbon or bow, intaglio eyes, mouth usually closed; spring-jointed wooden body; original or suitable clothes; all in good condition.

14–16in (35.6–40.6cm) $900-1000

"Baby Face": Ca. 1913–1930. Wooden head and fully-jointed toddler or bent-limb baby body, marked head and/or body. Painted hair, painted eyes, open/closed mouth, suitably dressed, nothing repainted, all in good condition.

MARK:

Baby body 15–16in (38.1–40.6cm)		$425-450
Toddler 16–17in (40.6–43.2cm)		400-425
11in (27.9cm)		450-500

ABOVE LEFT: 11in (27.9cm) Schoenhut Toddler. *H&J Foulke.*

ABOVE RIGHT: 15in (38.1cm) molded hair Schoenhut. *Grace Dyar.*

RIGHT: 19in (48.3cm) rare style Schoenhut Pouty, all original. *H&J Foulke.*

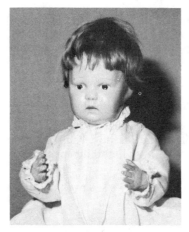

14in (35.6cm) Schoenhut Baby, all original. *Rosemary Dent Collection.*

16in (40.6cm) Schoenhut with "Dolly" face. *H&J Foulke.*

22in (55.9cm) Schoenhut Child with sleep eyes. *Esther Schwartz.*

"Dolly Face": Ca. 1915–1930. Wooden head and spring-jointed wooden body, original or appropriate mohair wig, decal eyes, open/closed mouth with painted teeth; original or suitable clothes; all in good condition.

     17–21in (43.2–53.3cm) $325-375

Walker: Ca. 1919–1930. All wood with "infant type" head, mohair wig, painted eyes, curved arms, straight legs with "walker" joint at hip; original or appropriate clothes; all in good condition. No holes in bottom of feet.

     11–13in (27.9–33.0cm) $350-400

Sleeping Eyes: Ca. 1920–1930. Used with the "Baby" or "Dolly Face" heads. Mouths on this type were open with teeth or barely open with carved teeth.

     17–22in (43.2–55.9cm) $600-625

Scootles

MAKER: Cameo Doll Products Co., Inc., Port Allegany, Penn., U.S.A.
DATE: Ca. 1925—on
MATERIAL: All-composition or all-bisque
SIZE: Many
DESIGNER: Rose O'Neill
MARK: All-bisque: "Scootles" on red and gold chest label; "Scootles"
and "Rose O'Neill" on feet

Scootles: Unmarked, all-composition, jointed at neck, shoulder and hips,
blue or brown painted eyes, closed smiling mouth, molded hair, eyes
to side, not dressed; doll in nice condition.

12in (30.5cm) $200-250
Black   300-350**

All-bisque jointed at shoulders only, molded hair and painted features.
All-bisque, 5—6in (12.7—15.2cm) Germany $450-500; Japan $175-200

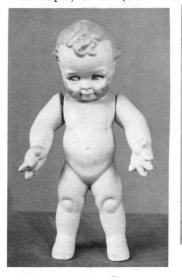
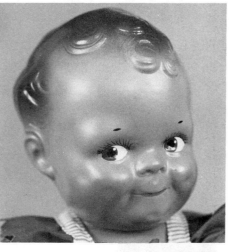

ABOVE LEFT: 7in (17.8cm) All-bisque "Scootles",
stamped Japan. *Mary Lou Rubright Collection.*

ABOVE RIGHT: 12in (30.5cm) black "Scootles",
all original, very rare. *H&J Foulke.*

RIGHT: "Scootles" wrist tag on composition doll.

Shirley Temple

MAKER: Ideal Toy Corp., N.Y., U.S.A.
DATE: 1934 to present
SIZE: 7½–36in (19.1–91.4cm)
DESIGNER: Bernard Lipfert
MARK: See individual doll listings below. (Ideal used marked Shirley Temple bodies for other dolls.)

All-Composition Child: 1934 through late 1930s. Marked head and body, jointed composition body, all original including wig and clothes. Entire doll in excellent condition. Came in sizes 11–27in (27.9–68.6cm)

MARK: On body: **SHIRLEY TEMPLE**
On head: **13**   **13**

SHIRLEY TEMPLE

11in (27.9cm)	$600
13in (33.0cm)	475-500
→ 18in (45.7cm)	475-550
22in (55.9cm)	600-650
25in (63.5cm)	700-750
27in (68.6cm)	800-850

On cloth label:

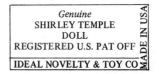

Genuine
SHIRLEY TEMPLE
DOLL
REGISTERED U.S. PAT OFF
IDEAL NOVELTY & TOY CO
MADE IN USA

22in (55.9cm) Shirley Temple, Texas Ranger outfit. *Rosemary Dent Collection.*

LEFT: 16in (40.6cm) composition Shirley Temple, all original. *H&J Foulke.*

Baby: 1934 through late 1930s. Composition swivel head with sleep eyes, open smiling mouth, dimples, molded hair or blonde mohair wig; cloth body, composition arms and legs. Appropriate clothes. All in good condition. Came in six sizes, 16–25in (40.6–63.5cm). Marked "Shirley Temple" on head.

18in (45.7cm) $650

15in (38.1cm) composition Shirley Temple Baby, not original. *Mary Lou Rubright Collection.*

Unusual Japanese-made Shirley with molded hair: From late 1930s. All-composition.
7½in (19.1cm) $150**

**Not enough price samples to compute a reliable range

10in (25.4cm) celluloid Shirley Temple, Made in Japan. *Mary Lou Rubright Collection.*

Vinyl and Plastic: 1957. Vinyl and plastic, rooted hair, sleep eyes, jointed at shoulders and hips, original clothes; all in excellent condition. Came in sizes 12in (30.5cm), 15in (38.1cm), 17in (43.2cm), 19in (48.3cm) and 36in (91.4cm)
    MARK: "Ideal Doll ST—12" (number denotes size)
12in (30.5cm) $65-75   19in (48.3cm) $200-225
17in (43.2cm) 150-175   36in (91.4cm) 1100-1250

Vinyl and Plastic: 1973. Vinyl and plastic, rooted hair, painted eyes, smiling mouth; jointed shoulders and hips; original clothes; all in mint condition.
      16in (40.6cm) size only $50 Boxed

Shirley Temple, 1972, vinyl, all original. *Rosemary Dent Collection.*

36in (91.4cm) 1957 vinyl Shirley Temple, all original in original box. *Maxine Salaman.*

12in (30.5cm) 1957 vinyl Shirley Temple, original slip. *H&J Foulke.*

Simonne

MAKER: F. Simonne, Paris, France
DATE: 1847–1878?
MATERIAL: Bisque head; kid or composition body
SIZE: Various
MARK: sticker or stamped on body

O PASSAGE DELORM
No. 1 à 13
SIMONNE
RUE PARIS
DE RIVOLI
1880

Simonne Lady Doll: Late 1860s–on. Bisque turning head on shoulder plate, kid body, bisque arms; paperweight eyes, closed mouth, wig, pierced ears; dressed; all in good condition.
18in (45.7cm) $2000**
Simonne Bébé: 1870s. Bisque head, composition and wood jointed body; paperweight eyes, closed mouth, pierced ears, wig, dressed; all in good condition. Rare.   20in (50.8cm) $3000 up**

**Not enough price samples to compute a reliable range.

18in (45.7cm) Simonne lady doll, all original. *Sheila Needle Collection. Photograph by Morton Needle.*

Simon & Halbig

MAKER: Simon & Halbig of Gräfenhain, Thüringia, Germany
DATE: Ca. 1880 s
MATERIAL: Bisque head; kid (sometimes cloth) or composition body
SIZE: Various
MARK:

$$S\ 13\ H$$
$$949$$

$$1079-2$$
$$DEP$$
$$S\ H$$
$$Germany$$

Child doll with closed mouth: Ca. 1880 s Mold numbers such as 719, 939, 949, etc. Bisque socket head on ball-jointed wood and composition body or on shoulder plate (swivel neck) and kid body with bisque hands. Glass set or sleep eyes, closed mouth, pierced ears, good wig; dressed; all in good condition.

#719, 939, 949 Composition body:*
  17–19in (43.2–48.3cm) $1500-1600
  24in (61.0cm)   2000
#905, 908
  12in (30.5cm)   1000
  18in (45.7cm)   1500
#950, Kid body:
  8–10in (20.3–25.4cm)   250-300

14in (35.6cm) S&H 949 child, closed mouth, swivel neck, kid body. *H&J Foulke.*

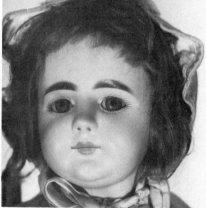

23in (58.4cm) S&H 719 child, composition body. *Mary Goolsby.*

Child doll with open mouth and composition body: Ca. 1889 to 1930s. Mold numbers, such as 1079, 1039, 1009, 550, etc. Bisque head, good wig, original ball-jointed composition body; sleep eyes, open mouth, pierced ears; very pretty clothes; all in nice condiiton.

#1009
  Swivel neck, fashion body
    20–22in (50.8-55.9cm) $500-550
  Composition body 16–18in
    (40.6–45.7cm)   350-400
#949, 939
    16–19in (40.6–48.3cm) 600-700
    24–26in (61.0–66.0cm) 850-950
#1079, 1009
    16–18in (40.6–45.7cm) 300-350
    21–24in (53.3–61.0cm) 400-450
    26–28in (66.0–71.1cm) 550-600
    37in (93.9cm)   1250

Baby Blanche
    22in (55.9cm)   400-450
Santa, #1249
    15–19in (38.1–48.3cm) 400-450
    25–26in (63.5–66.0cm) 650-700
#1039, walking body with flirting
  eyes, keywind mechanism
    20in (50.8cm)   850-900

Character Child:
  #151, 18in (45.7cm) $3000 up
  #1279, 14–16in (35.6–40.6cm)
                            750-800
         24in (61.0cm)   1500
  #1299, 18–20in (45.7–50.8cm)
                         700-800**
  #600, 12–14in (30.5–35.6cm)
                            600-700
  #1388, 24in (61.0cm)   7800*
  #1488, 18in (45.7cm)   2500**
  #1498, 18in (45.7cm)
                        1500-1800**
*A one-time auction price.

**Not enough price samples to compute a reliable range.

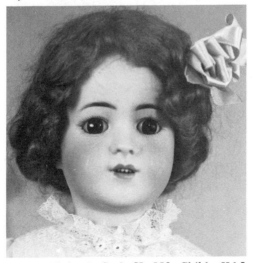

23in (58.4cm) S & H 550 Child. *H&J Foulke.*

11in (27.9cm) S & H 1269, composition body. *H&J Foulke.*

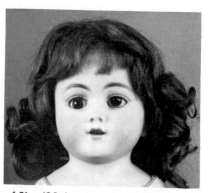

15in (38.1cm) S & H 1250, kid and composition body. *H&J Foulke.*

13in (33.0cm) S & H 1009, composition body. *H&J Foulke.*

14in (35.6cm) S & H 1248, composition body, all original. *Richard Wright Collection.*

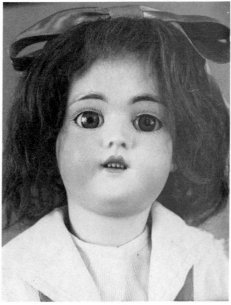

ABOVE: 23in (58.4cm) S & H "Baby Blanche". *H&J Foulke.*

RIGHT: 14in (35.6cm) S & H 1079, composition body, all original baby clothes. *H&J Foulke.*

15in (38.1cm) S & H
1109. *H&J Foulke.*

15in (38.1cm) S & H
1279. *H&J Foulke.*

28in (71.1cm) S & H "Santa".
H&J Foulke.

Child doll with open mouth and kid body: Ca. 1889 to 1930s. Mold numbers such as 1010, 1040, 1080, 1250, etc. Shoulder head with stationary neck, kid body, bisque arms; cloth lower legs, open mouth, sleep eyes, pierced ears; well costumed; all in good condition.

    #1040, 1080
     20–22in (40.6–55.9cm) $375-425
    #1250, 1260
     15–19in (38.1–48.3cm)   300-400

18in (45.7cm) S & H 600. *Mary Lou Rubright Collection.*

Tiny Child doll: Ca. 1889 to 1930 s. Usually mold number 1079 or 1078. Bisque head, composition body with molded shoes and socks, open mouth, nice wig, sleep eyes; appropriate clothes. All in good condition.

8—10in (20.3—25.4cm) $175-250*

*Allow more for fully-jointed body

9in (22.9cm) S & H 1079, tiny doll, fully jointed body. *H&J Foulke.*

So-called "Little Women" type: Ca. 1900. Mold number 1160. Shoulder head with closed mouth, glass set eyes, fancy mohair wig; cloth body with bisque limbs, molded boots; dressed all in good condition.

5½—7in (14.0—17.8cm)
$250-325
10—13in (25.4—33.0cm)
$350-450

8in (20.3cm) S & H 1160 shoulder head, original wig. *H&J Foulke.*

Character Baby: 1909 to 1930s. Mold number 1294. Bisque head, molded hair or wig, open or open/closed mouth, sleep eyes; composition bent-limb baby or toddler body; nicely dressed; all in good condition.

#1294, 18—20in (45.7—50.8cm) $450-500
#1428, 22in (55.9cm) 2200**

17in (45.7cm) S & H 1303 lady character. *Richard Wright Collection.*   24in (61.0cm) S & H 1159 lady. *Mary Lou Rubright Collection.*

Lady doll: Ca. 1910. Mold number 1159. Bisque socket head, open mouth, good wig, pierced ears, sleep eyes, lady body, molded bust, slim arms and legs, elegantly dressed; all in good condition.

#1159	14in (35.6cm)	$700-750
	18—20in (45.7—50.8cm)	1000-1200
	24in (61.0cm)	1300-1400

Lady doll: Ca. 1910. With closed mouth. Bisque head with set glass eyes, good wig, composition lady body, molded bust, slim arms and legs, nicely dressed; all in good condition.

#1469	14—15in (35.6—38.1cm)	$650-1200*
#1303	Closed mouth	
	15—18in (38.1—45.7cm)	4000 up**

**Not enough price samples to compute a reliable range
*Prices on this doll are not stable.

22in (55.9cm) S & H 1488 Toddler. *Esther Schwartz Collection.*

20 in (50.8cm) S & H 120 Character Girl. *Mary Lou Rubright Collection.*

Snow Babies

MAKER: Various German firms
DATE: Ca. 1890 until World War II
MATERIAL: All-bisque
SIZE: 1–3in (2.5–7.6cm) usually
MARK: Sometimes "Germany"

Snow Babies: All-bisque with snow suits and caps of pebbly-textured bisque. Painted features. Various standing, lying or sitting positions.

    1½in (3.8cm) $25 up depending upon action.
    4–5in (10.2–12.7cm) with jointed arms and legs $250-300
    7½in (19.1cm) shoulder head doll $250-300

ABOVE: Three Snow Babies 1in (2.5cm) tall on sled. *H&J Foulke.*

RIGHT: 7½in (19.1cm) rare Snow Baby shoulder head doll, cloth body, bisque limbs. *H&J Foulke.*

3 babies on sled $95
Santa on snow bear $200-225
2½in (6.4cm) smiling boy $85
3in (7.6cm) snow baby on bear $125

Steiff Dolls

MAKER: Fraulein Margarete Steiff, Würtemberg, Germany
DATE: 1894–on
MATERIAL: Felt, plush or velvet
SIZE: Various
MARK: Metal button in ear

Steiff Doll: Felt, plush or velvet, jointed. Seam down middle of face, button eyes, painted features, original clothes. Most are character dolls. Many have large shoes to enable them to stand. All in good condition.

10–15in (25.4–38.1cm)	$200-250
Characters	
15–21in (38.1–53.3cm)	450-650

21in (53.3cm) Steiff Character Man, all original. *H&J Foulke.*

Herm Steiner

MAKER: Hermann Steiner of Sonneberg, Thüringia, Germany
DATE: 1920s
MATERIAL: Bisque head, cloth or composition body
SIZE: Various, usually small
MARK:

15
ℋ
—————— Germany ——————
240

HermSteiner
ℋ
—————— Germany ——————

Herm Steiner Baby: Bisque head, cloth body, molded hair, sleep eyes,
dressed; in good condition.

6—10in (15.2—25.4cm) $175-225

Herm Steiner Child: Bisque head, jointed composition body, wig, sleep
eyes, open mouth, dressed; in good condition.

8in (20.3cm) $100-125
12in (30.5cm) 150-160

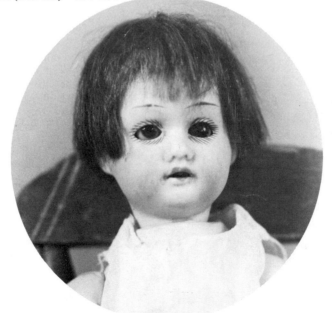

8in (20.3cm) Herm Steiner Baby, composition
body. *Joanna Ott Collection.*

Jules Steiner Bébé

MAKER: Jules Nicholas Steiner (and successors), Paris, France
DATE: 1870s—Ca. 1908
MATERIAL: Bisque head, jointed papier-mâché body
SIZE: Various
MARK: Various including incised on heads: $S^{TE}C^4$ or $\begin{smallmatrix}A\text{-}19\\PARIS\end{smallmatrix}$

on body: Paper label of child carrying flag

or

BÉBÉ "LE PARISIEN"
MEDAILLE D'OR
PARIS

Steiner Bébé: Marked bisque head, jointed papier-mâché body, good
French wig, closed mouth, beautiful paperweight eyes, lovely clothes,
all in good condition.

12—14in (30.5—35.6cm) $1800-2200
17—21in (43.2—53.3cm) 2500-2900
25in (63.5cm)   3300

Kicking, crying
18—20in (45.7—
  50.8cm)$1400-1600
Open mouth
19—21in (48.3—
  53.3cm) 1150-1350
Bourgoin
17—21in (43.2—
  53.3cm) 3200-3500

24in (61.0cm) incised
Ste C 5, wire eyes;
in red script J. Steiner
Sgdg J. Bourgoin.
Richard Wright.

23in (58.4cm) incised
FIre A 15 Steiner,
body with flag label.
Joanna Ott Collection.

19in (48.3cm) in-
cised A-13 PARIS,
LE PARISIENE,
open mouth with
two rows of teeth.
*Mary Lou Rubright
Collection.*

Superior Dolls

MAKER: Probably A. Fleishmann and Cramer; Müller and Strassburger; and G. Liedel, all from Sonneberg area of Germany
DATE: 1850s—1890s
MATERIAL: Composition head, cloth body, cloth or kid extremities
SIZE: Various
MARK: Label "M & S SUPERIOR 2015" or "G. L. 2015 SUPERIOR PERFECTLY HARMLESS" or "M & S SUPERIOR 4515", etc. Later ones also marked "Germany"

Superior Doll: Label on back of shoulder head; papier-mâché shoulder head, black or blonde molded painted hair; original cloth body, old kid arms and boots, quaint old clothing, brown or blue painted eyes; all in nice condition.

16—20in (40.6—50.8cm) $175-225
24—28in (61.0—71.1cm) 300-350

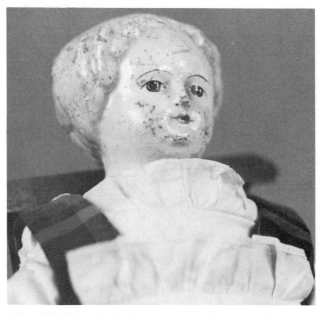

13in (33.0cm) M & S Superior doll, unusually small size. *Joanna Ott Collection.*

MAKER: Created by Morris Michton, later of Ideal Novelty & Toy Co., but made by a wide variety of American and German companies of which Steiff is probably best known.

DATE: 1902–on

MATERIAL: Plush

SIZE: Various

MARK: Generally only a paper label; Steiff bears have a metal button in the ear

---

Teddy Bear: Stuffed and jointed at neck with swivel joints at shoulders and hips, glass or button eyes, hump on back. Shows personality! Sometimes wears an old coat or sweater.

Early	$150 up
1930s	100 up

Celluloid-faced Teddy Bear. *Joanna Ott Collection.*

Terri Lee

MAKER: TERRI LEE Sales Corp., V. Gradwohl, Pres., U.S.A.
DATE: 1946–Lincoln, Neb.; then Apple Valley, Calif., from 1951–Ca.
1962.
MATERIAL: First dolls, rubbery plastic composition; later, hard plastic
SIZE: 16in (40.6cm) only
MARK: embossed across shoulders
First dolls: TERRI LEE   raised letters
          PAT. PENDING   Later dolls: TERRI LEE

Terri Lee Child Doll: Original wig, painted eyes; all original clothing and
accessories; jointed at neck, shoulders and hips. Mint condition.
Early model $125-135   Hard plastic $85

Tiny Terri Lee: 10in (25.4cm) tall. Inset eyes and lashes, original wig,
jointed neck, shoulders and hips. Original clothes, mint condition.
$75-80

Jerri Lee $100-110   **Tiny Jerri Lee** $80-90

16in (40.6cm) "Terri Lee" in
original dress. *H&J Foulke.*

10in (25.4cm) "Tiny Terri Lee",
original ballerina. *H&J Foulke.*

16in (40.6cm) early-type black "Terri Lee", all original. *H&J Foulke.*

322

Trudy
(Three-faced Doll)

MAKER: Three-in-One Doll Corporation, New York, N.Y., U.S.A.
DATE: 1946
MATERIAL: Composition head, arms and legs; cloth body
SIZE: Various
DESIGNER: Elsie Gilbert
MARK: On clothing (see below)

Trudy, Three-faced Doll: Composition head, arms and legs, cloth body, composition knob on top of head which turns faces. Original clothes, usually a felt or fleece outfit. "Sleepy Trudy, Smily Trudy, Weepy Trudy" in tiny pastel circles printed on white dress material. All fine condition.

      14in (35.6cm) $135
      Mint in box   225-250

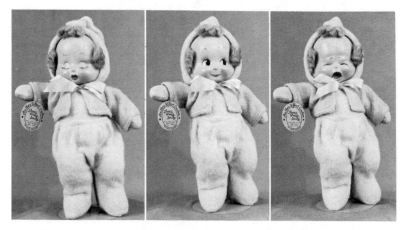

14in (35.6cm) "Trudy", all original with wrist tag. *H&J Foulke.*

Tynie Baby

MAKER: E. I. Horsman Co., New York, N.Y., U.S.A.
DATE: 1924
MATERIAL: Bisque head, cloth body, composition arms; also, composition head and all-bisque versions were made
SIZE: Various
DESIGNER: Bernard Lipfert
MARK:

© 1924
E.I. HorsMAN INc.
MAde in
Germany

Marked Tynie Baby: Bisque solid infant head with sleep eyes, closed mouth, slightly frowning face, cloth body with composition arms. Appropriate clothes. All in good condition.

12–13in (30.5–33.0cm) $550-600

All-bisque with swivel neck, glass eyes, wigged or solid dome head:

9in (22.9cm) $1000**

Composition head
  13in (33.0cm) $150**

**Not enough price samples to compute a reliable range

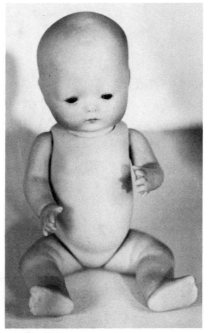

All-bisque version, swivel neck, glass eyes. *Richard Wright Collection.*

Uneeda Biscuit Boy

MAKER: Ideal Novelty & Toy Co., New York, N.Y., U.S.A.
DATE: Ca. 1914–1919
MATERIAL: Composition head, arms and legs; cloth body
SIZE: 16in (40.6cm)
MARK: Label on sleeve: "Uneeda Kid
Patented Dec 8, 1914
Ideal Novelty & Toy Co.
Brooklyn, N.Y."

Biscuit Boy: Composition head with molded brown hair, painted blue eyes, closed mouth. Cloth body with composition arms and legs. Wearing molded black boots, bloomer suit, yellow slicker, and rainhat and carrying a box of Uneeda Biscuits. All in good condition, showing some wear.   16in (40.6cm) $150*
　　　　　*Allow extra for molded hat

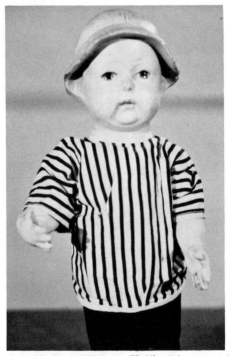

16in (40.6cm) "Uneeda Kid" with unusual molded hat. *H&J Foulke.*

Unis Dolls

MAKER: Société Française de Fabrication de Bébés et Jouets. (S. F. B. J.) of Paris and Montruil-sous-Bois, France
DATE: 1922–on
MATERIAL: Bisque head, jointed composition body
SIZE: Various
MARK:

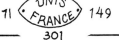

Also "Unis France 71 149 301"
"71 Unis France 149 60"

Unis Child Doll: Marked bisque head, papier-mâché body or wood and composition jointed body; sleep eyes, good wig, pretty clothes, open mouth; all in nice condition. 14–16in (35.6–40.6cm) $400-450
20–22in (50.8–55.9cm) 500-550

Unis Lady Doll: Marked bisque head, wood and composition body with molded bust and nipped in lady waist; sleep eyes, good wig, pretty clothes, open mouth; all in nice condition. 18in (45.7cm) $800-850

ABOVE: 3¾in (9.6cm) Unis Child doll, all original, *H&J Foulke.*

RIGHT: Unis Lady Doll, all original. *H&J Foulke.*

Costume Doll: Marked bisque head, glass eyes (painted eyes on tiny dolls), mohair wig, open or closed mouth; five-piece papier-maché body; original costume; all in good condition.

5—7in (12.7—17.8cm) $125-150
11—13in (27.9—33.0cm)   200-225
7—10in (17.8—25.4cm)
   fully jointed   250-300

Dark-skinned Costume Doll:
11—13in (27.9—33.0cm) $200-225

13in (33.0cm) Unis mulatto costume doll, all original except perhaps skirt. *H&J Foulke.*

13in (33.0cm) Unis 301 black costume doll, all original. *H&J Foulke.*

Vogue-Ginny

MAKER: Vogue Dolls, Inc.
DATE: 1937—on
MATERIAL: 1937—1948 composition; 1948—1962 hard plastic
SIZE: 7—8in (17.8—20.3cm)
CREATOR: Jennie Graves
CLOTHES DESIGNER: Virginia Graves Carlson
MARK: "Doll Co.", "Vogue Dolls" and "Ginny Vogue Dolls"; sometimes
stamped "TODDLES" on shoe.

Clothes label:

| VOGUE DOLLS, INC. |
| MEDFORD, MASS. USA |
| ® REG U.S. PAT OFF |

All-composition, sometimes called Pre-Ginny or "Toddles": Jointed neck, shoulders and hips; painted eyes looking to side, mohair wig. Original clothes. All in good condition.

7—8in (17.8—20.3cm) $65-75*

*Allow extra for special outfits

Hard Plastic Ginny: All-hard plastic, jointed at neck, shoulders and hips (some have jointed knees and some walk); sleep eyes (early ones have painted eyes; later dolls have molded lashes), nice wig. Original clothes. All in good condition. 1948—1954 dolls have painted lashes; 1955—1962 dolls have molded lashes; 1957—1962 dolls have jointed knees.

Painted eyes	$75-85*
Painted lashes	65*
Molded lashes	50-55*
Jointed knees	40-45*

*Allow extra for special outfits.

8in (20.3cm) composition "Toddles" boy, all original. *Beth Foulke Collection.*

**Hard Plastic Ginny
Baby:** Bent limbs.
Jointed at neck,
shoulders and hips;
painted or sleep
eyes, caracul wig.
Original clothes.
All in good condition.

8in (20.3cm) $65

8in (20.3cm) hard plastic
"Cowboy" and "Cowgirl" with painted lashes,
all original. *Beth Foulke
Collection.*

8in (20.3cm) hard plastic "Prince Charming",
all original. *Beth Foulke Collection.*

Izannah Walker

329

MAKER: Izannah Walker, Central Falls, R.I., U.S.A.
DATE: 1873
MATERIAL: All-cloth
SIZE: 15–24in (38.1–61.0cm)
MARK: *Patented Nov. 4th 1873*

Izannah Walker Doll: Stockinet, pressed head, features and hair painted with oils, applied ears, treated limbs, muslin body, appropriate clothes. In fair condition.

18–20in (45.7–50.8cm) $2500 up

Wax Doll-Poured

(Montanari or Pierotti-type)

MAKER: Various firms in England
DATE: Mid 19th century through the early 1900 s
MATERIAL: Wax head, arms and legs; cloth body
SIZE: Various
MARK: None

Unmarked Poured Wax Doll: Head, lower arms and legs of wax; cloth
  body, blue or brown glass eyes, blonde or brown set-in hair; original
  clothes or very well dressed; all in good condition.

    17—19in (43.2—48.3cm) $650-750*
      *Allow extra for a signed Pierotti, Montanari or
      Mrs. Peck

    Fashion lady, 16—18in (40.6—45.7cm) $475-500

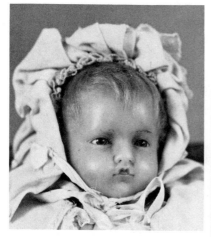

18in (45.7cm) poured wax baby,
all original. *Joanna Ott Collection.*

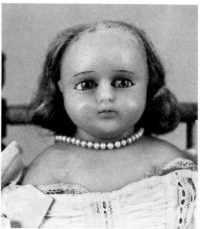

18in (45.7cm) poured wax doll,
all original. *Joanna Ott Collection.*

Wax Over Composition

MAKER: Numerous firms in England, Germany or France
DATE: During the 1800s
MATERIAL: Wax over shoulder head of some type of composition or papier-mâché; cloth body; wax over composition or wooden limbs
SIZE: Various
MARK: None

English Slit-head Wax: Ca. 1830–1860. Wax over shoulder head, not rewaxed, original cloth body with leather arms; human hair wig, glass eyes (may open and close by a wire); faintly smiling. Original or suitable old clothing. All in good condition.

      17–21in (43.2–53.3cm— $300-325
      26–28in (66.0–71.1cm)   375-400

Pumpkin Head Doll: Ca. 1850 to 1890. Wax over shoulder head, molded band in molded blonde hair pompadour, original cloth body, black, blue or brown glass sleep or set eyes; wax over or wooden extremities with molded socks or boots, nice old clothes, not rewaxed. All in good condition.

      16–20in (40.6–50.8cm) $250-300

18in (45.7cm) Wax over doll with flax hair and glass eyes. *Joanna Ott Collection.*

18in (45.7cm) pumpkin head. *Joanna Ott Collection.*

332

Wax Doll with wig: Ca. mid 19th century into early 20th century. Wax over shoulder head, not rewaxed, original cloth body, blonde or brown human hair or mohair wig; blue, brown or black glass eyes, sleep or set; open or closed mouth, any combination of extremities mentioned above; also arms may be made of china. Original clothing or suitably dressed; entire doll in nice condition.

15–17in (38.1–43.2cm)	$225-250
19–22in (48.3–55.9cm)	275-300
24–27in (61.0–68.6cm)	325-350

Bonnet Wax Doll: Ca. 1860 to 1880. Wax over shoulder head, original cloth body and wooden extremities; blue, brown or black set eyes; nice old clothes. All in good condition.

18–20in (45.7–50.8cm) $250-300

13in (33.0cm) Wax over with slit head, rare small size, all original. *Grace Dyar.*

Norah Wellings

MAKER: Victoria Toy Works, Wellington, Shropshire, England, for Norah Wellings
DATE: 1926–Ca. 1960
MATERIAL: Fabric: Felt, velvet and velour, etc. stuffed.
SIZE: Various
DESIGNER: Norah Wellings
MARK: On tag on foot: "Made in England by Norah Wellings"

Wellings Doll: All-fabric, stitch-jointed shoulders and hips. Molded fabric face (also of papier-mâché, sometimes stockinet covered), painted features. All in excellent condition. Most commonly found are sailors, Canadian Mounties, Scots and Black Islanders.

Characters
8–11in (20.3–27.9cm)
   Sailors $25-30
   Others   45-50 depending
       upon rarity
12–14in (30.5)35.6cm)
          $65-75
18in (45.7cm) Black, glass
   eyes $125-150

Children
14–16in (35.6–40.6cm)
       $150-175

10in (25.4cm) Wellings chubby girl, all original. *H&J Foulke.*

18in (45.7cm) Black native girl with glass eyes, all original. *H&J Foulke.*

10in (25.4cm) Wellings Scots girl with painted hair, all original. *H&J Foulke.*

10in (25.4cm) Wellings Little Pixie, all original. *H&J Foulke.*

Wood, Swiss

MAKER: Various Swiss firms
DATE: 20th century
MATERIAL: All-wood or wood head and limbs on cloth body
SIZE: Various, but smaller sizes are more commonly found
MARK: Usually a paper label on wrist or clothes

Swiss Wooden Doll: Wooden head with hand carved features and hair
with good detail (males sometimes have carved hats); all carved wood
jointed body; original, usually regional attire; excellent condition.

9–10in (22.9–25.4cm) $100-125   **Not enough price samples to
19in (48.3cm)   350-375**   compute a reliable range.

14in (35.6cm) Swiss carved wooden doll,
all original. *Sheila Needle Collection.*
Photograph by Morton Needle.

*A Short Study of Doll Bodies Part II**

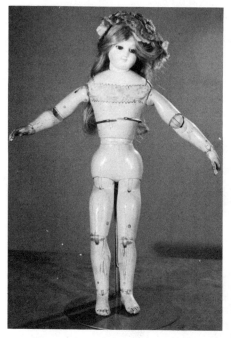

*For Part I, see the *3rd Blue Book of Dolls and Values,* pages 325—331

ABOVE: Fully jointed wood body of the type used with the French fashion-type heads. *Helen Teske Collection.*

LEFT: Unusual early Kestner body with torso, upper arms, and upper legs of kid. Lower limbs of composition with a ball joint which fits into a circular socket. *Elizabeth McIntyre.*

Body of the kind usually found with a Belton-type head. Note the elongated upper legs of turned wood, wooden upper arms, solid wrists, and cupped fingers.

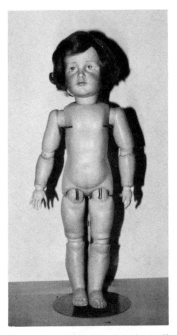

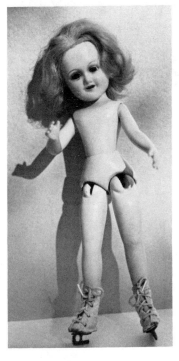

Kammer and Rinehardt ball-jointed child body, completely of composition; there are separate balls at the elbows and knees. (The head is marked K★R 114.)

Composition body with the swivel waist used for Alexander's 14in (35.6cm) *"Wendy Ann"* and *"Sonja Henie."*
Marked: WENDY-ANN
    MME ALEXANDER

338

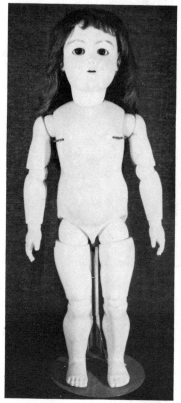

Fine quality German ball-jointed body all of composition. Note the separate balls at the hips and shoulders. (The head is marked 109, a number used by H. Handwerck.)

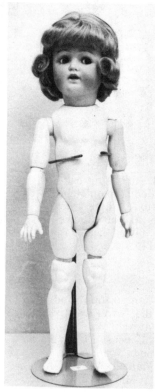

Teen-age-type composition ball-jointed body by Kestner. Torso, arms, and legs are all more slender than those of a typical child body. Knee joint is high so that the doll can wear a short skirt. (The head is marked JDK 260.)

LEFT:
A Jumeau body used with open-mouth and S.F.B.J. heads. Upper arms and legs are wood. Torso and lower limbs are a brown composition covered by a thick layer of flesh-colored paint which often peels in great chunks.

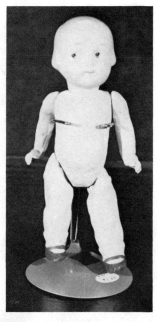

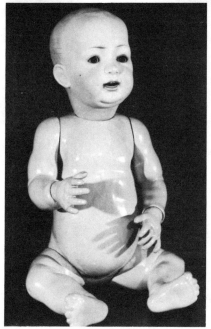

ABOVE: Inexpensive body of papier-mache generally used for googly-eyed dolls and some others of the same period. Shoes and socks are molded and painted. (The head is marked A.M. 210.)

German bent-limb baby body of composition with unusual jointed wrists. (The head is marked 151, attributed to Kestner.)

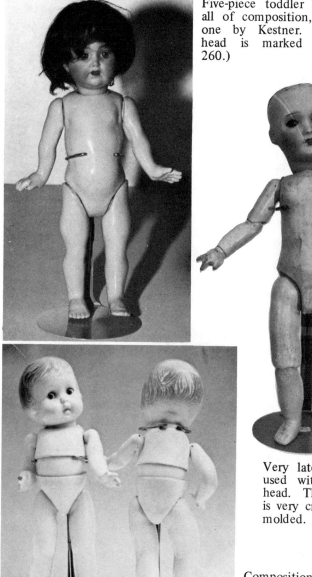

Five-piece toddler body all of composition, this one by Kestner. (The head is marked JDK 260.)

Very late French body, used with a Unis 301 head. The composition is very crude and poorly molded.

Composition bodies with a large ball-joint which allows the waist to swivel, of the type made by Amberg and Mme Hendren.

Cloth body designed by
Philip Goldsmith, marked
on the front under the
shoulder plate: PAT. DEC.
15, 1885. Torso is com-
posed of a red corset with
tan lacings; kid lower arms,
colored stockings, and shoes
with tassels. *Joan Kindler.*

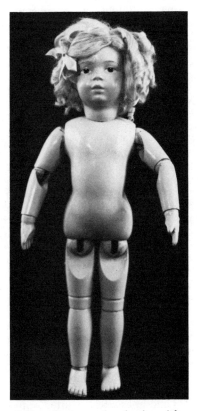

Schoenhut wooden body with
metal strung joints. Note the
extra joint at the ankle which
was lacking on the German
composition bodies.

Glossary

Applied Ears: Ear molded independently and affixed to the head. (on most dolls the ear is included as part of the head mold.)

Bald Head: Head with no crown opening, could be covered by a wig or have painted hair.

Ball-jointed Body: Usually a body of composition with wooden balls at knees, elbows, hips and shoulders to make swivel joints.

Belton-type: A bald head with one, two or three small holes for attaching wig.

Bent-limb Baby Body: Composition body of five pieces with chubby torso and curved arms and legs.

Biskoline: Celluloid-type of substance for making dolls.

Breather: Doll with an actual opening in each nostril; also called open nostrils.

Brevete (or Bte): Used on French dolls to indicate that the patent is registered.

Character Doll: Dolls with heads modeled to look lifelike, such as infants, young or older children, young ladies, and so on.

Crown Opening: The cut-away part of a doll head.

DEP: Abbreviation used on German and French dolls claiming registration.

D.R.G.M.: Abbreviation used on German dolls indicating a registered design or patent.

Embossed Mark: Raised letters, numbers, or names on the backs of heads or bodies.

Feathered Eyebrows: Eyebrows composed of many tiny painted brush strokes to give a realistic look.

Flange Neck: A doll's head with a ridge at the base of the neck which contains holes for sewing the head to a cloth body.

Flirting Eyes: Eyes which move from side to side as doll's head is tilted.

Frozen Charlotte: Doll molded all in one piece including arms and legs.

Ges. (Gesch.): Used on German dolls to indicate design is registered or patented.

Googly Eyes: Large often round eyes looking to the side; also called roguish or goo goo eyes.

Incised Mark: Letters, numbers or names impressed into the bisque on the back of the head or on the shoulder plate.

Intaglio Eyes: Painted eyes with sunken pupil and iris.

Kid Body: Body of white or pink leather.

Mohair: Goat's hair widely used in making doll wigs.

Molded Hair: Curls, waves and comb marks which are actually part of the mold and not merely painted onto the head.

Open-Mouth: Lips parted with an actual opening in the bisque, usually has teeth either molded in the bisque or set in separately and sometimes a tongue.

Open/Closed Mouth: A mouth molded to appear open, but having no actual slit in the bisque.

Painted Bisque: Bisque covered with a layer of flesh-covered paint, which has not been baked in, so will easily rub or wash off.

Paperweight Eyes: Blown glass eyes which have depth and look real, usually found in French dolls.

Pate: A shaped piece of plaster, cork, cardboard, or other material which covers the crown opening.

Pierced Ears: Little holes through the doll's ear lobes to accommodate earrings.

Pierced-in Ears: A hole at the doll's earlobe which goes into the head to accommodate earrings.

Pink Bisque: A later bisque of about 1920 which was pre-colored pink.

Pink-toned China: China which has been given a pink tint to look more like real flesh color; also called lustered china.

Rembrandt Hair: Hair style parted in center with bangs at front, straight down sides and back and curled at ends.

S.G.D.G.: Used on French dolls to indicate that the patent is registered "without guarantee of the government."

Shoulder Head: A doll's head and shoulders all in one piece.

Shoulder Plate: The actual shoulder portion sometimes molded in one with the head, sometimes a separate piece with a socket in which a head is inserted.

Socket Head: Head and neck which fit into an opening in the shoulder-plate or the body.

Solid-dome Head: Head with no crown opening, could have painted hair or be covered by wig.

Stationary Eyes: Glass eyes which DO NOT move or sleep; also called fixed eyes.

Stone Bisque: Coarse white bisque of a lesser quality.

Toddler Body: Usually a chubby ball-jointed composition body with chunky, shorter thighs, and a diagonal hip joint; sometimes has curved instead of jointed arms; sometimes is of five pieces with straight chubby legs.

Turned Shoulder Head: Head and shoulders are one piece, but the head is molded at an angle so that the doll is not looking straight ahead.

Watermelon Mouth: Closed line-type mouth curved up at each side in an impish expression.

Wax Over: A doll with head and/or limbs of papier-mache or composition covered with a layer of wax to give a natural, lifelike finish.

Weighted Eyes: Eyes which can be made to sleep by means of a weight which is attached to the eyes.

Wire Eyes: Eyes which could be made to sleep by means of a wire which protruded from doll's head.

Index

Text references are indicated in alphabetical and numerical order. Often there is a photograph to accompany the text reference. References to illustrations indicate that photographs appear on a different page.

A

ABG, 1
A.M. (see Armand Marseille)
A.T., 7
A.W., 8
Admiral Dewey, 67
Agnes, 98
Alabama Indestructible Doll, 9
Alexander, Henri, 153
Alexander-Kins, 25, 27
Alexander, Madame, 10-30
  Alexander-Kins, 25, 27
  Alice in Wonderland, 10, 17, 22
  Amy, 21
  Annabelle, 22
  Babies, 11
  Babs, 19
  Baby Jane, 14
  Baby McGuffey, 11
  Beth, 21
  Binnie, 23
  Bitsey, 11
  Bride & Bridesmaids, 17
  Butch, 11
  Carmen (Miranda), 18
  Caroline, 28, 29
  Cinderella, 19, 20
  Cissette, 25
  Cissette face, 25
  Cissy, 23
  Cloth Character Dolls, 10
  Coco, 27, 28
  Copperfield, David, 10
  Cynthia, 19
  Dionne Quintuplets, 12
  Dopey, 13
  Easter Doll, 28
  Edith, 26, 27
  Elise, 23
  Fairy Princess, 16, 17
  Fairy Queen, 19
  Flora McFlimsey, 14
  Foreign, 13
  Friedrich, 30
  Gibson Girl, 25
  Gidget, 28
  Glamour Girls, 21
  Godey, 25
  Godey Ladies, 21
  Godey Portrait, 27
  Grandma Jane, 28
  Greenaway, Kate, 15
  Gretl, 30
  Henie, Sonja, 19, 26
  Jacqueline, 25, 28
  Janie face, 30
  Jeannie Walker, 18
  Jenny Lind, 25, 28
  Jenny Lind & Cat, 28
  Jo, 21
  Karen Ballerina, 16
  Kathy, 22, 28
  Kathy Cry Dolly, 28
  Kathy Tears, 28
  Kelly, 25, 26
  Kelly face, 26
  Laurie, 25
  Leslie, 28
  Lewis, Shari, 24
  Liesl, 30
  Lissy, 24
  Little Colonel, 13

Alexander, Mme. continued
  Little Emily, 10
  Little Genius, 11, 26
  Little Granny, 28
  Little Men, 21
  Little Shaver, 11
  Little Women, 20, 21, 25
  Littlest Kitten, 30
  Louisa, 30
  Lucinda, 29, 30
  Madame, 28
  Madelaine, 17, 26
  Maggie, 21, 22
  Maggie face, 22
  Maggie Mixup, 24
  Margaret, 21
  Margaret face, 17, 19
  Margot, 25
  Marlo, 29
  Marme, 21
  Marta, 30
  Mary Ann face, 28
  Marybel, 26
  McGuffey Ana, 15, 28
  Margaret Rose, 19, 20
  Margot Ballerina, 19
  Meg, 20, 21
  Melinda, 25
  Miss Melinda, 26
  Nat, 21
  Nina Ballerina, 19
  O'Brien, Margaret, 19
  O'Hara, Scarlett, 16
  Orphant Annie, 28
  Peter Pan, 28
  Pinky, 11
  Polly, 29
  Pollyana, 26
  Polly face, 29
  Polly Pigtails, 22
  Portrait, 18, 26
  Portrettes, 25
  Precious, 11
  Prince Charming, 19
  Princess Elizabeth, 14, 15
  Renoir Girl, 28
  Riley's Little Annie, 28
  Sarg, Tony, 12
  Scarlett, 25, 28
  Sleeping Beauty, 24
  Smarty, 26, 27
  Snow White, 14, 28
  Sound of Music, 30
  Southern Belle, 25
  Special Girl, 19
  Storyland, 13
  Swiss, 12
  Wendy, 28
  Wendy-Ann, 15, 19, 20
  Wendy face, 17
  Winnie Walker, 23
  Withers, Jane, 18
Alexandre, Henri, 269
Alice in Wonderland, 10, 17, 22
All-Bisque Adults, 39
  Baby, 37, 41, 42, 72, 261
  Characters, 35, 38, 39, 41, 258
  Child Doll, 31-36, 39, 41, 43, 261
    Glass eyes, 32, 34, 35, 37, 40

  Molded clothes, 31, 32, 39, 43
  Painted eyes, 31, 36-39, 43
  Clown, 32
  Dolls (French), 40
    (German), 31-39
    (Made in Japan), 41, 42
    (Nippon), 43
  Flapper, 37
  French type, 32
  Googly, 149
  Hebee-Shebee, 160
  Immobiles, 39
  Kewpie, 218
  Lady, 62
  Mibs, 246
  Nodders, 38, 39, 41
  Piano Baby, 271
  Scooties, 299
  Snow Babies, 313
Alpha, Farnell's Toys, 45
Alt, Beck & Gottschalck, 1, 72, 79
Amberg, Louis & Son, 56, 246, 255
American Character, 46, 47
American Character Doll Co., 46, 47, 86
American Children, 123
American Doll & Toy Co., 47
American Dolls, 9, 10-30, 44, 46-52, 56, 58, 60, 61, 65, 70, 71, 72-74, 77, 79-81, 85-87, 90, 92, 101, 102, 104-107, 113, 116-129, 131, 136, 137, 146-148, 152, 158, 160, 161, 173, 174, 177-182, 195, 197, 219, 237-239, 242, 243, 246, 248, 249, 254, 255, 267, 270, 275, 296-302, 319-324, 327-328
American School Boy, 66
Amy, 21
Annabelle, 22
Anne Shirley, 122
Antoinette, Marie, 192
Armand Marseille, 2-4, 6, 64, 74, 102, 149, 150, 193
  Bergmann Character Baby, 64
  Bergmann Child Doll, 64
  Character Baby, 3
  Character Children, 4
  Child Doll, 2
  Fany, 4
  Floradora, 2
  Googly-Eyed, 149, 150
  Infant, 6
  Just Me, 193
  Lady, 6
  Maar, 4
  Queen Louise, 2, 3
Arnold Print Works, 74, 102
Arranbee Doll Co., 48-50
Art Doll, 173
Art Fabric Mills, 51
Auntie Blossom, 39
Aunt Jemima Family, 102
Austrian, 268

Autoperipatekikos, 52
Averill, Georgene Baby, 72
Averill Mfg. Co., 113, 161

B

B.F., 52
B.P. Character, 58
Babs, 19
Baby Bo Kaye, 54
Baby Blanche, 305, 307
Baby Bud, 43
Baby Dainty, 116
Baby Dimples, 173
Baby Dolls ABG, 1
  A.M., 3, 6
  Alabama, 9
  Alexander, 11, 14
  All-Bisque, 37
  All-Bisque, 2 faces, 41, 42
  American Character, 46
  Arranbee, 48, 50
  Baby Bo Kaye, 55
  Baby Peggy, 56
  Baby Sandy, 57
  Bergmann, 64
  Black, 68, 70
  Bonnie Babe, 72
  Bye-lo, 79-81
  C.P., 84
  Celluloid Dolls, 88
  Century Infant, 90
  Chase, 92
  Composition, 44
  Effanbee, 116, 119, 122
  Fulper, 136
  German Bisque, 140-142
  Heubach, Gebruder, 162, 166
  Heubach Koppelsdorf, 168, 169
  Horsman, 171-173, 323
  Hülss, A., 175
  Ideal, 177, 179
  Japanese Bisque, 185
  Kämmer & Reinhardt, 198, 200, 202, 206, 208
  Kestner, 211, 212, 214
  Kley & Hahn, 222
  Limbach, 236
  Metal, 243
  Molly-'es, 248
  Motschmann, 251
  New Born Babe, 255
  Oriental, 256, 257
  Orsini, 258
  P.M., 260
  Painted Bisque, 261
  Parsons-Jackson, 267
  Philadelphia Baby, 270
  R.A., 277
  Revalo, 381
  S&Q, 289
  Schmidt, Bruno, 291
  Schoenau & Hoffmeister, 295
  Schoenhut, 297, 298
  Simon & Halbig, 307, 311
  Steiner, Herm, 315
  Vogue, 328
  Wax, 330
Baby Grumpy, 116
Baby Jane, 14
Babyland Rag-type, 58

Baby Peggy (Montgomery), 56
Baby Sandy, 57
Baby Snooks. 177
Bähr & Pröschild, 59
Ballerina, 126
Barbie, 60, 61
Bathing Beauty, 62
Beauty, 143
Bébé B.F., 53
  B.L., 54
  L'Intrepide, 283
  Mascotte, 241
Belton-type, 63
Bergmann, C.M.,
  Child Doll, 64
  Character Baby, 64
Bertha, 98
Berwick Doll Co., 131
Bester Doll Co., 44
Beth, 21
Betsy McCall, 47, 180
Betsy Wetsy, 177
Betty Boop, 65
Betty Boop-type, 41
Billiken, 171
Binnie, 23
Biskoline, 267
Bucherer, A., 245
Bisque Dolls, 79-81, 254
Bisque Head, 1-8, 52-56, 59, 63, 64, 66-68, 72, 75, 76, 79-84, 90, 93-101, 103, 109, 111, 114, 130, 132-134, 136, 138, 145, 147, 149-151, 156, 157, 159, 166-169, 175, 184-195, 209-218, 222-225, 228, 236, 240, 241, 250, 252, 255, 258-260, 265, 266, 269, 277, 278, 282-286, 290-295, 303-310, 315-317, 323, 325, 326
Bitsey, 11
Black, 68-71, 169, 219, 295, 299, 321, 326, 333
  Bisque, 32, 41, 68
Black Hanna, 295
Blink, 87
Bonnie Babe, 72
Bonomi, 183
Bo-Peep, 50
Borgfeldt, Geo. & Co., 147
  Bonnie Babe, 72
Bottlotot, 48, 50
Boudoir Dolls, 73
Brandi, 182
Bride & Bridesmaids, 17
British Coronation Dolls, 235
Brother, 127
Bru Bébé, 75, 76
Brückner, Albert, 77
Brüchner Rag Doll, 77
Bru Jnè & Cie, 75
Brownies, 74
Bubbles, 117
Bucherer Doll, 245
Buddy Lee, 78
Butch, 11
Burggrub/Baby, 294
Buschow & Beck, 244
  Celluloid Dolls, 88, 89
Bye-lo Baby Dolls, 79-81
C
C.B. Multi-Face, 252

C.O.D., 82, 83
Cameo Doll Co., 55, 65, 79, 146, 219, 237, 239, 299
Campbell Kids, 85, 86, 172
Candy Kid, 128
Can't Break 'Em Characters, 171, 172
Carmen, 273
Carmen (Miranda), 18
Caroline, 28, 29
Carr, Gene Kids, 87
Catterfelder Puppenfabrik, 84
Celluloid Dolls, 55, 88, 89, 219, 301
Celluloid heads, 79
Century Doll Co., 90
Century Infant, 90
Ceremonial, 235
Chad Valley Co., 91
Change-O-Doll Co.. 131
Character Dolls ABG, 1
  A.M., 3, 4
  Alexander, 10
  All-Bisque, 38, 39, 41
  B.P., 58
  Bergmann, 63
  Black, 68, 70
  C.O.D., 83
  C.P., 84
  Carr, Gene, 87
  Composition, 44, 105, 106
  French Bébé, 132
  German Bisque, 141, 142
  Hendren, Mme., 161
  Heübach, Gebruder, 162
  Heübach, Köppelsdorf, 168
  Horsman, 171
  Japanese Bisque, 185
  K&K, 195
  K&W, 196
  Kämmer & Reinhardt, 198, 200, 201, 203
  Kestner, 211-215
  Kewpie-type, 105
  Kley & Hahn, 222, 223
  Liberty of London, 235
  Limbach, 236
  Orsini, 258
  P.M., 260
  R.A., 277
  Revalo, 281
  S.F.B.J., 288-290
  S&Q, 289
  Schmidt, Bruno, 291
  Schoenau & Hoffmeister, 295
  Schoenhut, 296-297
  Simon & Halbig, 305, 311
  Wellings, Norah, 333
Chase Dolls, 92
Chase, Martha Jenks, 92
China Heads
  Autoperipatetikos, 52
  Bald, 93
  Bangs, 93
  Brown Eyes, 94
  Common or Low Brow, 94
  Covered Wagon, 94
  Curly Top, 94
  Flat Top, 95
  Glass Eyes, 95
  Godey's Little Lady Dolls, 148
  Hatted, 96

China Heads continued
  Japanese, 100
  Madison, Dolley, 95
  Man, 96
  Motschmann-type, 97
  Patti, Adelina, 93
  Pet Name, 98
  Pierced Ears, 97
  Rohmer Fashion, 283
  Snood, 98
  Spill Curl, 99
  Wood Body, 99
Chinese, 112, 256
Choir Boy, 107
Cinderella, 19,20
Cindy, 104
Cinnamon, 182
Cissette, 25
Cissette face, 25
Cissy, 23
Clear Dolls, 101
Clear, Emma, 101
Cloth Dolls
  Alexander, Madame, 10
  Alice in Wonderland, 10
  Alpha, Farnell's Toys, 45
  Averill Mfg. Co., 113
  Babyland Rag, 58
  Black, 70, 71
  Chad Valley Co., 91
  Character, 10
  Chocolate Drop, 113
  Colonial Toy Mfg. Co., 113
  Dolly Dingle, 113
  Drayton, Grace G., 113
  Georgene Novelties, 137
  George VI, 45
  Hug-Me-Tight, 113
  Kewpie, 221
  Lenci-Type, 234
  Liberty of London, 235
  Little Shaver, 11
  Kruse, Käthe, 226
  Molly-'es, 248
  Motschmann, 251
  Philadelphia Baby, 270
  Pinky, 11
  Poir Dolls, 274
  Rag, 77
  Raggedy Ann & Andy, 280
  Walker, Izannah, 329
  Wellings, Norah, 333, 334
Cloth, Printed, 51, 74, 102, 110
Clowns, 103, 233
Cocheco Mfg. Co., 102
Cochran, Dewees, 104, 128
Coco, 27, 28
Cohen, David S. & Lyon, Joseph & Co., 52
Colonial Toy Mfg. Co., 44, 113
Columbia, 143
Composition
  Alexander, Madame, 11-20
  Amberg, Louis & Son, 246
  American Character, 46, 86
  Arranbee Doll Co., 48, 49
  Averill Mfg. Co., 161
  Berwick Doll Co., 131
  Bester Doll Co., 44
  Black Dolls, 70
  Boudoir, 73

Composition continued
  Bucherer, A., 245
  Buddy Lee, 78
  Cameo Doll Co., 55, 146
  Cameo Doll Products Co., 65, 237, 239, 299
  Carr, Gene Kids, 87
  Change-O-Doll Co., 131
  Choir Boy, 107
  Colonial Toy Mfg. Co., 44
  Co-operative Mfg. Co., 129
  Cuno & Otto Dressel, 170
  Effanbee, 116-128
  Freunditch Novelty Corp., 238
  Freundlich, Ralph, 57
  Happifats, 158
  Horsman, E.I. Co., 85, 86, 113, 160, 171
  Hoyer, Mary, 174
  Ideal Novelty & Toy Co., 177-179, 300, 301
  International Doll Co., 248
  Kewpie, 219, 220
  Mama, 106
  Miscellaneous, 105-107
  Monica Doll Studios, 249
  New Era Novelty Co., 44
  New Toy Mfg. Co., 44
  Oriental, 257
  Superior Doll Mfg. Co., 44
  Superior Dolls, 318
  Terri Lee Soles Corp., 320, 321
  Ventriloquist, 107
  Vogue, 327
Composition Mask Face, 151
Co-operative Mfg. Co., 129
Copperfield, David, 10
Coquette, 162, 281
Cowboy, 328
Cowgirl, 328
Creche Figures, 108
Cricket, 182
Crissy & Family, 182
Cutie, 105
Cynthia, 19
D
DEP, 109
Daisy, 98
Danel & Cie, 266
Darkey, 102
Darling, 143
Dean's Rag Book Co., 110
Debu Teen, 48, 49
Depose Bébé, 189
Diana, 244
DiDi, 258
Dina, 182
Dionne Quintuplets, 12
Dip, 284
Doll Bodies, 336-342
Dollar Princess, 143, 144
Dollcraft Novelty Co., 107
Doll House Dolls, 111
Dolly Dimple, 162, 164
Dolly Dingle, 86
Dolly face, 298
Dolly Reckord, 161
Doodle Dog, 219
Door of Hope, 112
Door of Hope Mission, 112
Dopey, 13
Dorothy, 98

Drayton, Grace G., 113
Dressel, Cuno & Otto, 82, 83, 194
Dressel & Kister Lady, 273
Duchess, 143
Dummy Dan, 107
Durbin, Deanna, 48, 177
Dutch, 268
Dy-Dee Baby, 122

E

Early Babies, 172
Earthenware, 157
Easter Doll, 28
E. D. Bébé, 114
Eden Bébé, 115
Edith, 26, 27, 98
Effanbee Doll Co., 116-128
  American Children, 123
  Anne Shirley, 122
  Baby Dainty, 116
  Baby Grumpy, 116
  Ballerina, 126
  Brother, 127
  Bubbles, 117
  Candy Kid, 128
  Cochran, Dewees, 128
  Dy-Dee Baby, 122
  Fields, W. C., 121
  Gibson Girl, 126
  Historical Dolls, 124
    Replicas, 124
  Honey, 128
  Lamkin, 122
  Little Lady, 127
  Lovums, 119
  McCarthy, Charlie, 124
  Marilee, 117
  Mary Ann, 118
  Mary Lee, 118
  Patsy, 120, 128
  Patsy Babyette, 119
  Patsy Family, 119
  Patsy Mae, 120
  Patsy Ruth, 120
  Pennsylvania Dutch, 123
  Portrait Dolls, 126
  Rosemary, 117
  Sister, 127
  Skippy, 121, 128
  Starr, Mae, 118
  Storybook-type, 126
  Suzanne, 125
  Suzette, 125
  Sweetie Pie, 128
  Tucker, Tommy, 125
E.J. Bébé, 189
Ellis, Joel, 129
Elisabeth, 151
Elise, 23
English, 45, 52, 91, 110, 234, 235, 276, 330-334
English Slit-head Wax, 331, 332
Esther, 98
Ethel, 98

F

F.G., 130
F.Y., 185
Fairy Princess, 16, 17
Fairy Queen, 19
Famlee Doll, 131
Farm Girl, 192
Fashion Lady, 187, 330
Felt, 230-234, 314, 333, 334
  faced, 110
F. G. Bébé, 130
  Fashion Lady, 130
Fields, W.C., 121

Flapper, 37
Fleischmann & Bloedel of Fürth, 115
Flexy Dolls, 177, 179
Flora McFlimsey, 14
Florence, 98
Florodora, 2
Foreign, 13
French Bébé, 132
French Dolls A.T., 7
  All-Bisque, 40
  B.F., 52
  Belton-type Child, 62
  Black, 68, 69
  Boudoir, 73
  Bru Bébé, 75, 76
  Celluloid, 88
  Clowns, 103
  DEP, 109
  E.D. Bébé, 114
  Eden Bebe, 115
  F.G., 130
  French Bébé, 132
  Fashion-type, 133, 134
  Gesland, 145
  Googly-Eyed, 149-151
  H.A., 153
  Hansi, 157
  J.V., 184
  Jullien Bébé, 186
  Jumeau, 187-192
  Lanternier Child, 228
  Leather, 229
  Lenci-Type, 234
  Marottes, 240
  Mascotte, 241
  Mon Trésor, 250
  P.D. Bébé, 259
  Paris Bébé, 266
  Phénix Bébé, 269
  Poir Dolls, 274
  R.D. Bébé, 278
  Rohmer Fashion, 282
  Roullet & DeCamps, 283
  S.F.B.J., 287-290
  Schmitt Bébé, 293
  Simonne, F., 303
  Steiner, Jules Bébé, 316, 317
  Unis, 325, 326
  Wax Over Composition, 331, 332
French Fashion-Type, 133, 134
Freunditch Novelty Corp., 238
Freundlich, Ralph, 57
Friedrich, 30
Frozen Charlotte, 135
Fulper Dolls, 136
Fulper Pottery Co., 136
Furga, 183

G

G.B., 143
G&S, 143
Gabby Joe, 107
Gallais & Co., Hansi, 157
Gans & Seyfarth, 144
Garland, Judy, 178
Gaultier, A., 130, 145
Gaultier, F. & Fils, 145
General MacArthur, 238
George VI, 45
Georgene Novelties, 137
Georgene Raggedy Ann & Andy, 280
German Bisque Dolly Faces, 143

German Dolls ABG, 1
  A.M., 2-6
  A.W., 8
  All-Bisque (see All-Bisque) 31-39
  American School Boy, 66
  Baby Peggy, 55
  B.P. Character, 59
  Bathing Beauty, 62
  Belton-type Child, 63
  Bergmann Character Baby, 64
    Child Doll, 64
  Bisque Dolly Faces, 143, 144
  Bisque Molded Hair, 66
  Black, 68-70
  Bonnie Babe, 72
  Bye-lo Baby, 79-81
  C.O.D., 82, 83
  C.P., 84
  Celluloid Dolls, 88, 89
  Century Infant, 90
  China heads, 93-99
  Clowns, 103
  Doll House Dolls, 111
  Frozen Charlotte, 135
  German Bisque, 138-142
  Googly-Eyed, 149-151
  Half-Bisque Dolls, 154
  Handwerck, Hunrich Child, 156
  Handwerck, Max Child Doll, 156
  Happifats, 158
  Hatted or Bonnet, 159
  Hebee-Shebee, 160
  Heubach, Gebruder, 162-166
  Heubach, Köppelsdorf, 167-169
  Highland Mary, 66
  Holz-Masse, 170
  Hülss, A., 175
  Hummel, 176
  Just Me Doll, 193
  Jutta, 194
  K&W Character, 196
  Kämmer & Reinhardt, 198-208
  Kestner, J.D., 209-217
  Kewpie, 218, 219
  Kley & Hahn, 222-223
  Kling Bisque Head, 224
  Krauss, 225
  Kruse, Käthe, 226, 227
  Lilli, 60
  Limbach, 236
  Little Annie Rooney, 237
  Marottes, 240
  Metal Heads, 244
  Milliner's Model, 247
  Motschmann, 251
  Multi-Faced, 252
  Oriental, 257
  P.M., 260
  Painted Bisque, 261
  Papier-Mâché, 263, 264
  Parian-Type, 265
  Peg Wooden or Dutch Dolls, 268
  Piano Baby, 271
  Pincushion Dolls, 272, 273
  Portrait, 67
  R.A., 277
  Revalo, 281
  S&Q, 289
  Schmidt, Bruno, 291

German Dolls continued
  Schmidt, F. Doll, 292
  Schoenatt & Hoffmeister, 294, 295
  Simon & Halbig, 304-311
  Snow Babies, 313
  Steiff, 314
  Steiner, Herm, 315
  Superior Dolls, 318
  Teddy Bears, 319
  Wax, 331, 332
Gesland, 145
Gesland, E.F. & A., 145
Gibbs, Ruth, 148
Gibbs, Ruth Doll, 148
Gibson Girl, 25, 126
Gidget, 28
Giggles, 146
Ginny, 327
Ginny Baby, 328
Gladdie, 147
Glamour Girls, 21
Godey, 25
Godey Ladies, 21
Godey Portrait, 27
Godey's Little Lady Dolls, 148
Goebel, 143
Goebel, William, 176
Governor, 219
Graduation, 254
Grandma Jane, 28
Great Ladies, 192
Greenaway, Kate, 15
Greiner Doll, 152
Greiner, Ludwig, 152
Gretl, 30, 157
Gypsy, 169

H

Half-Bisque Dolls, 154
Handwerck, Heinrich, 155
  Child Doll, 155
Handwerck, Max, 156
  Child Doll, 156
Hanna, 294
Hansi, 157
Happifats, 158
Harriett Hubbary Ayers, 180
Hartline, Mary, 180
Hatted or Bonnet Dolls, 159
H.B. Bébé, 153
Hebee-Shebee, 160
Hedda Get Bedda, 47
Helen, 98
Hendren, Mme. Character Dolls, 161
Hendren, Mme. Child, 161
Henie, Sonja, 19, 26, 49
Herm Steiner Dolls, 315
Hertel Schwab & Co., 79
Heubach, Ernst, 167-169
Heubach, Gebrüder, 151, 162-166, 271
Heubach Köppelsdorf, 167, 169
Hexe, 67
Highland Mary, 66
Historical, 124, 235
Historical Doll Replicas, 124
Holz-Masse, 170
Honey, 128
Horsman, E.I. Co., 57, 85-87, 113, 160, 171-173, 323
  Art Doll, 173
  Baby Bumps, 171
  Baby Dimples, 173

Horsman, E.I. continued
Babyland Rag, 58
Billiken, 171
Campbell Kid, 85, 86, 172
Can't Break 'Em Characters, 171, 172
Carr, Gene Kids, 87
Child Doll, 173
Early Babies, 172
Hebee-Shebee, 160
Peek-a-Boo, 113
Puppy Pippin, 113
Rosebud, 172
Tynie Baby, 323
Hoyer, Mary Dolls, 174
Hoyer, Mary Doll Mfg. Co., 174
Hug Me Kiddies, 151
Hug-Me-Tight, 113
Hülss, Adolf, 175
Hummel, 176

I

Ideal Novelty & Toy Co., 177-182, 319, 324
Ayers, Harriett Hubbard, 180
Baby Snooks, 177
Betsy McCall, 180
Betsy Wetsy, 177
Brandi, 182
Cinnamon, 182
Cricket, 182
Crissy & Family, 182
Dina, 182
Durbin, Deanna, 177
Flexy Dolls, 177, 179
Garland, Judy, 178
Kerry, 182
Little Miss Revlon, 181
Magic Skin Baby, 179
Mary Hartline, 180
Mia, 182
Miss Curity, 180
Miss Revlon, 181
Mortimer Snerd, 178
Peter & Patty Playpal, 181
Pinocchio, 179
Saucy Walker, 181
Shirley Temple, 177
Snow White, 178
Teddy Bears, 319
Toni & P-90 Family, 180
Tressy, 182
Uneeda Biscuit Boy, 324
Velvet, 182
Ideal Toy Corp. 300-302
Immobiles, 39
Infant (see Baby)
Indian, 102
Internationals, 248
Internaltional Doll Co., 248
Italian, 73, 108, 183, 230-234

J

J.V. Child Doll, 184
J.W., 185
Jacqueline, 25, 28
Jane, 87
Janie face, 30
Japanese
Bisque Caucasian Dolls, 185
China Heads, 100
Choir Boy, 107
Nippon, Happifats, 158
Traditional Girl, 256

Jeff, 245
Jerri Lee, 320
Jester, 103
Jiggs, 245
Jo, 21
Joy, 239
Jullien Bébé, 186
Jullien, Jenne, 186
Jumeau, 187-192
Antoinette, Marie, 192
Depose Bébé, 189
E.J. Bébé, 189
Fashion Lady, 187
Great Ladies, 192
Long-Face Bébé, 188
1907 Jumeau Child, 191
Phonograph Doll, 191
Portrait Jumeau, 188
Princess Elizabeth, 192
Tête Jumeau Bébé, 190, 191
Jumeau, Maison, 190, 187-192
Juno, 244
Just Me Doll, 193
Jutta Character Baby, 194
Jutta Dolls, 194

K

K&K, 195
K&K Toy Co., 55, 79, 195
K&W, 196
K&W Character, 196
Kamkins, 197
Kämmer & Reinhardt, 198-208
Baby, 198, 202, 206, 208
Character Babies, 198
Character Boy, 201
Character Children, 200
Character Girl, 203
Child Doll, 198, 201
Infant, 200, 206
Kaiser Baby, 198
Tiny Child Doll, 200
Toddler, 198, 205-208
Kampes, Louise R. Studios, 197
Karen Ballerina, 16
Kathy, 22, 28
Kathy Cry Dolly, 28
Kathy Tears, 28
Kaulitz, Marion, 253
Kelly, 25, 26
Kelly face, 26
Kerry, 182
Kestner, J.D., 55, 79, 105, 149, 209-218
Baby Bo Kaye, 55
Boy, 215
Bye-lo Baby, 79
Character 213
Character Baby & Toddler, 211, 212, 214, 215
Character Boy, 215
Character Child, 213, 215
Child Doll, 209, 210
Gibson Girl, 217
Girl, 213
Googly-Eyed, 149
Hilda, 216
Kewpie, 218
Lady, 217
Piano Baby, 271
Pouty, 209
Shoulder head, 209, 210
Kewpie, 105, 218-221
King George VI, 235

Kley & Hahn, 222, 223
Character Baby, 222
Character Boy, 222, 223
Character Child, 223
Character Girl, 223
Child Doll, 223
Walkure Child, 222
Kling & Co., 79, 224
Knickerbocker Toy Co., 280
Knoch, Gebruder, 143
Konig & Wernicke, 196
Krauss Doll, 225
Krauss, Gebruder, 225
Kreuger, Richard G., Inc., 221
Kruse, Käthe, 226

L

L H B, 143
L H K, 143
Lady Doll A.M., 5, 6
Bathing Beauty, 62
Chase, 92
C.O.D., 83
F.G., 130
Gesland, 145
Kestner, 217
Lenci, 230, 233
Simonne, 303
Simon & Halbig, 311
Wax, 330
Lamkin, 122
Lanternier, A. & Cie, 228
Lanternier Child, 228
Latex, 104
Laura, 232
Laurie, 25
Lawrence & Co., 102
Leather Dolls, 229
Lee, H.D.Co., Inc., 78
Lenci Dolls, 230-233
Child, 230, 231
Children, 230
Clown, 233
Farm Girl, 232
Glass eyes, 230
Ladies and novelty, 230
Lady, 233
Laura, 232
Lucia face, 230-232
Miniatures & Mascottes, 230
School Boy & Girl, 231
Lenci-Type, 234
Leslie, 28
Lewis, Shari, 24
Liberty of London, 235
Liedel, G., 318
Liesel, 30
Lilli, 60
Limbach, 236
Limbach Porzellanfabrik, 236
Lind, Jenny, 25, 28
Lind, Jenny & Cat, 28
Lissy, 24
Little Annie Rooney, 237
Little Colonel, 13
Little Emily, 10
Little Genius, 11, 26
Little Granny, 28
Little Lady, 127
Little Pixie, 334
Little Men, 21
Little Miss Revlon, 181
Little Shaver, 11
Little Women, 20, 21, 25, 310
Littlest Kitten, 30

Long-Face Bebe, 188
Lori, 284
Louisa, 30
Lovums, 119
Lucia face, 230-232
Lucinda, 29, 30

M

MB Baby Darling, 43
McCarthy, Charlie, 124
McGuffey Ana, 15, 28
Mabel, 98
Madame, 28
Madelaine, 17, 26
Madison, Dolley, 95
Maggie, 21, 22, 245
Maggie face, 22
Maggie Mixup, 24
Magic Skin Baby, 179
Majestic, 143
Mama Dolls, 161
Mammy, 71
Man Doll (China), 96
Margaret, 21
Margaret face, 17, 19
Margaret Rose, 19, 20
Margie, 239
Margot, 25
Margot Ballerina, 19
Marilee, 117
Marion, 98
Marlo, 29
Marme, 21
Marottes, 240
Marta, 30
Martin & Runyon, 51
Mary Ann, 118
Mary Ann face, 28
Marybel, 26
Mary Lee, 118
Mascotte, 241
Mason & Taylor, 242
Mattel, Inc. 60
May Freres Cie, 241
Meg, 20, 21
Melinda, 25
Metal, 243-245
Baby, 243
Head, 244
Mia, 182
Mibs, 246
Michton, Morris, 319
Midge, 60
Mike, 87
Milliner's Model, 247
MiMi, 258
Minerva, 244
Miniatures & Mascottes, 230
Miss Curity, 180
Miss Melinda, 26
Miss Revlon, 181
MOA Welsch, 143
Molded Hair, 66
Molly-'es, 248, 280
Molly-'es Raggedy Ann & Andy, 280
Monica, 249
Monica Doll Studios, 249
Montanari, 330
Mon Tresor, 250
Morimura Brothers, 185
Mortimer Snerd, 178
Motschmann, 251
Motschmann, Ch., 251
Mrs. Peck, 330
Mulatto, 326
Mulatto Bisque, 33
Muller & Strassburger, 318

Multi-Faced Doll, 42, 47, 252, 322
Munich Art Dolls, 253
Mutt, 245
Mutual Doll Co., 219
My Girlie, 143
My Sweetheart, 143, 144

N
Nancy, 48, 49
Nancy Ann Storybook Dolls, 254
Nancy Ann Storybook Dolls Co., 254
Nancy Lee, 49
Nancy Lee Brother, 49
Nanette, 50
Nat, 21
New Born Babe, 255
New Era Novelty Co., 44
New Mail baby, 102
New Toy Mfg. Co., 44
Nina Ballerina, 19
1907 Jumeau Child, 191
Nodder, 38, 39, 41, 43
Nursing Bru, 75

O
O'Brien, Margaret, 19
O'Hara, Scarlett, 16
O'Neill, Rose, 218-221
Ohlhaver, Gerbruder, 281
Oriental, 294
Oriental Bisque, 257
Oriental Composition, 257
Oriental Dolls, 256-257
Orphant Annie, 28
Orsini, 258

P
P.M., 260
Pansy, 143
Painted Bisque, 261
Papier-mâché, 70, 103, 152, 183, 254, 256, 262-264, 278, 331
Parian-Type, 265
Paris Bébé, 266
Parsons-Jackson Baby, 267
Parsons-Jackson Co., 267
Patsy, 120, 128
Patsy Babyette, 119
Patsy Family, 119
Patsy Mae, 120
Patsy Ruth, 120
Patti, Adelina, 93
Pauline, 98
P.D. Bebe, 259
Peg, Wooden, 268
Pennsylvania Dutch, 123
Peter Pan, 28
Peter & Patty Playpal, 181
Petit & Dumontier, 259
Petite Doll, 46
Petite Sally, 46
Phenix Bebe, 269
Philadelphia Baby, 270
Phonograph Doll, 191
Piano Baby, 271
Pierotti, 330
Pincushion Dolls, 272, 273
Pinky, 11
Pinocchio, 179
Plastic, Hard, 17, 19-30, 46, 47, 50, 60, 78, 128, 174, 180, 181, 183, 221, 227, 254, 320, 327, 328
Hard & Vinyl, 23, 24, 26-30, 46, 47, 122, 248, 302

Plush, 314, 319
Poir Dolls, 274
Eugenie, 274
Polly, 29
Pollyana, 26
Polly face, 29
Polly Pigtails, 22
Portrait Dolls, 18, 26, 126
Portrait Jumeau, 188
Portrettes, 25
Porzellanfabrik Burggrub, 294
P.Sch., 143
Poured Wax Doll, 330
Pouty, 296, 297
Pouty Baby, 289, 295
Precious, 11
Pre-Greiner, 275
Pre-Ginny, 327
Prince Charming, 19, 328
Princess, 143
Princess Elizabeth, 14, 15, 192, 295
Pumpkin Head, 331
Puggy, 46

Q
Queen Anne-Type, 276
Queen Louise, 2
Queue San, 43
Baby, 43

R
R.A., 277
Character Baby, 277
Child, 277
Rabery & Delphieu, 278
Rag Dolls, 71, 77
R.D. Bébé, 278
R.D. Mechanical Doll, 283
Raggedy Ann & Andy, 280
Recknagel, Th. of Alexandrinenthal, 277
Reinecke Baby, 260
Reinecke, Otto, 260
Renoir Girl, 28
Rex Doll Co., 219
Rheinische Gummi & Celluloid Fabrik Co.
Celluloid Dolls, 88, 89
Riley's Little Annie, 28
Rockwell, Grace Corry, 282
Rohmer Fashion, 283
Rohmer, Mad. Marie, 283
Rosebud, 172
Rosemary, 117
Rostal, Henri, 250
Roullet & DeCamps, 283
Roullet, J. & DeCamps, E. 283
Royal Children, 91
Rubber, 176
Rubber Heads, 122

S
S&C, 143
S&Co., 284
S&H Jutta Girl, 194
S&Q Character Baby, 289
Child Doll, 289
S.F.B.J., 40, 287-290, 325, 326
All-Bisque, 40
Character Dolls, 288-290
Child Doll, 287
Pouty Baby, 289
Tête Jumeau, 287
Toddler, 288, 290
Unis Child Doll, 325
Unis Costume Doll, 326
Unis Lady Doll, 325

S.F.B.J. continued
Walking & Kiss Throwing, 288
Sabu, 248
Santa, 102, 185, 290, 305, 308
Sarg, Tony, 12
Saucy Walker, 181
Scarlett, 25, 28
Scavini, Enrico & Signora, 230-233
Schmidt, Bruno, 291
Schmidt, F. Doll, 292
Schmidt, Franz & Co., 292
Schmitt Bébé, 293
Schmitt & Fils, 293
Schoenau & Hoffmeister, 294, 295
Schoenhut, Albert & Co., 296-298
Schoenhut Dolls, 296-298
Baby, 297, 298
Baby Face, 297
Character, 296, 297
Dolly face, 298
Molded Hair, 297
Pouty, 296, 297
Sleeping Eyes, 298
Smiling, 296
Toddler, 297
Walker, 298
School Boy & Girl, 231
Schuelzmeister & Quendt, 289
Scooties, 299
Scots Girl, 334
Selchow & Righter, 50
Sheppard, J.B. Co., 270
Shirley Temple, 177, 300-302
Silesia & Saxony
Celluloid Dolls, 88, 89
Simon & Halbig, 64, 194, 304, 311
Baby Blanche, 305, 307
Bergmann Child Doll, 64
Black, 69
Character Baby, 311
Character Child, 305
Child Doll, 304, 305, 309, 310
Lady, 311
Little Women, 310
Santa, 305, 308
Simonne, 303
Sister, 127
Skinney, 87
Skippy, 121, 128
Sleeping Beauty, 24
Sleeping Eyes, Schoenhut, 298
Smarty, 26, 27
Smith, D.M. & Co., 242
Smith, Ella Doll Co., 9
Snood, 98
Snow Babies, 313
Snowball, 87
Snow White, 14, 28, 178
Societe Francaise de Fabrication de Bebes & Jouets (see S.F.B.J.)
Sound of Music, 30
Southern Belle, 25
Special Girl, 19
Standfuss, Karl, 79, 219
Starr, Mae, 118
Steiff Dolls, 314
Steiff, Fraulein Margarete, 314, 319

Steiner Bebe, 316
Steiner, E.U., 143
Steiner, Hermann, 315
Steiner, Jules Nicholas, 316, 317
Bourgoir, 316
Kicking, Crying Doll, 316
LeParisiene, 317
Open Mouth, 316
Steiner Bebe, 316
Storybook Baby 254
Storybook Dolls/Storybook-type, 48, 126, 254
Storyland, 13
Stuart Baby, 162
Superior Dolls, 318
Superior Doll Mfg. Co., 44
Suzanne, 125
Suzette, 125
Sweetie, 105
Sweetie Pie, 128
Sweet Sue, 46, 47
Swiss, 12, 244, 335

T
Teddy Bears, 319
Teeny Weeny Tiny Tears, 46
Temple, Shirley (see Shirley Temple)
Terri Lee, 320, 321
Terri Lee Sales Corp., 320, 321
Tête Jumeau, 109
Bébé, 190, 191
Three-Faced Doll, 47
Three-in-One Doll Corp., 322
Tiny Tears, 46
Toddles, 327
Toni & P-90 Family, 180
Tonto & Lone Ranger, 107
Topsy Turvy, 77
Toto, 228
Traveler, 219
Trebor, 260
Trebor Child 260
Tressy, 182
Trudy, 322
Tucker, Tommy, 125, 291
Two-Faced Doll, 42
Tynie Baby, 323

U
Uncle Sam, 67
Uneeda Biscuit Boy, 324
Uneeda Kid, 324
Unis Dolls, 325, 326

V
Velvet, 110, 182, 314, 333, 334
Ventriloquist, 107
Verlingue, J., 184
Victoria Toy Works, 333, 334
Vinyl, 26, 30, 60, 181, 302
Viola, 143
Vogue Dolls, Inc., 327, 328
Vogue-Ginny, 327, 328

W
Walker, Jeannie, 18
Walker, Izannah, 329
Walker Schoenhut, 298
Walking Doll, 201
Walking & Kiss Throwing, 288
Walkure Child, 222
Wally, 236
Wax Dolls, 331, 332
Wellings, Norah, 333, 334
Wendy, 28, 291
Wendy-Ann, 15, 19, 20

Wendy face, 17
Whimsies, 46
Whistling Jim, 162, 163
Winnie Walker, 23
Wislizenus, Adolf, 8
Withers, Jane, 18
Wooden, 112, 129, 242,
  268, 276, 296-298, 335

Y

Yamato Importing Co., 185
Yerri, 157
Young Ladies, 248

Mold Numerals

1: 186, 198, 228, 260
3: 281
4: 255
5: 209, 316
6: 190, 209
7: 152, 189, 198, 209
8: 194, 209
9: 198
11: 194
13: 136, 300, 317
15: 315, 317
17: 236
23: 260
35: 181
38: 181
45: 195
50: 55
56: 195
60: 68, 195, 287, 325
69: 155
71: 192, 325
72: 236
79: 155
90: 180
95: 269
98: 196
99: 155, 196
100: 68, 198, 202
101: 200, 203
102: 200, 201
107: 200
109: 155, 200, 202
112: 200
114: 200, 203
115: 200, 202, 204
116: 198, 200
117: 200, 204, 205
118: 200, 205
119: 155
121: 198
122: 198, 206
125: 203
126: 68, 198, 206, 207
127: 200, 208
128: 198, 207
142: 211
143: 213, 215
146: 209, 210
149: 192, 230, 325
150: 35, 211
151: 305
152: 211, 213
154: 209, 210
159: 209, 210
162: 209
164: 209, 210
165: 150, 225
167: 210, 222
168: 210
169: 294, 295

171: 209, 210
173: 150
176: 222
183: 215
185: 215
192: 209, 210
195: 210
201: 84. 289
202: 252
208: 84
211: 211, 214
221: 150, 192
226: 211, 212, 288, 289
230: 287
231: 4
232: 284
234: 289
236: 287, 288
237: 211, 216
238: 290
239: 211
240: 315
241: 213, 215
243: 257
245: 211, 216
247: 211, 288, 290
248: 4
249: 215
250: 5, 167, 223
251: 288
252: 288, 289
253: 149, 150
256: 4
257: 211, 214
260: 211, 214
262: 168
263: 84
264: 84
267: 168
275: 167
300: 168, 230
301: 287, 289, 325, 326
306: 192
310: 193
320: 168
323: 150
326: 3
341: 6, 68
342: 168
349: 168
351: 6, 68
353: 257
362: 68
370: 2
377: 224
390: 2, 340
399: 68, 169
400: 5
401: 5, 6
403: 198
452: 169
500: 4
520: 223
525: 222
526: 223
531: 222
546: 223
550: 4, 5, 305
560a: 4
585: 58
590: 4, 5
600: 305, 309
604: 58
619: 58
624: 58

650: 150
678: 58
719: 304
769: 294, 295
886: 35
890: 35
914: 260
926: 208
939: 304, 305
949: 304, 305
950: 304
971: 3
985: 3
990: 2, 3
992: 3
996: 3
1009: 305, 306
1039: 305
1040: 309
1070: 196, 211, 216
1078: 310
1079: 304, 305, 307, 310
1080: 309
1109: 308
1159: 311
1160: 310
1248: 307
1249: 69, 305
1250: 306, 309
1260: 309
1269: 306
1272: 292
1279: 305, 308
1294: 311
1295: 292
1299: 305
1303: 311
1388: 305
1329: 257
1352: 1
1361: 1
1362: 1
1368: 72
1393: 72
1402: 72
1428: 311
1469: 83
1469: 83, 311
1488: 305
1498: 305
1500: 231
1857: 251
1894: 2
1909: 294
1970: 196
2015: 318
2033: 291
2048: 291
3200: 2
4515: 318
4900: 294
5500: 294
5636: 162, 166
5700: 294
5777: 162
5800: 294
6736: 164
6969: 162, 163
6970: 163
7602: 162
7604: 162, 165
7622: 162
7788: 162
7977: 162
8192: 162

8774: 162, 163
9355: 164
12386: 72
14303: 273
45520: 255
81971: 226
156/32: 175
163/1: 141
163-6: 150
982/2: 55
1005/3652: 72
1394/30: 54
173/6: 151
1a13: 303

Patent Nos.

2171281: 18
2675644: 45
1283588: 119
1857485: 122
800-060 (England): 122
723-980 (France): 122
585-647 (Germany): 122
142433 (Italy): 230

Copyright Dates

1892: 74
1910: 85
1914: 255
1921: 246
1923: 80
1924: 55, 117, 323
1958: 26, 60
1959-1962: 60
1962: 26
1963-1968: 60
1964-1966: 60
1965: 28
1966-1969: 60

Letters

A: 198, 228
AM: 193
BE: 181
D: 67, 184, 209, 210
F: 211
G: 181
L: 236
MB: 185
P: 180
S: 67

Selected Bibliography

Anderton, Johana. *Twentieth Century Dolls, More Twentieth Century Dolls*

Angione, Genevieve. *All-Bisque & Half-Bisque Dolls*

Angione & Wharton. *All Dolls Are Collectible*

Coleman, Dorothy, Elizabeth & Evelyn. *The Collector's Encyclopedia of Dolls, The Collector's Book of Doll's Clothes*

Desmond, Kay. *All Color Book of Dolls*

Foulke, Jan. *Focusing on Effanbee Composition Dolls, Treasury of Madame Alexander Dolls, Focusing on Gebruder Heubach Dolls — The Art of Gebruder Heubach: Dolls and Figurines*

King, Constance. *Dolls and Doll's Houses, The Collector's History of Dolls*

Merrill & Perkins. *Handbook of Collectible Dolls,* Vols. I, II, and III

Noble, John. *Treasury of Beautiful Dolls*

Shoemaker, Rhoda. *Compo Dolls Cute and Collectible,* Vols. I, II, and III

Jan Foulke, the author of *4th Blue Book Dolls and Values, Focusing Effanbee Composition Dolls, Focusing on Treasury of Madame ˙der Dolls,* and *Focusing on Gebruder Heubach Dolls.*